"Some of the strongest lives are forged in the courage to face what once felt unbearable. In Vulnerable, *Ed Cohen reminds us that healing begins the moment we stop hiding and start telling the truth. His story is a hopeful invitation to move beyond silence and discover that our greatest wounds can become our greatest source of purpose."*

—John O'Leary, No. 1 national best-selling author and inspiration of the film *Soul On Fire*

"This is a magnificent and courageous book that will help millions to break the silence and open their hearts and souls to the truth about their lives. It is the book I wish I had read when I was experiencing my own dark night of the soul; afraid to speak about my own abuse, neglect, and abandonment. It is also about those who suffer along with us, feel our pain, and are desperate to find a way through the barriers that keep us encapsulated and cut off. Ed not only breaks the silence so many live with, but he offers wisdom that can lead us to the freedom we long to know and the success that is not tainted by our hidden pain. I highly recommend Vulnerable. *It is a triumph of the human spirit."*

—Jed Diamond, PhD, author of *The Irritable Male Syndrome: Understanding and Managing the Four Key Causes of Depression and Aggression* and founder of MenAlive.com.

"Ed Cohen's contributions to the field of learning are countless. He has been a champion of human flourishing, resilience, and authentic leadership as long as I've known him. His new book, Vulnerable, *reveals the furnace in which those qualities were forged. This brave, raw story is a different kind of learning journey, but an important one: the journey of self-discovery, healing, and authenticity."*

—Tony Bingham, president and CEO of the Association for Talent Development

"Having known Ed for more than twenty-five years, I can attest to the truth and depth of this journey. In Vulnerable, *he transforms pain into purpose, offering a powerful invitation to reclaim worth, release shame, and love fully. Through his story, he encourages readers to speak their truth and recognize their inherent worth, sharing the simple guiding principles that helped him break free from feelings of unworthiness. Ed's honesty and vulnerability offer hope to anyone seeking freedom from shame and the courage to love fully."*

—Cheri Torres, PhD, founding executive of the CWH Institute and coauthor of *Conversations Worth Having*

"It's profound, important, and difficult work to break the destructive cycles from our past. This book is a story and a guide on how you might do that too."

—Michael Bungay Stanier, founder of Box of Crayons, and author of the best-selling book, *The Coaching Habit*

"To know Ed Cohen is to know a leader of immense warmth and capability, but Vulnerable *reveals the staggering emotional journey it took to get there. A masterpiece of resilience and authentic leadership. Ed Cohen's raw, courageous journey from trauma to triumph is a powerful reminder that our deepest wounds can become our greatest sources of strength and connection. I couldn't put it down."*

—Ann Herrmann-Nehdi, chair and chief thought leader at Herrmann

"Vulnerable *by Ed Cohen is a raw, unflinching look at what it takes to overcome parental failings and choose your own destiny. With grit and grace, Cohen explores the courage required to be seen and the transformative power of self-care. It's an essential read for anyone looking to turn their greatest wounds into their greatest source of purpose."*

—Monique Fai-son Ross, author of *Playing Dead: A Memoir of Terror and Survival*

VULNERABLE

VULNERABLE

One Man's Journey from Abuse to Abundance

by Ed Cohen

E&M PUBLISHING

Published in the United States by Evan and Nathan Publishing,
an imprint of Start Publishing, LLC, 830 Morris Tpke, Fourth Floor,
Short Hills, New Jersey, 07078.

Printed in the United States
Cover design: Jennifer Stimson Designs
Cover image: ruangrit junkong, shutterstock
Text design: Westchester Publishing Services

First Edition.
10 9 8 7 6 5 4 3 2 1

Trade paper ISBN: 979-8-8809-9999-6
E-book ISBN: 978-8-8809-9998-9

For those who carry pain in silence,
for those who live with its echoes,
and for those who walk beside survivors:
may you break the silence and heal.

CONTENTS

DISCLAIMER

The suggestions and recommendations made in this book are based on the author's knowledge, experience, and opinions. The methods described in this book are not intended to be a definitive set of instructions. Other methods and materials may accomplish the same end results. Results may vary. There are no representations or warranties, expressed or implied, about the completeness, accuracy, or reliability of the information, products, services, or related materials contained in this book. The information is provided as is, to be used at your own risk.

This book is not intended as a substitute for consultation with a licensed health-care practitioner, such as your physician. Before you begin any health-care program or make lifestyle changes in any way, please consult a physician or another licensed health-care practitioner to ensure that you are in good health and that the examples contained in this book will not cause any harm. If you or someone you know is suffering from addiction, depression/other mental health issues, eating disorders, or the like, please seek initial medical attention.

DISCLAIMER

For parts of this book related to real people and situations in my personal life, everything has been written as accurately as I remember it. Where appropriate, names have been changed out of concern for privacy.

INTRODUCTION

by TOM RATH,
New York Times* best-selling author of *StrengthsFinder 2.0
and *Are You Fully Charged*

After studying human behavior, well-being, and leadership for over three decades, I've come to believe one truth above all: what we refuse to face will eventually shape us. We can bury it, distract ourselves, or outwork it—but the most important work we do, the kind that actually transforms us, always begins from *within*.

That's why *Vulnerable* is such a vital contribution to the conversation around healing, leadership, and human growth.

Ed Cohen doesn't just recount what happened to him; he uses the raw material of his life: abuse, silence, ambition, addiction, and healing to build something that's useful to others. *Vulnerable* is both Ed's journey and a manual. It's grounded in lived experience, and it's guided by his five principles that offer clarity and action; not just inspiration, but direction.

One of the patterns I've seen over the years is how much energy we lose when we try to hide what's unresolved. That hidden pain affects our ability to lead teams, care for families, and build anything meaningful. Ed is not telling us to have it all figured out; he's reminding us that we don't have to be fully healed to contribute—we just have to be real.

This book gives us a language for that kind of honesty. It's not about perfection, it's about presence. About telling the truth to yourself and to others in a way that builds strength, not shame. That's what makes this book so timely—and so timeless.

If you're navigating your own healing, or walking alongside someone who is, this book offers a path forward. It's also a call to leaders everywhere: the days of leading from behind a mask are over. Trust is built through courage and clarity. Ed Cohen models both.

Vulnerable doesn't just show us what healing looks like. It shows us how to begin *and* how to keep going.

This isn't just a book; it's an invitation to live with more energy, more integrity, and more heart.

FOREWORD: WHAT IT MEANS TO STAY

By PRISCILLA D. NELSON,
wife, mother, sister, consultant, interior decorator, teacher, coach, and friend

The other morning, I saw Ed in the garden. He stood quietly, rubbing the back of his neck where the doctors had gone in to repair his spine. The air was still, and he looked peaceful. I knew though, that the pain remained—some days more than others. There is a kind of quiet he carries now; one I have come to recognize. It is the stillness of someone who has survived more than he ever should have. It is also the calm of someone who has learned, with time and intention, to endure and how to keep putting one foot in front of the other. He has learned to find abundance in the small things, and meaning in the ones that truly matter.

What I have learned, watching this man pay for it with his health, sleep, and body, is that he waited decades to end his silence and speak the truth he had buried, and it nearly undid him. I stayed beside him through it, but I also learned how easily silence becomes contagious. I had to find my own voice too, later than I would have preferred. I wonder if I was too patient sometimes; if perhaps I should have pushed more.

If you are reading this and you have been taught to hold it all in—to tough it out, to be strong, to be selfless—I want you to know that you are not alone. Especially if you are a man. I have seen, up close, how men are conditioned to stay silent. To protect others from their pain. To minimize what hurts. To believe that vulnerability makes them weak. I am here to tell you: silence is not strength. It is isolation. And healing cannot begin while you are still pretending.

That moment reminded me how far we have come—and how much we still carry.

This book is not a celebration of victory. It does not offer simple lessons or easy redemption. What you are holding is an invitation into one man's truth: the painful beginning, the long silence, the unraveling, and the rebuilding. From where I stand, this story begins with a single question:

What does it mean to love someone who has had to fight for their worth from the very beginning—and to keep loving them through every stage of their becoming?

When I first met Ed, I saw confidence that bordered on arrogance. We were both professionals, both leading our own businesses, and both navigating our lives with a sense of independence. He made me wait in the reception area for a meeting far longer than I felt I should have had to, and by the time he opened the door, I had already decided what kind of man he was.

What I didn't know then, was that I wasn't meeting the real Ed—I was meeting his *mask*; a carefully protected version, shaped by years of surviving in a world that hadn't been kind. He had learned how to command a room, but not how to trust one. What looked like distance was deep caution. What felt like control was fear dressed in confidence.

That mask did not come off all at once. It loosened slowly over time; over tears and thousands of conversations. The man beneath it was not the one I expected. He was gentler. More uncertain. Fiercely loving. And still carrying more pain than I could have imagined.

The story you are about to read belongs to Ed. I have walked beside it for more than three decades. I have seen him wrestle with ghosts, some remembered, others inherited. I have watched him break patterns passed down in silence, without reason or warning. I have sat with him in rooms thick with history, seen him rise after moments when he nearly vanished, and held his hand as he faced truths long buried. I have witnessed him choose honesty over comfort, even when the price was high.

You will read about some of those costs. You will feel what it is like when the body remembers what the mind has tried to forget. You will meet a boy who grew up learning to disappear, and watch how he slowly, and at times painfully, had come back into his own life. You will see how deeply family wounds can echo across decades, and how healing becomes possible only when those echoes are finally named aloud.

Now, more than thirty-six years later, I have shared life with a man who has poured much of his energy into learning how to stay—with his pain, with his truth, and with the world around him. That kind of staying did not arrive in a single moment. It came slowly, in layers—quiet, clumsy, and hard won.

There were days when staying meant holding space while he pulled away. Other days, it meant choosing not to walk out when everything inside me wanted to shut down and sometimes run away. Our life together has included distance, silence, and anger: his, mine, and sometimes both simultaneously.

There were moments when I questioned if I could stay: when the silence between us became too loud; when my own needs felt like they were dissolving inside his pain. I have known the ache of loving someone who is not always reachable. I have felt invisible inside a relationship that looked steady from the outside. Sometimes, I needed space—not to leave, but to *breathe*. The truth is, I had to learn how to hold on without losing myself. I had to learn how to speak up—not just for him, but for me.

This is a story about what it means to hold on through the seasons that could have unraveled us. It is about choosing to stay in the conversation, even when our voices trembled. It is about returning, over and over again, not because it was easy—but because something inside us knew we were not finished. It is about learning to speak each other's language, even when we were communicating from entirely different places. It was challenging at times, yet the simple changes and progress made by both of us cemented our efforts.

It included parenting while uncertain, growing even as we raised someone else, and challenging what we were taught about love—slowly, deliberately, rewriting it one difficult conversation and one unexpected breakdown at a time. Truthfully, it didn't always work. I can't tell you how many times we needed to invent a new solution to the same problem.

We entered our marriage with opposite wiring. I came from a home where conflict was buried, where silence was the currency of peace. Ed came from a world where conflict was direct and immediate; a way to survive. He could not tolerate silence. I could not endure pressure. When I retreated, he pressed harder. When he pushed, I disappeared. The result was always the same: we both ended up feeling alone, even when we were only inches apart.

Therapy gave us language. It gave us tools. It offered a new lens. We came to understand that we were not fighting each other. We were reenacting stories from long before we met—scripts shaped by trauma, fear, and longing. His urgency came from survival. My silence came from fear. It took time to name those patterns. So many times, it wasn't about us; it was simply a trigger for something one of us had felt in our life before meeting the other. It took longer to trust that we could choose something different.

The hardest moments were not the fights themselves. The deeper pain arrived in the quiet that followed—the question neither of us asked aloud: *Is this the one we won't come back from?* That question sat between us more than once.

But we always came back to each other, not quickly or easily, but slowly, stubbornly, and together. We kept showing up, not perfectly or cleanly, but consistently. That is what made healing possible.

During those early years, Ed struggled to stay emotionally and physically present. He loved our children deeply. At times, however, I could see him shut down. His distance did not reflect a lack of love. His emotions simply became too much to hold. If our daughter cried for too long, he would retreat. If the tension in the house rose, so did his anxiety. It was not indifference; it was overload. He could love us and still find it hard to stay in the room. That was a kind of heartbreak all its own.

Everything began to shift when Ed chose honesty. He started naming what was happening inside him instead of pretending nothing was wrong. He invited me in, and eventually, he invited the kids in too. Over time, they learned to trust that he would not disappear—not emotionally, not physically, not even when life became difficult.

Throughout our life together, I have carried memories that remain vivid in my heart.

I remember the night he brought me cold medicine in Florida, still convinced I had come out of obligation. I remember the way he gripped the steering wheel in London with both hands, as if the car might slip away if he let go. I remember when I was diagnosed with a rare form of uterine cancer and the radiation treatment I had to go through. He was almost numb talking about it, in complete disbelief for a while. He said, "They probably got your records mixed up with someone else."

The treatment was brutal and I lost my way for a time. Ed was at a new job, and the timing was horrible. I found myself pulling away and our youngest daughter said out loud one night, "I want my old mommy back, the one who dances with me so I can go to sleep. You aren't my mommy." I was fighting cancer, while Ed was fighting his demons and the thought that I might die.

I remember too, watching him stand in the spotlight, on global stages receiving praise he never fully believed he deserved. I remember walking beside him through unfamiliar streets in countries we never imagined we would visit, wide-eyed, exhausted, and somehow more alive than ever.

I remember our years in India, where the outside world slowed down even as something inside both of us began to stir and rise. That time changed us dramatically. My time there surfaced a familiar struggle. In the United States, I had worked hard to prove I belonged in leadership as a woman. In India, it felt like I was taking a step back. Men held most of the power, and women were often sidelined. When a group of women asked me to help create change, I agreed on one condition: I would support anyone facing bias, not just women. When I shared that with Ed, he gave me his full support. Each of those moments reminded me of who Ed was becoming—and who we were becoming together.

What I witnessed, over time, was something rare: a man who refused to stop becoming, even when it hurt. He was not always this open. In the beginning, I knew there was pain inside him. I did not understand how deep it went. I thought I was reacting to his moods or his silence. I did not realize I was brushing up against a childhood he was still trying to survive.

Eventually, something changed. Ed began learning a new way to work with his emotions—a practice that gave structure to his internal world and helped him move through pain rather than around it. He did not invent this practice, but he studied it. He practiced it. He made it his own. At first, I didn't fully understand it. Still, I could feel the shift. I saw it in the way he began to show up with more awareness, less defensiveness, and a deeper presence that reached everyone around him.

Even now, it resurfaces from time to time. I've always embraced change, while Ed has lived with so much uncertainty that change can still feel like a threat even though he dives right into it. When I went back to school for my second master's degree, when I started coaching more, when I added another evening class to my schedule, and later, when I returned to school again for design, each endeavor asked more of him. I'm independent by nature, and despite all the work we've done, I know it may have triggered an old fear of being left. For me, those choices were about continuing to grow and sometimes, it just takes a little time for a partner to see that.

The cost of silence was steep. Years of unspoken pain carved their way through Ed's body: irritable bowel syndrome, kidney disease, two heart attacks, and eventually, a diagnosis of sarcoidosis (a rare inflammatory disease). His physical suffering carried the weight of everything he had not yet spoken.

When Ed finally began to speak, honestly and fully, he also began to heal. His healing did not arrive in a straight line; it came slowly, deeply, and with fierce intention. It arrived in scenes you'll read in this book—some that tremble with heartbreak, others that shimmer with grace.

The pattern I have seen over and over again is one of resilience. Ed has always been a seeker. He has never been willing to settle for numbness. That is what moves me most. It continues to remind me that healing is not passive. Healing requires discipline. It demands devotion. It demands honesty with yourself, with others, and with your story.

Ed never waited for healing to come to him. He pursued it with everything he had, every time it mattered. When he finds a passion for something, he becomes a guru! There's no stopping him.

After thirty-six years of marriage, I no longer see just a survivor. I see someone who is fully alive. He breathes differently now. He speaks more gently. He holds space for others. He loves with his whole heart. Most importantly, he allows himself to be loved in return.

This is what it means to witness transformation: to stand beside someone not because they are perfect, but because they are becoming—still, always.

I have become more whole, in no small way, because of who we have chosen to be, *together*.

As you read this book, you will meet the man I have known in all his complexity. You will read stories that are raw and real. You will encounter truths that are painful, beautiful, and necessary. You will witness the silence, the unraveling, and the "almosts." You will walk with a boy through flames, with a young man through shame, and with a grown man through recovery. You will see what happens when someone stops running from their past and chooses to walk directly through it.

This is not just Ed's story—it is a mirror, a reminder, and a path.

It took Ed decades to speak what had never been spoken, and even longer to be willing to share his story with the world. I witnessed the toll that silence took—not just on his body, but on our connection, our parenting, and the trust he had to rebuild from the inside out. I also witnessed what speaking gave back. It gave us something honest to stand on. Something imperfect, but real. It gave him breath. It gave us possibility. It gave us a second chance at presence.

If you have been taught to hold it together, to say you are fine, to keep going no matter the cost—this book may stir something in you. That discomfort is not weakness. It is an opening. You are not broken for needing more. You are not less for feeling deeply. You do not have to wait until your body breaks down or your spirit goes quiet. You are allowed to begin *now*. To name what hurts. To ask for help. To stop pretending that silence is strength.

Especially if you were raised to believe that strength means swallowing your truth—please, let this book give you another way.

This is also your invitation, not just to observe, but to enter. To reflect. To ask your own quiet questions: *Who did you become to survive? What patterns are you still carrying? What might change if you let yourself be seen?* And, *what would it mean to stay—with your own story, with someone else's, with your truth?*

If you have ever carried pain in silence, if you have ever questioned your worth, or if you have ever stood beside someone whose story is heavy, then you will find yourself somewhere in these pages.

This is your permission to let the mask slip, even if just briefly. You are not alone in your pain, your questions, or your becoming. You are seen, even when you feel invisible. Even when you believe you do not deserve it, you do. Don't let the years pile up as Ed has done. He would want more for you, and if this book causes even one person to reclaim what they have a birthright to, then it will have been worth him coming forward and sharing his truth.

We are still here; that, too, is part of the healing.

PROLOGUE: BREAKING THE SILENCE

"There is no greater agony than bearing an untold story inside you."
—MAYA ANGELOU, *I KNOW WHY THE CAGED BIRD SINGS* (1969)

I stepped into the room where my father was lying, his eyes closed, chest unmoving.

I leaned in, expecting the stillness to remain, but his eyes suddenly snapped open—wide, dark, and alert.

Before I could move, his hands shot up, strong, fast, and clamped around my throat. I gasped and kicked, trying to scream, but no air came. No sound. No escape. His grip tightened, his thumbs digging deeper as my vision began to tunnel. He stared at me without emotion as I went limp.

Just like that, I was back on the cold floor of my childhood—small, trapped, and breaking in silence. That nightmare haunted me for years. Even after he died, he found his way back to me through dreams, flashbacks, and the unspoken residue of trauma.

But one day, the air around me felt different: warm, safe, and entirely *mine*.

It was my birthday, and the nightmares had long faded into the background.

We had gathered for brunch, surrounded by sunlight and the gentle clatter of silverware.

Everyone ordered what they loved most: coffee, mimosas, lemon bars; it wasn't anything fancy, but it felt perfect.

At the end of the meal, someone brought out a vegan carrot cake from a local shop; exactly how I liked it. My wife Pris sat beside me. Our daughter, MacKenzie, smiled at me from across the table. My childhood best friend Jay, our good friend Danny, and my cousins Elana and Mickey were all there too. MacKenzie began singing. Pris joined in, followed by Jay, and then the rest. Their voices were off-key, full of love and joy, rising in celebration. Even nearby diners clapped along.

I smiled genuinely. It wasn't the practiced smile I once wore to survive; it came without pretense. I didn't retreat inward. I didn't dissociate or disappear. I stayed, present, with them and with myself.

If you are in an abusive relationship, or have been abused, this story is for you. If you're still living in fear, healing from the past, or loving someone who's been hurt—please know you are not alone. You may see parts of your story here, or find language for something you haven't yet been able to name.

Whatever brought you to these pages, I hope they offer you presence, permission, and a sense of possibility. That is what healing can look like—not a dramatic transformation or a climactic ending, but a moment of presence. It is the quiet choice to remain open when love reaches toward you, and you choose to let it in.

There was a time when I couldn't imagine that possibility. I smiled on my birthdays, but it wasn't real. It was the mask I wore to keep others from seeing my pain. Smiling on my own birthday felt unreachable. Staying at the table, letting people in, allowing joy to exist alongside pain—it all seemed out of reach. Healing didn't begin with laughter. It began in darkness, shaped by silence,

Celebrating our marriage after thirty-five years with vow renewals in October of 2024. From left: my cousins, Mickey and Elana, and my daughter, MacKenzie.

shame, and survival. Getting to that birthday table required a lifetime of effort.

I had to grow through what I went through.

I had to accept support, even when I believed I didn't need it.

I had to keep learning, unlearning, and starting over.

I had to build relationships capable of holding both truth and tenderness.

I had to redefine purpose—not as a destination, but as a daily decision.

There was a time when birthdays were merely something to survive. Back then, silence was not peace—it was protection. Even kindness could feel like a trap.

Healing is not linear—the road bends back toward places we thought we had already passed. Sometimes, the past resurfaces in ways we never saw coming.

A year after that joyful birthday, I found myself unraveling.

Following months of chronic pain and limited mobility, I underwent cervical spine surgery to remove bone spurs that were compressing nerves in my neck. The pain had become unbearable. I had lost muscle in my left arm and my fingers were always tingling. Even sleep had become difficult. The procedure was a success, and I was sent home with post-operative instructions and medications that were described as "routine"—safe, necessary, and nothing to worry about.

During the first week, the pain was intense—aching bones, spasming muscles, deep nerve flares. I followed the instructions exactly. I took the prescribed medications on schedule, using alarms and tracking everything from blood pressure to mobility. I never asked for more. I never deviated. I just wanted to heal. By the second week, I learned to anticipate the pain. If I was late with a dose, it came back sharply and relentlessly. So, I stayed ahead of it.

By the third week, the pain had started to ease—but something else was shifting. I felt a lightness in my head that made me uneasy. That was when I realized it was time to begin tapering. I tried, cautiously and deliberately. Almost immediately, I spiraled into withdrawal: shaking; sweating; nauseous; the inability to calm myself. I was trapped inside a body I could no longer control.

When I called my surgeon, he told me I had reduced too quickly and recommended "catch-up" doses. His assistant offered a new taper schedule that would have stretched out over sixteen weeks. With my history of heart issues and kidney disease, I knew I couldn't navigate that plan on my own. Pris drove me to the emergency room in the middle of the night. They told me to increase my dosage and try again. I was sent home, still shaking.

By dawn, I was frightened, sick, and disoriented. Pris remained calm, but her concern was unmistakable, and my blood pressure had spiked to the level of a cardiac crisis. We went to a different ER, where a doctor finally listened. She said what no one else had: "You need to be admitted. You need to come off this safely."

Still, I hesitated. I was afraid of what being hospitalized might mean. I pictured the dramatic scenes from movies: seizures, restraints, and a total loss of control. I wasn't ready for that. Instead, I decided to wait until the morning to see a doctor she had referred me to.

After five minutes, he confirmed what the ER doctor had said: "You should be in the hospital." That was all we needed to hear. I went home, packed a bag, and we left. Within hours, I was in a hospital bed—monitored, treated, and, for the first time since surgery, *understood.*

When I shared what had happened and how I had gotten there, the nurse looked at me and said, "You're an accidental addict." That word hit me hard: *addict.* It was the word I had feared all my life. It was the word that described my father. I had spent decades distancing myself from that label. But despite my efforts, it had found me.

During my five-day hospital stay, I joined group sessions with others navigating their own recoveries. There, I saw what I had never allowed myself to see before: versions of the man my father might have been. Some were in their thirties, others in their forties, fifties, and sixties. Most had relapsed more than once. All spoke with trembling voices about their desire to stay sober. One man recounted every loss in his life and past arguments with family members. One woman said she only drank when alone because that's when it felt safest. Another man described decades of high-functioning success, even as he admitted how hollow and haunted he had become inside.

My father never stopped drinking. He drank in silence and in rage, in celebration and in shame. No moment was safe from it. Maybe he didn't fail because he didn't care. Maybe he failed because the world he came from offered him no path to healing.

He was born in 1924 and entered the military at eighteen, in the middle of World War II. But the drinking didn't start in the military; it started earlier, with his own father. The abuse and attempted escape from it were passed down, woven into the fabric of our family long before I was born.

His addiction unfolded from the mid-forties through the mid-seventies, during a time when alcoholism was treated as a personal failing instead of a cry for help. There were few options for support. Therapy was rare, and often carried a stigma. Vulnerability was punished. Silence was how men survived. There were no safe rooms. No language for generational trauma, and definitely no understanding of addiction as inheritance.

At that moment, sitting in a group of people working toward recovery, I realized he had likely never seen a space like that. Maybe he tried in the only way he knew how. Maybe it wasn't enough, but maybe he never had a real chance.

I had built my life around not becoming him, but for the first time, I considered the possibility that maybe he had tried. That awareness didn't erase the harm, but it helped me release the judgments I didn't realize I was still holding.

What began as a frightening detour became something else entirely: another layer of healing. And all because of a mismanaged recovery and a word that I never wanted to hear: *addict*.

Even after being discharged, I wasn't finished. I experienced weeks of rebound symptoms. To stay grounded, I returned to the methods I had spent a lifetime practicing: counseling, acupuncture, massage, breathwork, and body awareness.

Each of those tools helped me sit with the emotions that were rising to the surface; even the ones I thought I had already dealt with: grief, fear, anger, and compassion.

Healing is a spiral; a returning, a continuous journey that deepens with every step we take, forward or backward.

Through childhood trauma, marriage, family, a successful career, world travel, grief, and abundance, five principles emerged. They weren't invented; at first, they were instincts. Over time, they became practices. Now, they are the anchors by which I live:

1. Grow Through What You Go Through

   Every experience—whether born of pain or progress—holds the potential for transformation. Growth isn't a clean line. It's the courage to remain present through what cracks us open.
2. Value the Support of Others

   Healing never happens in isolation. The people who walk with us, who listen, who simply stay—those are the ones who carry us forward.
3. Pursue Lifelong Learning and Adaptability

   To stay resilient, we must stay curious. Relevance is rooted in humility. We grow by continuing to evolve—at any age, in any season.
4. Cultivate Meaningful Relationships

   Connection is a risk and a reward. The relationships that hold space for our truth, without trying to fix us, are the ones that help us thrive.

5. Stay Purposeful and Relevant

    Purpose is not a title or a goal; it's a daily return to what matters. We lead not through expertise alone, but through alignment—with ourselves, with others, and with what we value most.

You won't find these five principles spelled out in every chapter of this book, but they live in each one. They are present in every scar, every broken silence, and every moment I chose to stay. These principles no longer belong to me alone. They belong to anyone who chooses healing over hiding, to anyone still learning how to be present, and to anyone brave enough to speak.

These five truths didn't just help me survive; they are how I built a life of abundance.

This isn't just my story; it's a path—from trauma to truth, from abuse to abundance.

This is where mine begins. Maybe yours begins here too.

Either way, let's end the silence.

PART I

GROW THROUGH WHAT YOU GO THROUGH

Every experience, whether born out of pain or progress, holds the potential for transformation. Growth isn't a clean line. It's the courage to stay present through what cracks us open. It's awakening the spark, burning without breaking, and learning not to stay silent just because you were told "don't tell." It's finding the strength to take one brave step forward, to become the shield when no one else can, and to survive being trapped in the silence. Even when wearing the mask feels like the only option, growth still waits beneath it, quietly shaping the person you're becoming.

CHAPTER 1

AWAKENING THE SPARK

In the darkest moments, when we are forced to confront the very things we fear most, we often find the strength we never knew we had.

The smell of dinner still hung in the air: roast chicken, maybe potatoes. For a brief second, it almost felt like an ordinary night. But then:

"Get out of my sight before I really lose my temper!"

His voice exploded down the hallway, shaking our small duplex. Whiskey and smoke thickened the air. His words, sharp and hot, cut straight through me. The veins on his neck bulged as his eyes, wild with fury, locked onto my mother. Without warning, he shoved her hard. She cried out as she hit the floor. The sound of her fall echoed through the house.

"Please, stop! You're hurting me," she cried; her voice trembling as she crawled away.

"I'll leave you alone when I damn well please," he spat. "You're useless! Can't even make a decent meal!"

The untouched dinner sat on the table, cold and limp, like the promise of peace we never had.

I stood frozen, silent, and terrified; unable to move, and too young to fully grasp the horror of the situation, yet I felt its weight pressing down on me.

His eyes snapped to me, burning with anger and darkness.

"What are you looking at? Go to your room!"

His voice was thunderous, making my legs shake and my heart race. I backed away slowly, trembling, then turned and ran.

We lived in a cramped three-bedroom duplex just outside Chicago. My room was simple, with two beds: one for me, and one for my older brother, who was always out. The small bookcase in the corner held just a few items, none of which could protect me from the terror that filled our home. I carefully closed the door behind me, trying not to make any noise that would draw his attention. I pressed my back against the cool wood, my breath coming in shallow, rapid gasps. Through the thin walls, I could still hear his voice, each word another blow to my already fragile sense of safety:

"You're useless!" he shouted, his voice rising and falling with anger. "Why can't you do anything right?"

I sank to the floor, hugging my knees to my chest, trying to make myself as small as possible. My stomach was tight. My head buzzed. The world flipped upside down, and I could feel the terror in every muscle; every fiber of my being.

As I sat there, two thoughts ran through my mind: *Please don't hurt her,* and *why does she stay?* I didn't know love could look like that, or at least, that it shouldn't. When he said he loved me, I didn't believe him. That disbelief followed me, shadowed my relationships, and made it hard to trust kindness or accept love that didn't hurt.

* * *

While the world marched for justice, civil rights, women's liberation, and protests against the Vietnam War, I fought a different battle inside our walls. Their courage stirred something in me. If they could rise up, maybe I could survive.

As I listened to my father's rage and my mother's soft sobs, hope felt far away. My mother, despite everything, loved my father. She held onto the belief that if she showed him enough love and support, he might miraculously become the kinder, more loving husband she longed for. That shift never came. I wanted to comfort my mother and tell her it would be alright, but I knew better. My father's anger was unpredictable, and any attempt to help would only make things worse. Stepping in during one of his rages would only have led to more violence. I thought about running away all the time. I knew the police wouldn't help; in those days, they did not intervene, leaving families like mine trapped.

The neighbors had to hear the shouts, crashes, and cries. No one came. Maybe they were afraid. Maybe they just looked away. Either way, their silence made us feel even more alone.

Eventually, my mother's sobs subsided, and the house grew quiet. I closed my eyes, retreating to a place in my mind where I could be strong; where I could protect her. Even now, decades later, the memory of it still tightens my chest, a lingering reminder of the fear that once ruled my life.

Some nights, the fear followed me into sleep. I would dream that I could fly, only not with wings; just me, rising above the house, the streets, the people. I flew everywhere: schoolyards, neighborhoods, downtown crowds, but mostly inside our home. Quiet. Unnoticed. I watched people laughing, fighting, and living. They never saw me and I never landed. I hovered above them and felt safe. In those dreams, I was still part of the world . . . just not inside it.

When I awoke the next morning, the house was quiet. The sun streamed through the window, casting a warm glow on the walls. Daytime always felt safer; my father would either be sleeping off his hangover, or already at work. It was a small respite, and because I knew I would be in school, I also felt safe.

The bruises on my mother's face quickly shattered my illusion of normalcy. I was exhausted from not sleeping well. I put on a brave face, hiding my fear, and got ready for school. No one could know what happened behind our closed doors. As I left, I looked at my mother sitting at the kitchen table, staring blankly at her coffee, cigarette in hand. I gave her a small smile, hoping to offer some comfort. Still, her eyes were filled with resignation.

The bright sun outside felt wrong; too warm and too bright for the cold emptiness I carried inside. I wondered if anyone would notice the bruises beneath my skin; the ones that weren't on my mother's face. I felt the weight of every step as I walked to school that morning. The sounds of the world outside, like the chatter of kids walking and playing, felt muted, as if I were trapped in a bubble that muffled everything except the echo of my father's voice. As I approached the school, I paused, taking a breath. In front of me was my temporary escape from the storm at home.

The violence began early; my brother and sister endured it too. We were born years apart, but we all knew the pound of his fist, the sting of his belt, and the silence that followed. We all heard the horrifying sounds of our father beating our mother, and, like me, they too were repeatedly beaten with our father's belt buckle, and subjected to his violent rage time and time again.

My parents, Bernice and Jerry, met in Chicago and married in 1947, just after World War II had ended. Both families had fled the turmoil of Kiev in 1908, entering through Ellis Island and settling in Chicago. By coincidence, my grandparents came over on the same ship.

After they married, Bernice and Jerry moved to Gary, Indiana, with my older brother Phillip (who was five at the time), and opened a small grocery store. Beneath the surface, my father was already troubled: drinking to numb his pain, and gambling to escape reality. When their finances collapsed, they lost the store.

Jerry took a job with a major airline. Soon, they moved back to Chicago. Bernice joined a typing pool in suburban Chicago. The move did not bring healing. Jerry's anger turned violent—first words, then fists. Desperate to save the marriage, Bernice had another child. My sister Diane was born eight years after Phillip, then I came along two years later, in 1959.

The postwar promise of prosperity was a lie inside our house. My father's discontent deepened, leaving him drawn to alcohol, gambling, and affairs. Our home became a war zone.

Outside, America was rising. The Montgomery Bus Boycott had just ended a few years prior, and Dr. Martin Luther King, Jr. had emerged as a national voice for justice. Civil rights marches filled the streets. Betty Friedan's *The Feminine Mystique* would soon spark the second wave of feminism. Following that, protesters locked arms across the Edmund Pettus Bridge in Selma, Alabama. I watched Dr. King speak on our black-and-white TV, his voice full of power and grace. If they could face hatred with courage, maybe I could survive the war at home.

I'll never forget the night he pressed a knife to her chest. The air reeked of stale dinner, cigarettes, and something worse: pure fear. When he pushed it in, it felt like it pierced me too. I froze. Time cracked open. I couldn't move or scream, just watch.

The fear never left me. Every day, I braced for the moment his anger might erupt again, louder, worse, final. Our walls were thin, but no one heard. Or if they did, they never came. I carried that silence everywhere. Yet, something inside me held on. I don't know what it was. Maybe stubbornness. Maybe hope. Maybe simply survival.

I didn't just fear for my mother's safety; I feared for my own life. Each night, I lie awake, straining to hear the softest sound of footsteps or the murmur of voices, wondering if it would be the night when things would go too far. It felt like my entire childhood was spent holding my breath, waiting for the next explosion—never knowing when or how it would come.

I didn't know it then, but change was coming. Something powerful enough to shift the ground beneath me.

That night didn't end the violence. It didn't rescue me, or teach me how to fight back, but something shifted. A flicker deep inside fragile, but real. I didn't have words for it yet, but I just knew I wasn't ready to disappear. Not completely. Not yet.

CHAPTER 2

BURNING WITHOUT BREAKING

Like a flame tempered by wind, each challenge makes us stronger. The fires we face forge our resilience, teaching us to adapt and rise from adversity.

I was six and I just wanted to play and have fun. Isn't that what all kids want? It was January of 1966, and the snow in our Chicago neighborhood piled high against the sidewalks. I didn't mind the cold. I had my dog Lassie, and when I was with her, I felt safe. I wasn't allowed to tell anyone what was happening. So, I told Lassie. She always listened.

"Mom, can I take Lassie for a walk?" I asked, excitement bubbling in my voice.

"Sure, just bundle up," she replied, glancing at the snow-covered landscape outside.

I nodded eagerly and rushed to get dressed. My blue coat went on over my sweatshirt, and I tugged on my snow boots, the snug fit promising to keep my feet dry and warm. That afternoon, I stepped outside into the snow, not knowing that everything was about to change.

"It's freezing out, so don't stay out too long," Mom reminded as I grabbed Lassie's leash.

My father insisted I call her "Mom," and him "Dad," because: "Only babies call their parents, 'Mommy' and 'Daddy'."

"Okay, Mom!" I called back, already halfway out the door with Lassie bouncing beside me.

The cold stung my cheeks, but I didn't care. I had my boots, my coat, and Lassie. That was enough.

"Come on, girl!" I urged, laughing as Lassie darted forward, her nose buried in the snow, searching for hidden treasures.

As I walked along, the sounds of the neighborhood surrounded me: the distant hum of a car engine, the occasional bark of a dog, and the laughter of the older kids sliding around on the frozen creek nearby. Their carefree play contrasted the tension I often felt at home. I watched them with a mix of envy and longing, remembering my father's stern warnings about not playing on the ice. Lassie, eager and curious, tugged on the leash, her nose still in the snow.

The older kids, with their colorful scarves and mittens, slid across the frozen creek with reckless abandon, their laughter echoing through the air. They glided effortlessly, performing tricks and racing each other; the ice reflecting their joy like a mirror. One boy, tall and lanky, attempted a daring spin, only to lose his balance and tumble to the ground, his friends' laughter mixing with his own. Another girl, her cheeks flushed with cold and excitement, skated gracefully. She moved like the ice itself, fluid and fearless. They seemed invincible; their world a perfect blend of ice, laughter, and light, so different from my own cautious steps.

"Hey, Eddie! Come join us!" a boy called out, waving.

"I can't," I replied, my father's warnings echoing in my ears. "I'm walking my dog."

The snow kept falling. Lassie kept pulling.

As we walked along the creek, a plume of smoke rising in the distance caught my attention. The smell of burning wood and paper drew me to the source. It was a neighbor burning their trash in a large barrel. The older kids continued their play. Curious, I approached the fire with Lassie by my side. I picked up a few sticks and threw them into the can. The crackling flames mesmerized me. Its warmth was a welcome relief from the cold. The orange and red hues flickered against the gray sky, casting dancing shadows on the snow.

I knew better than to get too close. The flames flickered and danced; teasing, beautiful. A spark shot into the air and landed on my sleeve. I swatted, expecting it to die. Instead, it bloomed into a full flame, hot and *fast*. Panic surged through me, not just at the sight of the flame, but at the thought of the trouble I'd be in for damaging my coat.

I tried to put it out on the ground. Then, I felt the pain sear into my back and the heat rise up my neck: I was *on fire*. My heartbeat pounded in my ears, drowning out all other sounds. Instinct took over and I ran. They didn't teach "stop, drop, and roll" back then, and child safety laws for clothing were still a thing of the future.

I ran toward the creek. Frantically I pulled off my coat, but it was too late. My sweatshirt was consumed by the flames. Pain exploded through me. I couldn't see. Couldn't breathe. I screamed, louder than I knew I could. Terror swallowed me whole. Even then, some part of me knew it wasn't the end of the story, it was the beginning of a battle I would have to fight one breath at a time.

Panic turned to dread. I was *burning*. My father was going to be so angry at me.

The older kids, momentarily stunned, stopped sliding and stared in horror as I ran toward them, the flames growing higher with each step. Their laughter twisted into shouts of panic and confusion.

"Someone help him!" a girl screamed, her voice shaking with fear.

Roy White, one of the older kids, jumped into action.

"Hang on, kid!" he yelled, leaping toward me.

He tackled me hard, knocking the wind out of me. The cold snow stabbed my skin, then smothered the flames. I barely registered the impact through the searing pain. Roy grabbed fistfuls of snow, packing them onto my back. Each handful burned with relief. The fire hissed and sputtered out, leaving behind the stench of burnt fabric, charred flesh, and singed hair; thick in the air, sickening and inescapable.

"Are you okay?" Roy asked, his voice trembling as he brushed the remaining snow off me. He stared at my back, blackened and oozing, his face pale with shock.

I couldn't speak. The pain was raw. I could feel the wetness of my back where the skin had peeled away, sticking to the inside of my coat. Every breath burned. Every step Roy took sent a jolt through my body. I clenched my teeth, trying to scream without sound.

Tears streamed down my face from the pain, and from the fear. I had almost died. I should have felt lucky to be alive. Instead, I was already bracing for my father's reaction. His voice. His anger. The ruined coat. The broken rule.

Roy carried me piggyback, careful to avoid my back. My clothes had fused to my skin. Each movement was a fresh wave of agony. With every step toward home, the dread deepened.

When we reached the house, my mother's face drained of color. "Eddie! My God, what happened to you?" Her voice cracked as she ran to me.

"He was near the trash fire. His jacket caught," Roy said quickly, lowering me gently.

"Please don't tell Dad," I whispered. "Where's Lassie? Is she okay?"

He knelt beside me, calm and steady. "Lassie's fine. She ran to the creek. One of the kids went after her."

Almost on cue, a girl appeared, leading Lassie by the leash. "She's okay, Eddie," she said softly.

Lassie pressed her wet nose into my hand. I let out a shaky breath. The pain was still there. Something in me eased anyway.

In the middle of fire and fear, Roy gave me something I had rarely known: protection without punishment. He carried me when I couldn't carry myself.

My mother didn't call an ambulance. She grabbed the car keys and rushed me to the hospital herself. I lay across the back seat, sobbing, each breath jagged. My back felt like it was melting. Every bump in the road tore through me. *I'm in so much trouble,* I thought. *He's going to kill me. He's never going to forgive me.*

My father met us in the emergency room parking lot. One look at his face, and I knew he was already furious.

"Why didn't you take him to the other hospital?" he hissed at my mother as we stepped inside.

"I—I didn't know," she stammered, still gripping the car keys. "This one was closest."

"You're useless," he muttered.

A nurse tried to guide me toward a room. "We need to assess him quickly."

"That's my son!" my father roared. His voice cracked through the sterile air like a whip. "You better take good care of him!"

Staff froze. Patients turned. His rage filled the entire corridor, thick and suffocating.

"Sir, lower your voice," a doctor said, calm but firm. "We're doing everything we can."

"I have every right to know what's happening!"

"We understand you're upset," the nurse said. "Yelling isn't helping your son. Please, step back."

As they wheeled me down the hall, their words faded. I could hear everything: my father's rage, the beeping machines, the scrape of the gurney wheels; but it all blurred together. Yet, I couldn't make sense of what was happening. My body was on fire. My mind was unraveling.

The doctor leaned over. "He needs to be transferred. A hospital with a pediatric burn unit has the right resources."

"He needs to stay here!" my father barked. "Why are we wasting time?"

"We've stabilized him," the doctor said. "Now we have to move him, *fast*."

An ambulance came and I was loaded in. My parents followed behind. Every bump made me want to scream. A paramedic stayed by my side.

"We're almost there, buddy. Hang in there," he said, his voice like a warm hand on my shoulder.

At the new hospital, a team rushed in. They started peeling away the burned clothing. The smell of charred fabric and flesh filled the room. I couldn't move. I couldn't speak. I floated above it all trapped inside my body. They worked carefully, stripping away the dead skin, layer by layer. The pain was unbearable, but I had no more strength to cry. Third-degree burns had torn through my back and right arm, down to the tissue. My body went into shock. Fluids drained from me. Blood pressure dropped. I couldn't keep warm. I couldn't fight.

The doctors tried everything. They stabilized me. They prepped me. They worked with urgency and precision.

But my body began to fail anyway.

Within a week, infection set in; the open wounds welcomed it. The bacteria found their way into my bloodstream, and soon, sepsis spread. My system couldn't keep up.

My mother stayed kind. Thanked the nurses. Clung to hope.

My father snapped at everyone. Demanded updates. Yelled until the staff told him, more than once, that he was interfering with my care. He backed down, but only because he had to.

Meanwhile, my first-grade teacher, Mrs. Hanson, began showing up every afternoon. She tutored me to make sure I didn't fall behind, and on days when I wasn't strong enough, she simply sat beside me—sometimes reading, sometimes talking about my dreams, and sometimes just being there in silence. After a few weeks, Cook County sent a tutor to replace her. When the woman walked into my room, Mrs. Hanson stood up, looked her in the eye, and said firmly, "I will take care of my student, thank you very much." Then she closed the door behind her.

Her presence gave me more than academic help. In the middle of fear and chaos, she became my lifeline—someone who saw me, believed in me, and made learning feel like a safe place.

One afternoon, the doctor pulled my parents aside to a small conference room outside the Intensive Care Unit where I had been moved during the night.

"Mr. and Mrs. Cohen," Dr. Andrews began, his voice steady, "Eddie's condition has become critical."

"What does that mean?" my father asked, sharp and immediate.

"The burns triggered a serious infection," Dr. Andrews explained. "It's entered his bloodstream. We call it sepsis. His body is overwhelmed and struggling to respond."

My mother gasped, eyes filling with tears. "What can you do for him?" she asked, her voice barely holding together.

"We're doing everything we can," Dr. Andrews said gently. "He's receiving strong antibiotics. We've increased his fluid intake and are supporting his blood pressure with medication. He's in the ICU, and his vitals are being monitored continuously. Still, his organs are under extreme stress."

My father stepped forward, fists clenched. "Why wasn't this caught earlier?" he demanded.

"Sepsis can develop very rapidly," Dr. Andrews replied. "Even with excellent care, sometimes it moves faster than our ability to control it. Right now, our focus is on stabilizing Eddie and supporting his vital functions."

"So, what's the plan?" my father asked, his voice tight with urgency.

"We're continuing with fluid resuscitation, adjusting medications as needed, and watching him closely. Every decision is being made to give him the best chance of recovery," Dr. Andrews answered.

"Is he going to make it?" my mother asked softly, barely above a whisper.

Dr. Andrews paused before responding, "The next twenty-four to forty-eight hours are critical," he said quietly. "Eddie is very sick. We are doing everything in our power but I need to be honest. We must prepare for all possibilities."

A nurse entered the room and whispered something to him. Dr. Andrews nodded, then turned back to my parents.

"Eddie's condition is deteriorating," he said, voice low. "He's slipped into a coma. This is the body's way of protecting itself from overwhelming infection and stress."

"A coma?" my father echoed, his voice breaking. "What does that mean for him?"

"It means his system is shutting down nonessential functions to redirect energy toward healing," Dr. Andrews explained. "Our job is to keep him stable and support him while his body fights."

My mother broke into tears, her body shaking. My father stood frozen, his eyes wide and glassy, the strength drained from his face.

"Please," he said, voice cracking, "you have to save him. He's just a boy."

Dr. Andrews met his eyes. "We won't give up on him," he said with quiet conviction. "He's in the best possible hands. We're with him every step of the way."

I don't know if it was real or not. I saw people, faces I couldn't name, smiling, welcoming me. I heard my mother's voice, and others too, calling my name. I tried to answer, but I couldn't.

I drifted for six days in silence. No time. No edges. No pain. Just the endless sensation of floating.

I moved through a space without color, without shape. I wasn't cold. I wasn't warm. I wasn't anything I could describe. I couldn't move. I couldn't speak. My body was still somewhere else, but a part of me flickered on and off, like a light struggling to stay lit.

Voices came and went, soft, strained, slipping through a thick, invisible wall. Some sounded close. Some felt like echoes from another world.

Sometimes I saw faces, some familiar, some unknown, hovering at the edge of awareness. None of them stayed long. None of them answered the questions I didn't know how to ask.

I wasn't fully here. I wasn't fully gone. I was caught between two places, one I had left, and one I wasn't sure I could return to.

* * *

When I opened my eyes, the world came back in fragments, light too bright, shapes too blurry, sounds too far away. Then I felt it.

A tube down my throat.

I couldn't breathe. I couldn't speak. Panic surged through me. I tried to move, tried to scream, but nothing came out.

Then, her hand.

Warm. Steady. Real.

My mother leaned in close, her eyes full of tears she was trying not to let fall. Her voice came soft, but urgent.

"It's okay, Eddie. I'm right here."

I tried to focus on her face, anything to anchor myself to something I knew. My heart pounded. I couldn't swallow. I couldn't ask where I was or what was happening.

"You're going to be okay, sweetie. Just breathe. Stay with me."

She gripped my hand tighter. Her voice was shaking now, trying to sound stronger than she felt.

"Look at me, honey. You're safe now. The doctors are taking good care of you. I'm not going anywhere. I'm right here."

I couldn't hold her hand back. I couldn't say I was scared. I couldn't say I didn't understand.

The nurses moved quietly, their hands efficient, their eyes kind.

"You're doing great, Eddie," one whispered as she adjusted the lines in my arms. Another leaned over me, checking the machines.

"Just breathe easy, sweetheart. We're right here with you," she said, her words a thread of calm through the storm inside me.

My mother's voice kept coming, like a lifeline.

"You're so strong, Eddie. I know this is scary, but you're doing so well."

She brushed hair off my forehead. Her eyes never left mine.

"We're all here for you. Just relax, sweetheart. You're not alone."

I blinked slowly, trying to hold on, trying to stay where her voice could reach me.

Then she said gently, "They're going to help you breathe better now, okay?"

The nurse nodded. "We're going to give you something to help you sleep, Eddie. When you wake up again, the tube will be gone. You'll feel much better."

I closed my eyes, not because I wanted to but because I had to. Everything inside me was raw. I was trying so hard to hold on.

Her hand never left mine.

The brief moments of consciousness were a blur of confusion, discomfort, and vulnerability. Each second felt like an eternity as the sedation took hold, and the world faded into darkness once more. My mother's comforting words lingered, a soft anchor in the overwhelming sea of sensations.

* * *

In 1966, performing skin grafts was delicate, painstaking work; the only real option for treating severe burns. Once my condition stabilized, the doctors prepared to take skin from my legs to repair the wounds on my back and arm.

Before the surgery, Dr. Andrews gathered my parents in the waiting area.

"Mr. and Mrs. Cohen," he began, voice calm but serious, "we're preparing to perform a series of skin grafts on Eddie. This is a complex and vital procedure for his recovery."

My mother clutched my father's hand, her knuckles white. "How long will it take?" she asked, barely above a whisper.

"Four to six hours," Dr. Andrews said. "We'll harvest thin layers of healthy skin from Eddie's upper legs using a dermatome. Once removed, the skin will be grafted onto the burns on his back and arm. The grafts will be dressed and immobilized to give them the best chance to take. It's essential he remains still after surgery."

My father nodded tightly. "Is there a risk?"

"There's always risk," Dr. Andrews said gently. "Infection, graft failure, scarring. But we'll monitor him closely every step of the way."

"How long will recovery take?" my father asked, his voice losing some of its edge.

"Weeks in the hospital, followed by months of rehabilitation," Dr. Andrews explained. "There may be additional surgeries. Physical therapy will be needed to restore movement and strength."

I didn't really understand what was coming. No one explained it to me in words I could grasp. I just knew that maybe if I stayed still, if I was strong, I could go home.

When I woke from the surgery, I was lying on my stomach. The pain was staggering. Tears ran down my face. I couldn't think. I couldn't breathe right. I just hurt.

My mother was there. Her eyes were red and full of love.

"Mom," I whispered, choking on the words. "It hurts."

"I know, sweetheart," she said softly, stroking my hair. "You need to stay still so the grafts can take. The doctors are doing everything they can."

My father stood at the foot of the bed, arms crossed, face unreadable.

Only one visitor was allowed at a time. My mother stayed as long as she could. Her voice calmed me. Her touch grounded me.

"Uncle Bert is here too," she said gently. "He's waiting to see you."

"Can I see him?" I asked, the thought giving me something to hold onto.

She smiled. "Of course. I'll go get him."

She started to leave.

"You'll see him later," my father said, stepping in. His tone was sharp. "Right now, you need rest."

"I really want to see him," I said, voice trembling.

His face hardened. "You don't always get what you want, Eddie. Uncle Bert can wait."

I looked away. The physical agony blurred with something deeper; disappointment, and helplessness.

"Okay," I whispered.

He sat next to me for a few minutes, stiff, unmoving. "You need to focus on getting better," he said. "Be strong."

I nodded, silent. I wanted my mother back.

Eventually he left, and she returned.

"I'm sorry, Eddie," she said softly. "Your father wanted to see you first."

"I just wanted to see Uncle Bert," I murmured.

"I'll bring him in now," she said, squeezing my hand.

A moment later, Uncle Bert entered. His smile, warm and gentle, was like sunlight through a cracked door.

"Hey there, champ," he said, sitting beside me. "How are you feeling?"

"It hurts," I whispered, tears returning.

"I know," he said, his voice low. "You're tough, Eddie. You'll get through this."

We talked quietly for a while. He didn't try to fix it. He just stayed.

As days became weeks, the pain stayed constant. So did the emotional weight. My mother's comfort and Uncle Bert's calm presence were lifelines. My father's expectations hovered, unspoken but heavy. The grafts were watched carefully. Any infection or rejection could undo it all. My parents rotated at my side. The nurses did their best to ease the pain. I tried to stay still.

A few days later, Roy came to visit. A local reporter showed up too. They took a photo of me in the hospital bed, handing Roy a twenty-five-dollar savings bond. It ran in the paper the next day.

Years later, in the early eighties, I saw Roy again in Chicago. After that, we lost touch. I am still searching, hoping to thank him one more time.

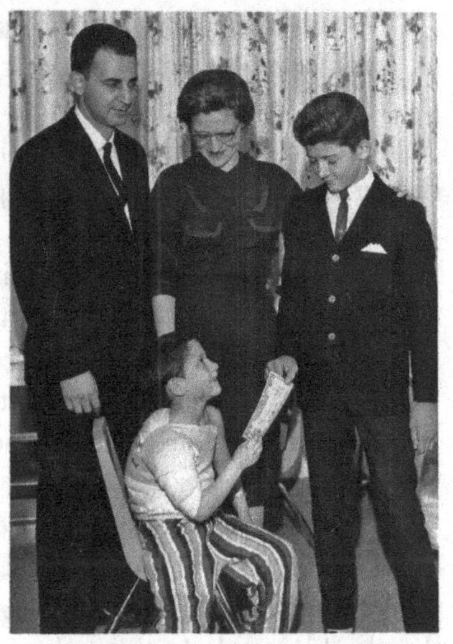

Presenting Roy White with an honorary savings bond (1966). From left: my father, my mother, Roy, and myself.

The physical scars stayed with me to this day.

The deeper wounds were the fear, the shame, and the longing for comfort.

At six years old, I didn't have the words for trauma. I only had the pain and the silence that followed it.

* * *

I woke up sweaty and shaky. The doctor was concerned it could be an infection. My temperature was high, and I was still so weak.

"We need to keep him here," I heard someone say. "It's too soon for him to go home."

My father wasn't having it. "He's fine," he snapped. "We're done here."

The nurses pushed back, and so did the doctor.

Once he made up his mind, no one changed it. Not even them.

So, they signed the papers and released me; just like that, I was going home.

It was February twenty-first, Aunt Audre's birthday.

Aunt Audre was always nice to me. She smiled big and real, not fake like some people. Her hugs were soft, and not too tight. I liked her. They threw a party; for her birthday and for my homecoming. Two reasons to celebrate. Two reasons to pretend everything was okay.

That afternoon, the house was packed, full of mostly adults. Grown-ups everywhere, talking, laughing, and holding drinks. Trays of food crowded every surface. Music blared from the small stereo speakers. Elana and Paul, cousins closest to my age, attended. My brother and sister were there too, drifting through the crowd like nothing had happened.

The air was thick with cigarette smoke and alcohol. It clung to my skin and made me dizzy. Just a room full of mostly adults who didn't know how to see a kid unless he was smiling.

"He's home!" someone said, like I was an unexpected guest. I didn't feel welcome. I felt small. Tired. Like I wanted to disappear.

I went to my room, hoping it would feel the same: my bed, my books, my pillow; it didn't. The walls looked off. My bed was hard. My toys seemed unfamiliar. I had changed. Everything had. Except *him*.

The door flew open. My father stood there with those same angry eyes. Same mean mouth. The fire hadn't touched any of that.

He didn't say a word. Just hit me. Quick. Sharp. Right on the cheek. "What are you doing in here?"

"I—I'm tired. I don't feel good," I whispered. My face burned, but I didn't cry. I tried to never cry in front of him.

"You're ruining the party. Get out there. Smile. Be good."

I nodded. "Yes, sir." Big boys always said, "yes, sir" and "yes, ma'am."

The slap stung. His words landed deeper. I had almost *died*. Nothing had changed.

Back in the living room, the noise swelled. Glasses clinked. Smoke floated like ghosts. My father laughed by the stereo like he hadn't just hit me.

Then he looked over. One eyebrow lifted. That was the signal.

So I smiled.

"Thank you," I said when they called me strong. "It's good to be home; I feel better."

My legs ached where they had taken the skin. The grafts were raw, and still bandaged. Every step sent pain shooting through me. I felt weak and feverish. I should have been in a hospital bed. No one noticed, not in the way I winced, or how I kept searching for a chair. Not my cousins. Not my siblings. Some people were kind. Some meant it. Their words slid off me like water on glass. They couldn't touch the part of me still hurting. The burns were on my back but that's not where it hurt most. It hurt in that house, in that room, and in the way my father's shadow swallowed everything. Even the party felt like punishment wrapped in noise.

The music played. The laughter rose. My father acted like nothing had happened.

I stood there, sick, sore, and silent. I wanted to lie down. I wanted someone to notice. I just smiled. It was easier than trying to explain the kind of pain that doesn't bleed.

CHAPTER 3

DON'T TELL

When chaos is your constant companion, holding onto the truth, "I'm not crazy" becomes your lifeline.

I was still healing when it happened. The bandages had come off, but I hadn't found my footing. Just when I thought the worst might be over, another wound came for me. That's how trauma worked in our house. But it didn't wait its turn; it layered itself; one terror stacked on top of the last, before the bruises even had time to fade.

I didn't have time to scream. His weight slammed into me, knocking me to the floor.

Then, pain. Sharp. Sudden. His teeth tore into the side of my face.

The snarling. The terror. Everything blurred, except the pain.

My brother kicked the dog off me and scooped me into his arms. "I've got you, Eddie. I've got you." His voice was shaking, but his arms didn't.

I remember him running. I remember my mother's voice, panicked, high-pitched, yelling as she pulled open the car door, loaded me in, and peeled out of the driveway.

At the hospital, they stitched my face. The right side was torn and swollen, a jagged line of trauma running from my cheekbone to my jaw. Thick bandages wrapped around my head like a mask.

When I looked in the mirror, I didn't recognize the boy staring back. Stitched and swollen. Eye half shut. Lip bruised. I looked broken, and I felt worse.

Then, they sent me home.

Just hours earlier, we were at my great Uncle Joe's house for an end-of-summer family picnic. Folding chairs scattered across the grass, paper plates piled high, the smell of grilled hot dogs and burgers filled the air.

Inside the house, chained in a narrow hallway, was a large German shepherd. Every time we carried something in or out, we had to pass him. I was careful; I always was. I was walking back inside, balancing a plate of leftovers, when he lunged. That's how fast it happened. That's how everything changed. My father had left the picnic early to go to work. When he came home, he walked into my room. I waited, bruised and bandaged, aching for something. A touch. A word. *Anything.*

He just looked at me. A long, cold stare that said everything and nothing at the same time. Then he turned and walked away.

No "Are you okay?" No "I'm sorry." Just silence.

The door clicked shut behind him, and with it, something inside me did too. I had nearly died, again, and all I got was his back. I didn't cry. I learned something colder than pain. I learned what it meant to be invisible.

* * *

His temper stayed unpredictable. Living with an alcoholic was like tiptoeing through a minefield, each step loaded with the threat of explosion. Any mistake could become a catastrophe. By the time

Christmas came, whatever innocence I had left felt like it had been burned off, stitched over, and silenced.

Despite our Jewish heritage, we clung to the story of Santa Claus. Not because it made sense, but because we needed something to believe in. Something kind, mysterious, and hopeful.

That year, the house was filled with tension, not joy.

"Eddie, keep your room spotless," my mother whispered. "We mustn't give your father any reason to be angry."

"Yes, Mom," I said, already holding my breath.

"Do you think Santa will bring that toy you wanted?" Diane asked me that night. She was nine; still hopeful.

"I hope so," I whispered back; and he did.

On Christmas morning, Santa brought me a Creepy Crawler gummy maker oven. For a brief moment, the house felt lighter. My mom smiled. Diane leaned in with wonder. My brother knelt beside me. Even my father seemed calm, almost playful.

"Here, Eddie," he said, handing me the machine. "Pour it carefully."

My hands shook. I leaned over the table, trying so hard not to spill. I wanted to get it right.

Then, my fingers slipped.

The liquid splattered.

His face hardened.

"You idiot!" he shouted, grabbing the toy from my hands and hurling it against the wall. The plastic shattered. The room froze.

"You're useless," he spat.

Tears stung my eyes. "You broke my present from Santa . . ."

That's when he looked at me, furious and disgusted. "You know Santa isn't real, right? It's all a lie. Just like everything else in this house."

His words hit harder than his hands ever did.

I looked down at the broken pieces. Whatever magic was left in me, whatever I had been holding onto, leaked out like the ruined candy mix across the floor.

My mother stood frozen. Diane's face crumpled. My brother clenched his fists, helpless.

"Go to your room!" my father roared, pointing sharply. His eyes blazed with fury; his face twisted in anger.

I didn't dare argue. I hurried away, leaving behind the broken pieces of my toy and carrying my shattered innocence with me. In my room, I sat on my bed, feeling the weight of his words pressing down on me. For the first time I whispered the words: "I'm not crazy; he is!" At the same time, I fought against the creeping doubt that maybe, just maybe, I was the one at fault. I had to believe it. I had to hold onto that one small truth, or else risk being swallowed by the chaos.

I began scratching into the wall beneath my bed; a spot only I knew about. Each letter was jagged, my small hands trembling as I fought to keep the line straight. The effort took all my focus, and for those moments, the act of writing became my entire world. The fear of getting caught only made me more determined. My heart pounded louder with each scratch as the letters began to take shape, giving me purpose amidst the chaos.

I, I wrote, taking extra care to make the letter straight; *m,* then *n, o, t . . .*

As I etched each letter, the words slowly formed: *I'm not crazy; he is!*

When I finished, I sat back and looked at the crude, uneven letters. Those hidden words became my secret refuge; a lifeline in the storm. I whispered them whenever the chaos surged, reminding myself that the madness wasn't mine. It was survival and the first seed of something profound. I didn't know it then, but those words were my first act of reclaiming truth, my first quiet step toward healing. I repeated them when his rage surged, reminding myself the problem was his. It gave me a sliver of control in an uncontrollable world.

Later that evening, as I lay quietly in my bed, my father entered without knocking, his shadow stretching across the floor like a dark omen. He closed the door behind him with a deliberate click, the sound heavy in the silence.

He leaned against the wall, his body swaying slightly, the sharp smell of alcohol and cigarettes wafting through the air. His eyes fixed on me with a hard stare. "You listen to me," he began, his voice low and with a sharp, threatening edge. "You better not tell any of the other kids that Santa isn't real. Do you hear me?"

I nodded, my heart pounding in my chest. The stench of alcohol mixed with the tension in the room made me feel sick. There was no room for questions, no space for the hurt that swelled inside me, and certainly no apology from him.

"If you do," he continued, his tone growing colder, "you'll ruin it for them. You don't want to be the one to ruin *everything*, do you?"

His words stung because of the threat they carried and what they revealed. He didn't care that Santa was ruined for me, that he had taken something precious and irretrievable from my sister and me. It was clear he cared about all the other children, about preserving their innocence. That contrast, his indifference toward us and concern for others, spoke volumes, cutting deeper than any punishment.

I could only shake my head; my voice was trapped behind the lump in my throat.

"Good," he said, straightening up, clearly satisfied with my silent submission, as he added, "Remember, this stays between us.

Now go to sleep." His commanding voice left no room for argument as he raised one eyebrow, a gesture that always made it clear he meant business. I hadn't even had lunch or dinner, but I didn't dare argue. I just nodded again, my stomach churning.

He turned and left the room, the door closing behind him with a final, heavy thud. I was left alone, with the secret of what was happening to us behind the walls of our home, and with the painful understanding that the magic of Santa was just another shattered illusion, one I had to hide, even as it lay in pieces around me.

A little while later, I heard a soft knock on the door before it gently creaked open. My mother stepped in, holding a sandwich on a small plate.

"Eddie," she whispered, her voice barely audible, as if she were afraid of my father hearing. She closed the door behind her with a quiet click and walked over to the bed where I sat.

She sat down beside me, her movements slow and deliberate, as if she were trying not to startle me. "I brought you something to eat," she said softly, offering the sandwich with a small, weary smile.

"Where's Dad?" I asked.

"He's sleeping," she replied, her voice a mixture of relief and caution.

I took the plate from her hands, my fingers brushing against hers. The simple gesture of kindness made the knot in my chest loosen just a little. As I chewed, she reached out and gently brushed a strand of hair from my face. "I'm sorry, honey," she murmured, her voice heavy with sadness. "I know it's been a hard day."

I nodded, unable to find the words to respond. The simple act of eating brought a fleeting sense of normalcy; a brief escape from the weight of the day.

She sat with me in silence for a moment, her presence a small comfort in the heavy quiet that had settled over the house. Then, with a soft sigh, she began to tell me a story, her voice gentle and soothing, trying to mend what had been broken.

"Once upon a time, there was a brave little boy who faced many challenges but never gave up," she began, her voice wrapping around me like a warm blanket. "You know," she continued softly, "that brave little boy, he had a heart full of courage. No matter what happened, he always found a way to keep going. And do you know why? Because he knew that even when things were hard, there was always something good waiting for him, just around the corner."

She then brushed my hair back gently, her fingers soothing against my forehead. "You're just like that little boy, Eddie," she went on. "You're stronger than you know. Every time you face something difficult, you grow a little bit more. One day, all the strength you're building inside will help you overcome everything that stands in your way."

She finished by placing a soft kiss on my forehead. She gently tucked me into bed, smoothing the covers and making sure I was comfortable. Then, in her soft, reassuring voice, she had me repeat the same comforting words her mother had spoken to her when she was a child: "Good night, sleep tight, wake up bright, to do what's right, before the night."

With those words lingering in the air, she quietly left the room. I repeated them silently as she did. They became more than just a lullaby; they became a moral compass. In a world of chaos, they were a thread of clarity I could hold onto.

* * *

Even with the constant fear and turmoil, there were rare, fleeting moments of joy, brief respites that reminded me life could hold something other than pain. One such moment came on my cousin Elana's sixth birthday. Aunt Audre took a group of us to see the movie *Born Free* to celebrate. She and I shared a special bond. My release from the hospital happened on her birthday, February twenty-first. That day had been complicated, but what stayed with me wasn't the pain. It was Aunt Audre's warmth, the way she lit up the room, the way she made me feel seen.

It was the first movie I had ever seen in a theater, and sitting next to Aunt Audre, I experienced a rare surge of excitement and anticipation. As the lights dimmed and the movie began, I felt a wave of awe wash over me. The lioness Elsa's journey from captivity to freedom wasn't just a story; it awakened something deep inside me, a desperate yearning for escape. Sitting beside Aunt Audre, I felt a fleeting sense of what freedom might feel like: warmth, safety, and the possibility of a world beyond my father's rage. I didn't have the words then, but the feeling ran soul deep: the ache of being trapped, the hunger to be free. That afternoon in the theater, I felt what it meant to be seen, to be safe, and to matter.

My bond with Aunt Audre felt sacred. Her love never hurt. She was one of the first people I could truly trust and her kindness became a lifeline.

I glanced at her during the movie, her face glowing in the flickering light. She was absorbed in the story, and her presence made me feel safe and seen. Elsa's journey mirrored my own: the longing to be free from fear.

Afterward, we excitedly shared our favorite parts. She listened with genuine interest, smiling gently. "Wasn't Elsa so brave?" she said, squeezing my hand. "Just like you, Eddie."

I often dreamt of living with her and Uncle Bert. Those small moments of joy were rare but they gave me hope. Enough to keep going. Their home felt happy and safe. Not quiet, but the kind of loud that made you feel alive. Audre was always larger than life, laughing from the gut, talking with her hands, and filling every room with energy. Uncle Bert was steady—calm and warm, the kind of man who listened when you spoke and never raised his voice. In their home, I felt seen. I felt wanted. Those small moments gave me something I didn't find anywhere else.

Hope.

One night, I overheard my parents talking in low voices outside their bedroom door; fragments like "tests," "not good," and "soon." I wasn't supposed to hear any of it. No one explained anything. They just carried on, pretending everything was normal.

Then one day, Uncle Bert was gone.

No goodbye and no explanation. No funeral for the kids, just a quiet erasure.

After that, my father continued to unravel.

He would sit in the dark, smoking, the room thick with the smell. Always with a drink in hand: sometimes from a glass, sometimes straight from the bottle. It didn't matter. The ashtray filled up either way.

He talked to himself, to the past, to the silence. Then out of nowhere, he'd explode.

"Why not me?!" he shouted once, slamming his hand on the table. "Why him?!"

Sometimes, he didn't have to say a word. He'd just stare at me, eyes narrow, unreadable. Not with love. Not with grief.

As if he was asking, "Why not *you*?"

I felt it in my spine.

His gaze would land hard—piercing, distant. *Why not you?*

That stare never left me.

It was not love.

I was seven.

That's when I stopped looking for safety. I stopped expecting rescue.

Every day and every night, I whispered to myself, "I'm not crazy; he is." It was the only thing that made sense. The only thing I could hold on to.

That mantra became my lifeline.

Soon something else would crack through the darkness.

A flicker, a moment, a spark.

Just a few years later, on a sweltering night in Miami, the world looked up—and so did I.

CHAPTER 4

TAKING ONE BRAVE STEP FORWARD

Each step you take toward growth is a personal leap toward resilience. Like walking on the moon, learn to navigate your own path, even in the dark.

I was not prepared for the spark of hope on that hot Miami evening. The world was on the brink of a historic achievement, and for a moment, it felt as though anything was possible, even for a boy like me.

The Miami heat was intense that night, but it couldn't dampen my excitement. Just a few weeks past my tenth birthday, I felt the thrill of something extraordinary in the air. The cramped apartment seemed less important as we gathered around the TV, waiting for history to unfold. The space was tiny: just one bedroom, with an old, dirty smell that clung to everything. My sister and I slept on the sofa, and though the apartment was just a few blocks from our grandparents, it felt like a world away from the life we had left behind in Chicago. We had moved only two weeks earlier, filled with excitement and hope that the change would bring the new beginning my father had promised.

The show was interrupted by a live broadcast. Walter Cronkite appeared, his steady, reassuring voice breaking through the noise, announcing the historic moment that was about to unfold.

It was close to eleven at night on July 20, 1969, when Cronkite's voice crackled through the tiny speaker: "The Eagle has landed." His excitement was palpable, even through the black-and-white images on the screen. We all held our breath as Neil Armstrong began his descent from the lunar module, each careful movement magnified by the bulky suit. The world seemed to stand still as he paused at the bottom rung, his boot hovering just above the moon's surface.

"That's one small step for man," Armstrong's voice echoed through the transmission, slightly distorted but clear enough to sear itself into our memories. As his boot finally touched the lunar dust, he continued, "One giant leap for mankind." The screen showed the historic moment as his foot pressed into the powdery surface, leaving an imprint that would be remembered for generations.

I watched in awe, completely captivated by what was happening. For that brief moment, it felt like anything was possible. If a man could walk on the moon, then maybe the wildest dreams really could come true. As I sat there, glued to the screen, as a spark of hope flickered within me, a hope that maybe, just maybe, the promises my father made about our new life in Miami could come true as well.

He had told us that moving there would be a fresh start; that we would be happier, safer, and more secure. The thought of living in a home free from constant fear, where my father's anger wouldn't dominate every moment, where my sister and I could sleep peacefully through the night; it didn't seem so far-fetched in that instant. Watching Neil Armstrong take those first steps on the moon, I allowed myself to believe, even if just for a fleeting moment, that a better life was possible for us too. Maybe, like the astronauts, we could navigate the unknown and land safely in a place where we could finally thrive.

As quickly as that hope appeared, reality began to creep back in. The excitement of the moon landing was undeniable, and so was the unpredictability of my father's temper. Still, in that brief moment of wonder, I clung to the possibility that for once, things might truly change for the better.

While the world was captivated by that monumental achievement, my reality was far removed from the celebrations taking place across the globe. By the time the moonwalk ended, my father, as usual, was drunk. His appearance was disheveled, his eyes bloodshot, and his movements unsteady. He slurred his words as he stumbled through the small apartment. When he looked at me, he raised one eyebrow, a gesture I had come to recognize as a sign of his anger. "You don't respect me," he spat into my face. My heart pounded, fear gripping me as I braced for what might come next. The contrast between the awe-inspiring event I had just witnessed and the impending dread in my living room was almost too much to bear.

In a moment of desperate defiance, my voice trembling, I blurted out, "I respect you, but I'm afraid of you."

He stared at me in silence for what felt like an eternity, his expression unreadable. Then he said, "Afraid of me? If you're afraid of me, I'll give you something to be afraid of." Then he commanded me to scrub the bathtub with my toothbrush.

At midnight, the moon landing was still playing in the background, with the voices of Walter Cronkite and the astronauts providing a surreal soundtrack to my thoughts. I fetched my toothbrush and knelt beside the old, stained tub. The toothbrush felt absurdly small in my hand, like everything else I had to face with tools far too fragile, but I began scrubbing with all my might, determined to meet the impossible challenge. The task felt monumental, as if I were trying to scrub away not just the dirt but the fear and helplessness that had taken root inside me.

At around one in the morning as I continued my futile efforts, the broadcast announced the end of the moonwalk. The astronauts were back inside the lunar module, their historic mission almost complete. There, in that small bathroom, my own mission felt far from over.

I worked and repeated my mantra silently, over and over: "I'm not crazy; he is!" I felt a surge of strength with each repetition. "I'm," I whispered fiercely, pressing the toothbrush harder against the grime. The resistance of the dirt only fueled my determination. "Not," I continued, my grip tightening, my movements becoming more aggressive. The grime began to yield under the force of my resolve.

"Crazy," I muttered through gritted teeth, scrubbing with renewed vigor. The rhythm of the mantra synchronized with the motions of my hand. The dirt and stains slowly faded, revealing the white porcelain beneath. I felt a small triumph with every speck of grime that disappeared.

"He is," I repeated, a surge of energy coursing through me. The mantra was more than just words; it was my anchor, my shield against the chaos around me. I scrubbed every inch of the tub with unwavering dedication, each stroke empowering my inner strength. Despite my exhaustion, my mantra kept my energy fueled. Nonetheless, I was scared, terrified that he would inspect the tub and find a single flaw, something that would set him off all over again.

It took nearly two hours to scrub the tub clean. My hands were raw, my arms aching. Still, I kept going.

"I'm not crazy; he is!" I whispered it over and over as I worked, the toothbrush moving like it had something to prove.

The grime faded. The porcelain gleamed. The mantra steadied me.

I was terrified he'd inspect it and find something wrong, that he'd explode all over again. When I finally stepped out of the bathroom, the house was silent.

He was passed out. Loud snores echoed from the bedroom.

I stood there for a long moment, toothbrush still in hand, watching him sleep.

I had finished the job. He never even checked.

A few months later after we settled into our home in Northwest Miami where we continued to live in fear, his cycle of drinking, rage, sickness, and remorse became even more frequent. School offered a partial respite, though my struggles to concentrate tainted it. I was always obsessed with whether or not my father would be home when I got there and what trouble awaited. I fruitlessly yearned for approval at home, so I sought it from teachers. With so many students in the classroom, they were oblivious to my struggles. I struggled academically, distracted by the turmoil at home and the constant fear that a bad grade would cause a major reaction.

Each morning, I carried a knot in my stomach to school, worry packed tight beside my homework. I wanted to learn, grow, and matter, but my mind kept drifting home, back to the war I wasn't sure I'd survive. The anxiety was a constant companion, making it difficult to focus on my lessons. My mind would wander, replaying the scenes of my father's outbursts, and I would catch myself glancing at the clock, dreading the end of the school day.

The fear of bringing home a bad grade was paralyzing. I would stare at my assignments, my hands trembling, imagining my father's angry face. The pressure to do well was immense. The constant stress and fear made it nearly impossible to succeed. I was trapped in a vicious cycle, unable to escape.

* * *

One evening, after another one of his outbursts, he cornered me in the kitchen. His breath was heavy with the stench of alcohol, his eyes wild, and I knew in that moment that there would be no escape from his wrath.

"Why can't you do anything right?" he slurred, his voice laced with venom. "You're *useless*, just like your *mother*."

That line hit harder than the slap. He didn't just attack me; he erased her too. In that moment, I knew: his cruelty was bigger than me.

I stood there, trembling, unable to respond. His words sliced into me. No matter how hard I tried, it was never enough. The more I attempted to appease him, the more his fury seemed to grow, feeding on my fear and desperation. I felt myself shrinking under the weight of his hatred, my spirit crumbling with every word he hurled at me.

"Answer me!" he commanded, his voice sharp and demanding, making me flinch.

"I don't know," I finally whispered, my voice barely audible, overwhelmed by the intensity of his anger.

"If you don't know, who does?" he snapped back, his words cutting through me like a knife. The question hung in the air, heavy and oppressive, as if demanding an answer I could never give.

Finally, having drained every ounce of venom he had, he shoved me to the floor. The impact sent a sharp pain through my side, but I didn't cry out. I just lay there, avoided his eyes, and waited for the next blow. He slapped me across the head so hard that my ears rang, and I felt my head spin.

I tasted blood where my teeth had cut into my lip, but I didn't dare wipe it away. My whole body ached. The physical pain was nothing compared to the emotional torment that gnawed at my insides. His words kept echoing in my mind, each one reverberating like an unyielding drumbeat: "Useless . . . disappointment . . . stupid . . ."

He spat on me, the warm, wet saliva landing on my face, mingling with the tears I could no longer hold back. The disgusting taste and smell of stale cigarettes and alcohol made me gag, my stomach churning with a mix of revulsion and helplessness. My vision blurred as I watched him turn and stumble away, his anger spent for the moment. The sound of his heavy footsteps faded as he left the room.

For a long moment, I didn't move. I couldn't. My body felt numb, paralyzed by a mixture of pain and disbelief. How had it come to this? How had I become so small, so powerless in the face of his relentless cruelty? I wanted to scream, to cry out for help. I knew it would do no good. No one would come; no one ever did.

Slowly, I picked myself up off the floor, every movement sending a jolt of pain through my bruised and battered body. As I made my way to the bathroom, I repeated my mantra in my mind: *I'm not crazy; he is!* The words were like a lifeline; something to cling to in the aftermath of his rage. I washed myself off as best as I could, scrubbing away the traces of blood and spit, though I knew the stains of his words would linger long after the physical marks faded. "I'm not crazy; he is!" I whispered to myself, letting the words rise above the ache. It wasn't healing yet, but it was the beginning of holding onto something true; something *mine*.

I went to bed, curling up under the covers as though they could somehow shield me from the darkness. I repeated the words with a steady rhythm in my mind. I felt degraded, small, and unloved; the weight of his words pressing down on me like a leaden blanket. As I lie there in the dark, the tears came again, silently soaking into my pillow. I cried from the pain and for the aching loneliness that filled every corner of my heart. Even as the tears fell, my mantra persisted, a quiet rebellion against the despair.

Unlike before, hope felt like a distant memory. I had come to terms with the grim reality that one day he might go too far. The only thing I had left was my mantra, a thin barrier against the inevitable. I repeated the words with a fragile shield against the darkness. As I drifted into a restless sleep, I clung to those words, "I'm not crazy, he is," the only part of me that still felt whole.

CHAPTER 5

THE SHIELD

The presence of someone who understands can turn fear into courage and despair into hope; the quiet support of a single person can make all the difference.

While the world celebrated progress beyond Earth's bounds, I was learning how to survive in a world where fear ruled every corner of my home. My growth wasn't inspired by triumph, it was forged in silence, shaped by pain, and carved out of necessity. I didn't know it then, but every terrifying moment was quietly building something inside me: the strength to adapt, the instinct to protect, and the refusal to let it become my legacy.

My father's punishments were frequent, arbitrary, and always foreshadowed by the chilling phrase, "Wait until we get home." Those words were enough to send a cold shiver down my spine; a prelude to the pain that awaited.

There's one instance that stands out more vividly than the others, etched into my memory with a clarity that time can't erase. We were out with friends, and my father had a strict rule: children should be seen and not heard. We were meant to be his trophies; silent and obedient. I never could do that. I wanted to be part of everything happening around me, so I began speaking in that excited voice that only a ten-year-old can muster when they are truly engaged in a conversation.

I felt the atmosphere shift. My father's gaze bore into me like a laser, his raised eyebrow a silent warning. My heart skipped a beat. Then, with a forced smile still plastered on his face, he leaned over and whispered in a tone that was cold and cutting, "Wait 'til we get home."

The meaning behind his words was all too clear. Dread settled in my stomach, heavy and cold, as if I were already feeling the blows that were to come. Before I could even process it, he reached out, gripping my arm with just enough pressure to make his point without making a scene. "Come with me," he said, standing up abruptly.

He guided me to a secluded corner, away from prying eyes and curious ears. I looked up at him, my heart pounding. His expression was unreadable, a mask of stern authority. "What have I told you about speaking?" His voice was low, measured, and laced with anger.

"I—I'm sorry, Dad," I stammered, my voice trembling. "I just wanted to be part of it."

His eyes narrowed. "It's not your place," he growled in a low voice so only I could hear. "You know what I told you; children should be seen and not heard! What part of that do you not understand?"

I nodded quickly, tears pricking at the corners of my eyes.

He leaned in closer, his face inches from mine. "When we get home, you're going to remember why you need to follow the rules."

The ride home in the backseat was unbearable, the silence heavy with the unspoken punishment that awaited me. I sat there, my hands clenched in my lap, knowing my destiny. Every bump in the road felt like a countdown to the pain that would soon come.

"Get over here," he commanded.

I shuffled forward, my legs trembling. "Please, Dad," I whispered, tears already forming in my eyes. "I didn't mean to . . ."

"Quiet," he snapped, cutting me off. "You know the rules. Children should be seen and not heard! Now, bend over and touch your toes."

Standing in the living room, with my pants down, I bent over and touched my toes as ordered, bracing myself for the inevitable sting of the belt buckle against my bare skin. The room seemed to close in around me, every breath heavy with the knowledge of what was about to happen. The living room, with its dim lighting and heavy curtains, became a chamber of horrors. Any sign of pain or defiance, such as crying too soon or not soon enough, only escalated the severity of the beatings, creating a lose-lose situation fraught with fear and dread. The moments before the first strike were the worst, as my heart raced and my stomach churned, knowing there was no escape.

I obeyed, feeling the cool air on my exposed skin. He slowly reached for his belt and unbuckled it slowly. The leather slid through the loops with a sharp hiss. Then he folded it in half; tight, deliberate, and creaking with tension. He stood over me, a towering figure of rage and authority. His face was twisted in anger, eyes burning with fury as he glared down at me.

"Do you know why you're being punished?" he demanded, his voice low and menacing.

"Yes," I managed to choke out, my voice barely a whisper as tears threatened to spill over.

"Speak up," he growled. "I can't hear you."

"Yes, sir," I said louder, the words trembling as they left my mouth.

"Good," he said, almost mockingly. "This is going to hurt me more than it will you."

I squeezed my eyes shut, trying to brace myself for the pain. The moments stretched into what felt like an eternity. The anticipation was almost worse than the beating itself. My heart pounded in my chest, my breath coming in short, panicked gasps.

"Don't you dare cry," he warned. "Not until I say you can."

The first strike landed with a searing pain that ripped through my body. I bit my lip, stifling a scream. The belt came down again and again, each blow worse than the last. Tears streamed down my face, but I fought to keep quiet, knowing that any sound would only make it worse.

"You're going to learn to listen to me," he snarled between strikes. "Do you hear me?"

"Yes, sir," I sobbed, the words barely intelligible through my tears.

I stayed bent over, too afraid to move until he gave me permission. The pain was unbearable; the emotional sting of his words cut even deeper. He was trying to explain away his behavior, to make me feel sorry for him. Poor Dad *had* to spank his worthless kid.

"Get up," he said, his voice devoid of any emotion.

I slowly straightened, my body trembling. He stood there, watching with a look of disdain.

"Pull your pants up," he ordered. "And remember this the next time you think about talking when you don't have my permission."

I hurried to obey, my hands shaking. As I dressed, he turned and left the room, leaving me standing there, alone and in pain. The living room was a place of fear and dread.

Every time I heard the sound of his belt, the memories would flood back. It was a cycle of terror that I couldn't escape, no matter how hard I tried.

He forced my sister and mother to watch. Diane turned away. My mother stood silent, eyes hollow, powerless to stop it. My brother had already moved out, escaping the chaos. The guilt of not being able to intervene hung over us all.

* * *

Recently, my childhood friend Jay shared that he had witnessed one of these ritual beatings. Though I have no memory of him being there, the event remains vivid in his mind even after more than fifty years.

Jay looked at me with a mixture of sadness and determination in his eyes. "Ed," he began, his voice steady, laced with emotion, "I've never forgotten. It's haunted me all these years."

I could see the pain in his expression as he recounted the event. "Both you and Diane had done something that upset your father. I don't even remember what it was, but he was furious."

Jay paused, taking a breath, building the courage to continue. "When your father started, I felt horrible. I didn't want to be there. I wanted to go into your bedroom so I wouldn't have to watch. Your father commanded me to stay. He didn't just want to punish you; he wanted to make sure I saw it too."

Jay's eyes watered as he continued. "I remember standing there, paralyzed with fear and helplessness. He made you stand in the middle of the living room, pull down your pants, and bend over. The look on your face, Ed . . . it was like you were bracing yourself for the worst."

Jay clenched his fists, his voice breaking slightly. "He stood over you, and then he struck. The sound of the belt buckle hitting into you was sickening. You cried out in pain, and he growled at you to stop crying and hit you again."

He wiped a tear from his cheek. "I cried that night, Ed. I cried for you, for Diane, for the injustice of it all. I was so angry with myself for not stopping it, but what could I have done? I was only twelve. I felt so powerless. There was nothing I could have done to stop him. Nothing."

I hadn't remembered it the way Jay had, but hearing the pain in his voice all these years later hit me in a place I hadn't touched. Jay's memory reminded me: I wasn't completely invisible. Even back then, someone saw what was happening, and never forgot. Sometimes, just knowing you were seen can become a quiet form of support that stays with you, long before you recognize its power.

Jay's tears mirrored the pain I had carried for so long. His account revealed how far the abuse affected not only my immediate family but also the few who witnessed it from the outside. It was a reminder that the cycle of pain rippled out, touching everyone around it.

From my father's perspective, it was discipline. He believed that children needed to be corrected harshly to learn their place. "They need to learn respect," he would often say. "They need to understand consequences."

There were times when I had difficulty sitting in my seat in class due to the injuries. The welts and open wounds on my skin were a constant reminder of the violence I endured. I never told anyone. He said that if I told anyone, I would be punished again. The secrecy was suffocating; a heavy burden I carried alone.

The pain was excruciating. Worse was the psychological torment of expecting each beating; a slow, dread-filled wait that gnawed at my soul.

I adapted before I even knew that's what I was doing. Watching his footsteps, the flicker in his eyes, the tightness in his jaw; these weren't school lessons. They were survival skills and strangely, they became part of a skill set I would carry forward in life, using them to navigate tough meetings, cultural divides, and the unpredictability of leadership.

The belt being unbuckled and the slow, menacing swoosh of the leather as he removed it and prepared to strike were sounds that echoed in my nightmares. Each blow felt like fire against my skin, leaving welts that would later turn into open wounds and bruises.

Many nights, I lie in bed unable to sleep on my back; the physical pain of welts and wounds a constant reminder of the violence endured. Each night brought its own kind of torment, as the pain of the day's beatings throbbed relentlessly, and the fear of what tomorrow might bring loomed larger. The darkness of my room offered no respite, only a space to replay the horrors and dread the future. In those dark moments, I clung to the words I had scratched into the wall beneath my bed when we lived in Chicago: *I'm not crazy; he is!* Those hidden words were my refuge, a small but vital defense against the overwhelming fear and pain.

To shield my sister, I often took the blame. That quiet loyalty, the kind born in silence and pain, became our bond.

Despite the overwhelming fear, a part of me still held on to *hope*. My sister and I didn't talk much, but we shared one unspoken understanding: survive. We each tried, in our own way, to avoid his fury, and sometimes, that meant silently shielding each other. My mother, though fearful and scarred, did her best to put on a brave face for us.

The bruises faded, but the emotional damage stayed, shaping how I saw the world and myself. The fear and dread seeped into every corner of my life, becoming an inseparable part of who I was. Over time, though, something shifted. The same memories that once held me back eventually became the fuel for purpose. The shadows still followed me, but so did the fire to make sure they wouldn't consume someone else. I didn't just survive; I carried the scars forward as reminders of why I speak up now. My pain would not be wasted.

I didn't know it then, but I was already living the truth that would shape my life: grow through what you go through. The words came later, but the lesson had already taken root.

CHAPTER 6

TRAPPED IN THE SILENCE

Courage isn't the absence of fear but the determination to push forward even when the shadows threaten to consume us.

Our three-bedroom house was split down the middle, my sister and I on one side, our parents on the other. The true divide wasn't walls; it was fear.

We had no real furniture, just lawn chairs. Poverty perched where comfort should've been. Every door was broken, wrecked by my father's fury. The sound of splintering wood was our home's anthem. From the outside, it looked like any other house. Inside, it was a fortress of fear. Every shattered door reminded us: danger didn't knock, it lived there.

Labor Day weekend in 1971 was a time when the unbearable Miami heat and suffocating humidity pressed in on us from all sides. Without air conditioning, the heat inside our home was stifling; amplifying the tension that was always simmering just beneath the surface. The atmosphere inside our home mirrored the stifling weather. Already on edge, my father erupted in fury over a hot meal my mother had prepared. He called us into the room, his voice laced with venom, as he berated her for what he saw as an unforgivable mistake.

"You call this dinner? I work all day, and this is what I come home to? A hot meal on an even hotter day? What are you, crazy?" he roared, his face flushed with anger, already having had several drinks.

Her silence only fueled him. He shoved her so hard she hit the floor, knocking the breath out of her. Then came the flash of red, a switchblade, flicked open, cold and gleaming.

Then, he pressed the blade into her chest. A thin line of red bloomed. I froze. The heat pressed in. She didn't move. For a terrifying second, I believed she was gone. In my mind, I screamed over and over: *My father killed my mother!*

His voice pulled me out of my daze, demanding that we fetch bandages from the cabinet. After crudely patching her up, he got up off of her and stormed out of the house, heading for the bar. The sound of his angry footsteps faded, replaced by the heavy silence of our sweltering home.

As my father got in his car, I watched from the window. His movements were erratic, driven by a toxic mix of rage and alcohol. The car roared to life, and he screeched down the street, heading to the local bar, his familiar refuge where he could drown his anger in more drinks.

My mom lay on the floor, the pain in her chest throbbing, her mind struggling to process the horror of what had just occurred. We stood frozen, eyes wide with shock, having just witnessed our father stab our mother.

In that frozen moment, I wasn't just a boy in shock, I was a child forced into growth. Survival demanded it. Every trauma expanded the well of strength I didn't know I had. It would be years before I understood it, but that moment marked the beginning of a truth I now live by: we don't grow in safety, we grow in the fire.

She wanted to comfort us, to tell us it would be okay, but the words caught in her throat, suffocated by the weight of fear.

"He'll be back," I whispered, my voice trembling with fear. I looked at my mother, desperation in my eyes. "Please, Mom, we have to call the police."

She shook her head weakly, tears streaming down her face. "They won't help us, Eddie," she whispered, her voice filled with fear and resignation. In those days, they just didn't do anything when it came to domestic violence.

"But he hurt you," I pleaded, my voice breaking. "He can't get away with this."

My mother winced as she tried to sit up, each movement making the pain in her chest and body more unbearable. "I know, honey," she said softly, reaching out to hold my hand. "But if we call them, it will only make things worse. He'll be even angrier."

I felt a surge of anger and helplessness. "We can't just do *nothing*!" I cried, tears of frustration welling up in my eyes. "We have to do something!"

"Edward, listen to me," her voice was firm despite her pain, she only called me Edward when she was angry or wanted to be sure to have my attention. "We have to be smart about this. We have to find a way to protect ourselves without making him angrier. Calling the police won't help. They won't come. If they do, they'll just leave, and he'll come back even more furious."

I looked at her, my heart aching with the weight of her words. "What are we going to do then?" I asked, my eleven-year-old voice small and defeated.

"We'll get through this," she said, trying to muster a reassuring smile.

"But *how*?" I whispered, feeling the hopelessness creeping in.

"I don't know yet," she admitted, her eyes filled with tears. "But we'll figure it out. We have to. For now, when he gets back, we need to stay quiet and try not to make him angry."

She squeezed my hand, her grip weak. I did not feel any comfort.

As we sat there, the fear and uncertainty weighing heavily on us, I made a silent vow to protect my mother and find a way to escape the nightmare we were living in. The road ahead was uncertain and filled with danger; I knew we could not give up.

* * *

When he left, I knew exactly where he was headed. Although I was just a child, he had brought me there many times before, so I could see it play out in my mind as if I were watching it happen again.

The Mint Lounge was an old, dim bar with a flickering neon sign and a reputation as worn as its lighting. Inside, smoke clung to the ceiling, mixing with the sharp reek of alcohol, cigarettes, and who knows what else. The smell alone could cling to your clothes for days. Nearly naked dancers swayed under tired spotlights, scanning the room for someone to charm.

I had been there enough times with him to know every corner. The sticky carpet under my shoes, the sting of smoke in my eyes, the rattle of glasses against the bar. No one dared point out that a kid my age had no business being there. They simply looked the other way.

I pictured him at the bar, fist slamming down. "Whiskey. *Neat.*"

The bartender, a burly man with a grizzled beard who had worked there for years, didn't flinch, just poured without comment. The first sip would have burned his throat, but it was never enough. Drink after drink, he tried to drown the fire inside him.

But the haze didn't soften him; it sharpened the edges. He glared at the stage, unmoved by the dancers' painted-on smiles. One of them, a tall blonde with practiced eyes, sauntered over, hips swaying.

"Hey there, handsome," she purred. "Want some company?"

He smirked, slurring. "Maybe. You always this friendly?"

"Just trying to make a living," she said, fingers brushing his glass. "Rough night?"

"Rough life."

She smiled. "Maybe I can help."

He leaned in, drunk enough to believe her. "It's been hell. But things are looking up."

She flagged the bartender. "Another?"

"Keep 'em coming," he said, puffing up with false charm.

They drank and flirted. Her laugh was soft, perfectly timed. His hand grazed hers, and she let it. He believed she meant it.

"You're something special," he muttered.

"You're not so bad yourself," she replied.

As the bar thinned out, so did the illusion.

"Got plans after your shift?" he asked.

"Maybe," she teased. "Stick around."

He grinned, convinced. The bartender finally approached, eyes firm. "Time to go."

"Yeah, yeah," he grumbled. He looked back at the blonde. "See you around?"

"Take care," she said with a smile that meant nothing.

Outside, the night air was heavy. The neon sputtered and went dark. I could see him standing there, blinking, bitter, and boiling. The whiskey hadn't helped. The attention hadn't helped. Nothing helped.

He stumbled toward his car, each step heavier than the last. The drive home was a blur of honking horns, swerving tires, and shouted curses. Red lights were insults, other drivers, enemies.

When he pulled into the carport, the sight of the house reignited his fury. He sat gripping the wheel, knuckles white, hatred rising like steam. Years of resentment hissed inside him.

He got out, fumbling with the keys. The lock gave way. He stepped into darkness. Silence. The hum of the refrigerator. His own breath.

I wasn't there that night, but I didn't need to be. I had lived it enough times to know exactly how it would have unfolded, and exactly what it meant when he came back through that door.

* * *

It was after two in the morning when I heard the door open as he stepped inside. The dim rays from the carport light outside cast long shadows across the room, making the house feel even more oppressive to him. He stood there for a moment, taking in the familiar surroundings: the living room filled with lawn furniture because that was all they could afford, and the ragged carpeting; they were all reminders of a life filled with disappointment and turmoil.

I had seen it countless times—the way his eyes narrowed when he staggered through the door, scanning the room like he was looking for someone to blame. His jaw would tighten as he ground his teeth, and I could almost feel the heat of his anger before he said a word. My stomach knotted, and my chest tightened as I braced myself. I already knew what was coming.

His steps were heavy and uneven, yet each one carried a terrible certainty. There was never an escape. The storm inside him always broke over us. He would make sure we carried his pain, frustration, and rage.

I tried to disappear into the smallest version of myself, barely breathing, hoping he might not notice me. The silence of the house cracked under the weight of his voice. Low, sharp, and filled with menace, it cut through the stillness:

"I'm home."

His words dripped with fury and warning. My body froze. Every muscle tensed with the anticipation of the first strike.

With that, the night descended into greater darkness, and the fragile few hours of peace shattered. He stumbled from room to room, the heavy scent of alcohol and cigarettes preceding him. His presence filled the house with fear. He was more volatile, more unpredictable. The night stretched on, a never-ending nightmare as he ranted and raged, creating a house of horrors that left us all traumatized. The oppressive heat, the violence, and the fear became a permanent part of my memories, a dark cloud that loomed over that Labor Day weekend.

I could hear him muttering to himself, the slurred words of a man lost in his rage and alcohol. I lay in my bed, unable to sleep. The heat pressed down on me, mingling with the fear that gripped my heart. Sweating from head to toe, my body was enveloped in fear. The door to my room busted open. He stood there, the dim light casting shadows on his menacing face. A storm of emotion raged in me. I hated him, but a small part still ached for the father I never had.

Then the blade touched my throat. His voice was flat, his eyes empty. "I already took care of your mother and sister," he said. "Are you ready to die?"

Inside, I was screaming, *Do it already—just end it!*

Outside, I whimpered, "Please, Dad. Don't. I want to live."

My mind spun, clinging to the only thing that made sense: *I'm not crazy; he is.*

I could feel the tension in the air, the moment teetering on the edge of life and death. Then, without a word, he pulled the blade away, leaving me trembling with fear and disbelief. He turned and left, his footsteps fading as the reality of what had just happened began to sink in.

He returned three or four times throughout the next two days repeating the same actions. In between, I didn't dare leave my room, except for brief, terrified trips to the bathroom, navigating the house in a state of paralyzing fear.

The Jerry Lewis MDA Telethon blared in the background: jokes, songs, and tearful appeals for compassion. Its cheerful host rallied the nation to support children with muscular dystrophy, filling the screen with hope and unity. Meanwhile, our house was imploding. The laughter and applause felt like a cruel joke, echoing through rooms soaked in silence and fear.

America was raising millions for strangers; we couldn't get help inside our own walls.

Every upbeat song, every touching story only deepened the contrast. It was surreal, like the television existed in another universe where people cared, where kindness lived. In our universe, we were hostages. No donations. No rescue. Just dread, hiding in plain sight.

That weekend, the telethon became more than background noise. It became a taunting reminder of everything we didn't have: safety, comfort, and witnesses. It asked people to care, yet no one cared about us.

Early Monday morning, the house was unnervingly quiet. I stepped out of my room and crept across the narrow hallway to my sister's door. For a moment, I froze, unsure if I would find her dead or alive. I pushed the door open just enough to see her chest rise and fall in sleep. Relief washed over me, but only for an instant.

I turned toward the living room, the space that had so often been our chamber of horrors. The thin carpet barely softened the cold cement beneath it, and each step pressed the silence deeper into my chest. Memories clung to that room like shadows. Moving carefully, I crossed to the far side of the house, toward my parents' bedroom.

Each step felt like an eternity, the weight of the previous days' events pressing down on me. I had no idea where he was or if he was even home. The door to their room was open. I hesitated in the doorway as my heart pounded; every fiber of my being urged me to turn away. The curtains blocked out some of the morning light, but then, as my eyes adjusted, I saw them: my mother and father, cuddled in bed. His arm was draped over her protectively. The sight was surreal and totally different than the violence and fear that had consumed us just hours before.

My mother's eyes opened, and she looked directly at me. Her gaze was filled with exhaustion and resignation, silently pleading for understanding and forgiveness. The sight of her awake, aware, and yet lying there in his embrace as if nothing had happened, shook me to my core.

As my heart raced even faster, I ran back to my room, closed the door, and leaned against it as I tried to process what I had seen. My mind reeled, struggling to reconcile the abnormal horrors I had witnessed. *I'm not crazy; he is,* I reminded myself, trying to steady my thoughts. The dissonance between the nightmare we had lived through and the unsettling calm of the morning left me feeling disoriented, numb, and utterly alone.

On Tuesday morning, I woke up, showered, brushed my teeth, and got dressed. I packed my bag, trying to bury the memories clawing at me. Routine became a mask, fragile and thin, but better than nothing. In the mirror, I saw a pale, tired face that didn't look like mine. I forced a smile, hoping it might make things feel normal. It didn't.

As I walked out the door, the weight of the past few days pressed heavily on my shoulders. It was a burden only I could carry. I learned early how to wear a mask, to move through the world like nothing had happened. School became a place where I practiced pretending. In the contrast between chaos at home and the structure of school, I started to learn how to bend without breaking.

Jay lived just down the street. As I did every day, I stopped at his house on the way.

"Hey, Eddie, where were you this weekend?" he asked, concern in his voice. "You all right?"

I nodded, not trusting myself to speak.

As we walked, I hesitated, then whispered, "Jay . . . I need to tell you something."

He looked at me, frowning. "What is it? You look sick—are you okay?"

"My dad . . . he hurt my mom. It was bad. He stabbed her."

Jay's eyes widened. "What? Are you serious?"

I nodded. "Right in front of us. I didn't know what to do."

He slowed, hand on my shoulder. "Man, I'm so sorry. Do you want to come over after school? You can stay with us."

I shook my head. "If I don't go home, he'll know I told someone. It'll just make it worse."

"You sure?"

"I have to be careful."

He nodded. "All right. Just know—you can count on me."

Jay's kindness was a lifeline I couldn't grab, but knowing it was there mattered.

We got to school late. Jay headed to junior high, and I walked into sixth grade.

Mrs. Turner stood at the door, arms crossed.

"Eddie, why are you late? Goofing off again?"

"No, Mrs. Turner. Sorry."

"Take your seat. We'll talk later."

The other kids snickered as I passed them. I kept my head down.

The day passed in a blur. I did the assignments, but my mind stayed trapped in fear. Every noise made me flinch. I dreaded the final bell.

The walk home felt longer than ever. Kids laughed and played around me, but I was somewhere else. I kept repeating, *I'm not crazy; he is.* It became my shield.

At the door, I paused. *I'm not crazy; he is.* Then I stepped inside.

The house was quiet, the kind of silence that didn't offer comfort, but *warning.* I braced myself, hoping for peace, but prepared for the storm.

That weekend left no visible bruises, but it scarred everything. I didn't know it yet, but it planted something in me: a vow to break the silence, to give voice to the pain, to help others find their way out.

Summer turned into fall. The heat broke, but the weight stayed. On the outside, we looked calm. On the inside, the storm never left.

CHAPTER 7

WEARING THE MASK

Each challenge is a reminder that finding relevance in your actions, no matter how small, is key to navigating through the storm.

By January, the oppressive heat of that Labor Day weekend had given way to a different kind of pressure, one born from the grind of everyday life. Even in the mundane routines, there was no peace. Only tension, simmering just beneath the surface.

It was January 16, 1972, in Miami. Gas was thirty-six cents a gallon, and my father co-owned a Mobil station with full-service attendants. At the age of twelve, I worked weekends there for fifty cents an hour—but never saw a penny of it.

* * *

My mother shook me awake around midnight, her voice strained but controlled. "Get up. We need to go to the station."

That night was heavy and still, the kind of Miami humidity that made everything feel quiet and suspended. As we drove through the dark streets, she spoke quickly, her eyes fixed ahead. "Your father's been drinking again. He's made a mess. He called and said he was going to burn the place down."

Her words came in fragments, and I tried to piece them together. I could almost picture him—sitting in the small office behind the counter, hunched over the big brown desk, the rickety chair squeaking beneath him. The black-and-white TV would have been blaring Super Bowl VI, the Cowboys crushing the Dolphins. I imagined the ashtray overflowing, the bottle half empty, and his temper rising with every touchdown. When someone pulled up for gas—*ding ding*—he would have slammed his glass down, cursed, and stomped outside, furious that anyone dared to interrupt him.

By the time we reached the station, the smell of gasoline hit us before the lights came into view. The pavement glistened under the fluorescents, slick with fuel. My father stood by the pumps, cigarette in hand, muttering, "Damn Dolphins," over and over. My mother went straight to him, her voice calm but steady.

"Please, come home," she said. "You don't want to do this."

He wavered, jaw clenched, eyes glassy. "This is all I've got," he said softly.

She kept talking until, finally, he let her lead him to the car.

When they drove away, I was left standing there—an eleven-year-old surrounded by the pungent, suffocating smell of gasoline. I turned off the glowing OPEN sign, dragged the orange cones across the drive, and picked up the hose. Water hissed as it hit the pavement, sending ribbons of rainbow fuel sliding toward the drain.

The fumes stung my eyes. My arms ached. The only sounds were the faint buzz of the station lights and the occasional car passing on the road beyond. I kept rinsing, careful and slow, until the danger seemed to fade, until the ground looked normal again, even though nothing about that night felt normal.

When I finally finished, I called my mother, and she came back for me. She locked up while I stood there, exhausted and reeking of gasoline. At home, I showered and scrubbed my skin as hard as I could, trying to wash the smell away. Even after dressing for school, I could still smell it on me—and I knew others would too.

As I sat in class that same day, the buzz of chatter and the scrape of pencils against paper felt surreal, like watching a scene from a life that wasn't mine. My classmates laughed and whispered secrets, while I struggled to keep my eyes open, the weight of the night before pressing down on me like a heavy blanket. The transition from chaos to normalcy was jarring; the classroom felt like an alien world; a safe bubble far removed from the events of the night before. Adapting between two realities, school and survival, became my curriculum. I was learning far more than textbooks could teach: how to stay invisible, how to read danger, and how to function on empty.

Other students' biggest worries were math tests and playground gossip, while my mind replayed scenes of gasoline-soaked fear and the threat of fire. The noise of the classroom reverberated around me, but I felt disconnected, as if watching everything from a distance, unable to share the trauma I had endured. When the final bell rang signaling the end of the school day, a mix of relief and dread washed over me. Relief that school was over, but dread because the walk home meant facing the uncertainty that awaited me. When I met up with Jay, our usual lighthearted banter was absent. That day, silence spoke louder than words.

As we walked, Jay noticed my silence. He shot me a concerned glance and asked, "What happened this time?"

I hesitated, the weight of the night before still heavy on my mind. I knew I couldn't keep it all bottled up. I took a breath, deciding to share the burden I carried. "Last night, my dad almost burned down the gas station."

Jay's eyes widened in shock, his expression shifting from concern to disbelief. "What? Seriously?"

I nodded, my throat tightening as I recalled the chaos. "Yeah, he was drinking and got really mad when the Cowboys won. He went outside and started messing with the gas pumps. He was so drunk, he sprayed gas all over the tanks and the bay."

Jay's face paled, his steps slowing as he absorbed what I was saying. "That's insane! What happened next?"

"My mom calmed him down and took him home," I continued, my voice growing quieter. "But I had to stay up all night hosing the place down, trying to clean up the mess he made and make sure nothing would catch fire. The smell of gasoline was everywhere, and I could barely keep my eyes open by the time I finished."

Jay was silent for a moment, processing everything. His usual carefree demeanor was replaced by a serious, almost protective look. "That's messed up, man. Are you okay?"

I shrugged, trying to downplay the turmoil that had become normality. "I guess. I just keep thinking about what could have happened if my mom hadn't shown up when she did. It's scary, you know? He's so unpredictable."

He nodded, his voice softening. "I can't imagine dealing with that. You shouldn't have to."

I looked down at my feet as we walked, feeling a mixture of gratitude and frustration. Grateful that he was there to listen, but frustrated that I couldn't escape the cycle I was trapped in. "Thanks for listening, Jay. It helps to talk about it."

Jay's presence reminded me that I didn't always have to carry the weight alone. Even if I couldn't fully accept help, just knowing it was offered gave me strength. Our conversation continued, with Jay offering words of comfort and trying to lift my spirits. Beneath the surface, I could feel myself growing more cautious, always anticipating the next outburst, always ready to respond to a new crisis.

Those experiences began to influence every aspect of my life. At school, I became more vigilant, always on guard, always bracing for something to go wrong. I developed a resilience that helped me cope with the chaos at home. It also made me more withdrawn and isolated. I avoided drawing attention to myself by hiding in the shadows, not wanting anyone to see the cracks in my armor.

I was in a constant state of alert; never fully relaxed, and always bracing for the next storm. Alone with my thoughts, the weight of it all threatened to crush me.

Even then, something in me kept searching; for meaning, for a reason, for a way to make it matter. Maybe that quiet voice was the earliest whisper of purpose.

The beatings paused, but he hadn't changed. He just found new ways to hold on to his power.

PART II
VALUE THE SUPPORT OF OTHERS

Healing begins when we stop hiding. By unveiling secrets, we start finding our ground, and the moment someone sees you, the weight gets lighter. We learn to let go of false promises, to embrace the unfinished, and to grieve our way to strength. In time, through connection and courage, we find freedom through learning, and through each other.

CHAPTER 8
UNVEILING SECRETS

Even in the face of betrayal and fear, the courage to choose loyalty over manipulation can lead to the liberation of our true selves.

Marta was the wife of my father's business partner; sixteen years younger than him, and sixteen years older than me. Their affair was already in full swing by the time he pulled me in, not as a bystander, but as a confidant. He began revealing everything, confiding in me as if I was his equal. It wasn't a bond; it was a burden. The secret sat on my chest like a weight I couldn't set down. I wasn't just carrying his betrayal; I was part of it.

In exchange for my silence, my father became kinder, almost as if he were rewarding me for my complicity. The beatings that had been a constant in my life abruptly ceased. His newfound kindness was jarring, disorienting, and welcomed. I found myself torn between relief and guilt, struggling to reconcile the gentler version of my father with the man who had inflicted so much pain.

My new role was clear: I was to be the lookout. Each time they met, I stationed myself outside the front door, every sense heightened, listening intently for any sign of my mother or Marta's husband. The tension was palpable, a knot of anxiety twisting in my stomach as I carried out my duty. My ears strained to catch even the faintest sound of approaching footsteps, ready to alert them at a moment's notice.

Each time I played lookout, I felt a part of myself slipping away. The guilt gnawed at me, yet my silence was a powerful reward. For the first time in years, I didn't flinch at every sudden movement, and the constant fear that had taken up residence in my chest began to ease. I knew it was wrong, but I couldn't walk away from the one thing I had always longed for: peace.

The weight of the secret was crushing, but the silence came with its own reward. My father began confiding in me; he had plans for a life with Marta, far from everything we knew. I nodded along, torn between fear and the strange hope that the new version of himself would remain.

"I can't wait for us to move to Atlanta," he would say, his eyes lighting up with a rare spark of enthusiasm. "Marta and I have found a beautiful house there. You'll love it, Eddie. Fresh start for all of us."

"That sounds nice, Dad," I replied, forcing a smile. "I'm sure it will be great." His words reminded me of similar conversations when we moved to Miami.

He wanted me to live with him after the divorce. I pretended to be excited, and told him I couldn't wait. Inside, the idea filled me with dread. Living with him was the last thing I wanted. I knew I had to play along until the divorce was final.

"Dad, will I have my own room?" I asked one evening, trying to sound excited.

"Of course, you will. We'll set it up just the way you like it," he responded, ruffling my hair. "Marta is looking forward to having you with us. She thinks you're a great kid."

"That's good," I lied, my voice barely above a whisper as my heart pounded with trepidation.

* * *

The same day my parents signed the divorce papers, we went to the courthouse for my dad and Marta's wedding. Her kids, her parents, and I stood witness. Afterward, we returned to her house marked SOLD.

As the celebration was starting to wind down, I summoned the courage to speak my truth. He was sitting in the living room of her place, going through some paperwork. I approached him, my hands trembling.

I steadied my nerves. It was time for me to enact my own plan. "I'm not going with you to Atlanta," I said, my voice steady but my heart racing. "I'll be staying with Mom. She needs me."

His reaction was immediate and fierce. He was enraged, his face contorting with fury. "What do you mean? We had a deal. If you don't come with me . . . ," he pointed a trembling finger at my chest, ". . . then you're dead to me." The kindness he had shown during the affair vanished in an instant, replaced by the familiar anger I had known. Hearing his harsh words, Marta and her parents looked over at us.

"Mom needs me here. She can't manage on her own," I said without much emotion, trying to reason with him and definitely not wanting to tell him the truth: that I never had planned to live with him, ever. Why would I, when I finally had an opportunity to escape?

"I don't care! You are coming with me and that's final," he roared, standing up and towering over me.

I stood my ground, my fear turning into a quiet resolve. "No, Dad. I'm staying. Mom needs me."

His face twisted with rage. "You're an ungrateful little bastard!" he spat. "After everything I've done for you, this is how you repay me?" I flinched at his words and didn't back down. He raised his hand, the threat clear in his eyes, but then, with everyone watching, he lowered it. He turned away, muttering curses under his breath, leaving me standing there, shaken yet not broken.

I left Marta's house and walked the mile plus to my home, uncertain how things were going to play out. Finally, I had stood my ground. By the time I got home, he was already there, shouting at my mother.

"He's coming with me!" he screamed into her face. She had no idea what he was talking about and looked at me, questioning as I walked into the house.

"I told you already, I'm not going. I'm staying here with Mom," I said firmly.

His eyes held the same menacing look I had seen many times before. This time, I wasn't going to be his victim. I ran next door to the Cole's house, where my friend Kenny lived. He was a year younger than me, and had a younger brother and two younger sisters. Their father, Mr. Cole, was a large man who did construction for a living. Our mothers were friends, so they knew about the divorce.

"He's going to hurt her," I cried out as they opened the door. "We need your help!"

Mr. Cole didn't hesitate. He followed me back to my house, and I could hear the angry shouts from my father even before we stepped inside. Kenny and his siblings had been told to stay inside, but the shouting had drawn them to the windows. Curiosity and concern got the better of them, and soon they were at the fence, peeking through the gaps, wide-eyed and silent. They'd never seen their father like this, so serious, so determined. Their little sister clung to Kenny, her eyes filling with tears as she watched the scene unfold. They were scared too, not knowing what might happen next, but they couldn't look away.

Inside, my father was shoving my mother, his face twisted in rage. My stomach churned with fear. Mr. Cole, strong and unafraid, gave me a glimmer of hope. My sister Diane stood off to the side, her face a mask of confusion and fear. She hadn't been part of the secret plan, and now she was witnessing the storm unfold with no understanding of why. Her eyes flicked between them, confused and scared, searching for something that made sense.

Mr. Cole immediately positioned himself between my parents. My mother stood frozen. She had been on the receiving end of his anger for years, but this time was different; she wasn't alone. She could see the fear in my eyes, and it shattered her. When Mr. Cole spoke, calm and unwavering, she felt a flicker of hope. It was a feeling she hadn't known in a long time: safety.

Diane, on the other hand, was still processing the scene. The way Mr. Cole stepped between them, protecting us, made her realize something was terribly wrong. She felt small, helpless, and unsure of who to turn to.

"It's time for you to leave, Jerry," Mr. Cole said resolutely. My father protested, claiming she was keeping me from going with him. Mr. Cole stepped forward and repeated, "It's time for you to leave."

When the neighbor confronted him, I saw for the first time what a coward my father truly was. It was one thing for him to bully a child or his wife, but it was clear that he was intimidated by Mr. Cole and backed down. My father, seething with anger, balled his fists and glared at the neighbor.

"Stay out of this," he growled.

Mr. Cole didn't flinch. "Not this time, Jerry. You've done enough. Now, leave." He had dealt with men like my father, bullies fueled by fear. One wrong move, and it could all fall apart.

Furious, my father's expression distorted. Outmatched, he hesitated, his eyes darting between my mother, Mr. Cole, Diane, and me. Diane's eyes met his, and for a moment, he saw the fear and confusion there, and perhaps it dawned on him that he was losing his grip on his family. Finally, he turned and stormed out of the house, slamming the door behind him.

As he drove away, seething with humiliation, I could almost hear him swearing revenge under his breath. He wasn't going to let it go. That moment marked a turning point. I wasn't just surviving anymore, I was choosing; real strength comes from finally saying no.

My mother nearly collapsed with relief. Diane stood quietly, still trying to process everything she had seen. She felt like her world had been turned upside down, and she wasn't sure how to make sense of it.

Mr. Cole waited until he was sure my father was gone, then turned to us. "You did the right thing," he said, his voice calm and steady. Then, looking directly at me, he added, "You were brave today." He glanced at Diane, who still looked shaken, and gave her a reassuring nod, as if to tell her that everything would be okay.

We spent the afternoon at Mr. Cole's house, still tense, still watching the street, still bracing for the sound of my father's return. But something had shifted. For the first time, help had come from outside our walls. Someone had seen, stepped in, and stayed.

It didn't fix everything, but it changed *something*.

That moment was more than relief; it was when I began to understand what support could look like. Sometimes it looks like a neighbor standing between you and the storm. Sometimes it looks like someone simply refusing to walk away. That day, we weren't alone.

* * *

For years, my grandparents stopped speaking to us. My father had severed the bond, cutting us off completely. The visits, the shared stories, the warmth of our grandparents' home; everything was lost. Each holiday and birthday passed in silence, a stark reminder of the control he still exerted over our lives, even from a distance. The void left by their absence was a constant, painful reminder of the power he wielded.

There were times when I would pick up the phone, hoping to hear their voices again. I would dial their number, with a mix of hope and dread; the familiar sequence of digits bought back a flood of memories. The phone would ring, and I would wait, holding my breath, imagining what I would say when she answered. As soon as my grandmother heard my voice, she would hang up. There was no pause, no moment of recognition, just the sharp click of the receiver and the hollow silence that followed.

Each time it happened, I would stand there, phone in hand, the dial tone echoing in my ears, as the reality sank in further. She didn't fail to recognize me; she chose not to. She chose silence. The bond we once shared stood no chance against the control he held over her; over all of us.

The rejection was a confirmation of the control my father still had, even when he wasn't there. He had managed to extend his reach, to make sure that the silence was complete, unbroken by even a word of comfort from those who used to love us. The silence became a part of life, a constant companion, just as his control remained a constant shadow over everything.

Years later, my grandfather told me what really happened during that time. After my father left, he had called his parents, Mary and Les, and pulled them into his vendetta.

"If you have anything to do with them," he warned, "you're dead to me too."

His voice, my grandfather said, was icy and unwavering, the same tone that had silenced so many before.

"Jerry, you can't mean that," my grandfather protested, his voice full of shock and sadness. "They're our grandchildren. You can't expect us to cut them off."

"I do mean it, Dad," my father replied coldly. "If you keep seeing them, you won't be part of my life anymore. It's as simple as that."

My grandmother had pleaded softly, "Jerry, this isn't fair. They're innocent in all of this. We love them, and they need us."

"I don't care, Mom," he snapped. "You either choose them or me. If you choose them, consider yourself dead to me."

My grandfather told me that when the call ended, my grandmother's hands trembled as she turned to him.

"What are we going to do, Les?" she asked, her voice breaking.

He paused. With his face etched with anguish he replied, "I don't know, Mary. We can't lose our son—but this is tearing me apart."

She wept softly. "He's our only living son, Les. We've already lost our other two boys. I can't bear to lose Jerry too."

They had agreed to do what he said, hoping one day he would change his mind.

By the time my grandfather told me this years later, I had already known how far my father's control reached, how fear could twist love into silence. His anger had forced them into complicity, just as it had bound us for so long.

I had stood with my mother and sister, recognizing that we were all victims of his actions. Together, we made the decision to start breaking free from his hold, determined to reclaim our lives from the shadow he had cast over us.

As we moved forward, it became clear that the end of one chapter in our lives was just the beginning of another. The shadow of my father's influence began to fade. We were ready to rebuild; however, we knew that some pieces of our lives would always be missing.

In that brokenness, we found *our* beginning. Not in reclaiming the past, but in shaping a future on our own terms.

Healing isn't linear. His absence didn't erase the damage he left behind.

CHAPTER 9

FINDING YOUR GROUND

In the struggle to reclaim our lives, we discover that our strength lies not in the absence of pain, but in the determination to rise and rebuild despite it.

The aftermath of my father's departure didn't free us from his grip; it only tightened it in new, insidious ways. Every unpaid bill, every echo of his voice reminded us, he was still there. The broken doors spoke of past violence. The debt was suffocating; a daily reminder of the damage he left behind.

We were forced to confront the shattered remnants of our home and the fragments of our fractured identities. That is when I first learned what resilience really means. It's not about bouncing back to what was, it's about stepping into what's next, even when your footing feels unsure. "Grow through what you go through" became more than a phrase; it was survival. We weren't just behind on bills. We were broken, and we had to rebuild.

Living with my mother after the divorce brought relief and new challenges. The absence of my father's anger was a welcome change, but even with him gone, his presence lingered. It was there in every debt he left behind, in the broken family ties, and in the depression that consumed my mother.

She couldn't navigate the wreckage of the life she once knew. My father had been her only love for more than twenty-five years. Their relationship had been built on abuse and control, but even so, the thought of living without him felt impossible to her. As days turned into weeks and weeks into months, her sadness only deepened.

She would stay in bed all day, exhausted and crying, a shadow of the woman she used to be. I spent hours by her bedside, pleading with her to get up, to come outside for just a moment of sunlight. I tried everything to shake her from the darkness that had taken hold. Nothing worked. Her self-esteem had crumbled, her will to fight snuffed out like a candle in the wind.

Sometimes, I found her sitting silently by the window, staring into the distance, lost in a fog of memories and pain. Watching her fade away left me feeling helpless, a silent witness to her slow unraveling. Her friends visited less and less, their attempts to revive her spirit defeated by the depth of her sorrow.

One morning, I found her still in bed, the curtains drawn tightly shut, blocking out the morning light. The room was thick with an oppressive silence, broken only by her soft, uneven breathing. I stood in the doorway, frustration and determination bubbling up inside me. I couldn't let it continue any longer.

"Mom," I called, my voice sharper than I intended. "You can't just stay here all day. It's time to get up."

She remained motionless, her eyes staring blankly at the ceiling. The sight of her like this, day after day, drove me to the edge.

"Come on, Mom," I pressed, stepping closer. "This isn't helping anyone. Don't you even care?"

Pain crossed her face, and I felt a pang of guilt. I pushed on. "We need you, Mom. I need you. You can't just give up. Get out of bed and do something. At least try."

She turned her head slowly to look at me, her eyes brimming with tears. The sight of her so broken made my anger and frustration bubble up even more.

"I don't know how to, Eddie," she whispered, her voice trembling. "I feel so lost, so alone."

I crossed my arms, trying to keep my resolve. "He's gone, Mom. Get up and start your life. You don't need him."

She shook her head, her voice trembling. "I'm nothing without him," she protested, her words laced with despair.

"That's not true," I countered, my voice firm. "You're so much more than what he made you believe. You don't have to do it alone, but you can't just lie here and expect things to get better. You have to get up and face the day. We need you to at least try."

She closed her eyes, and for a moment, I feared she would retreat back into herself. Then she sighed, a sound so heavy it seemed to carry all her sorrow.

"Okay," she murmured, her voice barely audible. Then she shifted her weight, sat up slowly, and swung her legs over the side of the bed. She reached for the curtain and pulled it back, letting some light into the room for the first time in weeks.

A wave of relief and triumph washed over me. "Good. We'll figure this out. It starts with you getting out of bed. Come on, let's go."

I turned and walked out of the room, not waiting to see if she followed. Anger surged, fueled by the unfairness of having to take charge at just twelve years old, while still drowning in my own pain. Looking back, maybe I believed that pushing her, forcing her to feel how much we needed her, might be what finally helped her fight back. There was no compassion, no kindness; just a kid struggling to keep everything from falling apart. It was all I knew how to do.

Over time, my mother found small joys in daily activities, rediscovering the person who had been buried under years of abuse and grief. She found solace in going out with Jay's mother Blanche for coffee or walks. Blanche didn't try to fix her, she just showed up. Sometimes that's all we need. "Cultivating meaningful relationships" isn't just about surrounding yourself with people, it's about being open to those who hold space for your pain without judgment. Blanche did that. She reminded my mother and me that connection heals. They even joined a group for single parents, which provided some support and social experiences like weekly dances.

Her recovery was not linear; there were setbacks and days when the darkness threatened to swallow her again. But she kept pushing forward, driven by the need to care for us and to reclaim her life from the shadows of the past. Her smiles, though rare at first, gradually returned, bringing small bits of warmth back into our home, reminders that even in the darkest of times, light can find its way back in.

The path to healing was neither easy nor straightforward. As my mother slowly emerged from the depths of her grief, she realized we couldn't do it alone. The trauma we had endured as a family had left invisible wounds that needed more than time to heal. She insisted we go to therapy, alone and together. That decision marked a turning point: we would face the pain, not bury it.

Therapy was difficult. It forced us to face the very things we had spent years trying to escape, and confront the truth of our experiences head-on. In those sessions, we began to unravel the tangled web of our emotions, to understand the depth of the damage that had been done, and to start the process of rebuilding ourselves from the ground up.

We were provided with a safe place to name our pain, and to speak freely about the things that had happened. It drained us. We weren't chasing happiness, we were chasing stability, healing, and a sense of self beyond survival. Resilience isn't always loud. Sometimes it's an exhausted whisper of "okay" when someone says, "Let's try again tomorrow."

CHAPTER 10

SOMEONE SEES YOU

The strength to rebuild comes not just from within, but from the unwavering support of those who walk with you through the challenges.

Healing didn't come all at once. It came in pieces, hard won and uneven. Even as progress came, nothing felt guaranteed. Life continued to test us, just in new ways.

My mother's newfound resilience laid the groundwork for a new period in our lives. Graduating high school at sixteen wasn't just an academic milestone, it was a testament to my mother's determination to rebuild. Since the divorce, she never let up. We relied on food stamps and welfare, and my mother found small ways to earn extra money, such as conducting phone surveys. Her resolve to create a better future for us, even while grappling with her own past, became an obsession.

One evening, as my mother sifted through bills at the kitchen table, I watched her, my heart heavy with concern. The dim light from the lamp showed her tired face, illuminating the lines etched by years of struggle.

I took a breath and asked, "Mom, are you sure about this?" My voice trembled with a mixture of fear and worry.

Her gaze met mine. Despite her exhaustion, her eyes held a fierce determination. "Eddie, I have to do this. For us. I need to prove to myself and to you that we can have a better life," she replied, her tone firm and unyielding.

The weight of her past struggles and the mountain of debt she faced were enormous. Her new resolve was even stronger.

Her past burdens gradually lifting, she decided to take a bold step toward reclaiming control over our lives: enrolling in college. This decision symbolized a fresh start, a chance to break free from the cycle of hardship and build a new future.

The drive to campus took us through Liberty City, an area known for poverty, crime, and unrest. For my mother, every trip meant pushing through fear just to keep moving forward. In the early seventies, Liberty City was a hotbed of high crime rates and social unrest. The aftermath of the 1968 Miami Riot had left scars, exposing severe racial discrimination and economic exploitation. The neighborhood was filled with dilapidated buildings, occasional police sirens, and a pervasive sense of danger and instability.

She insisted I come with her on those drives, partly for safety, partly for courage. As we drove through Liberty City, I could see how nervous she was.

"Mom, are you okay?" I asked, trying to gauge her level of discomfort. The city's bleak surroundings mirrored the worries etched on her face.

She forced a smile. The anxiety in her eyes was unmistakable. "Just keep your eyes open, Eddie. We'll be okay. This is all part of making a better life for us," she reassured me, though her voice carried a note of strain. Her courage taught me perseverance, though it took years before I understood just how much.

That was the first time I realized learning could happen even while you're afraid. My mother wasn't just seeking a degree; she was rewriting our future. Her determination taught me that education isn't just about books. It's about reclaiming your power.

That became one of my guiding principles: Pursue Lifelong Learning and Adaptability.

I watched my mother juggle college, two kids at home, and mounting bills. She adapted because she had to. Sitting beside her in class, I started to understand: adaptability wasn't just a skill, it was survival. School became my safe place, the one structure in all the chaos.

Once we arrived at the college, the atmosphere was charged with anticipation and tension. My mother's determination was clear as she prepared for her classes. One day, as I sat quietly in the back of the classroom, Professor Thompson approached me with a curious glance and a faint, surprised smile.

"Ed, if you're going to be here, you might as well follow along," he said, handing me a textbook.

He called me *Ed*—not Eddie. That mattered. I'd started asking people outside the house to use the name. It felt like a small act of growing up, of reclaiming something for myself. Hearing it from him, without hesitation, made me feel seen.

I took the textbook and opened it up to the first pages. The material inside was challenging and intriguing. As the class went on, I found myself absorbed in the formulas and fascinated by the numbers. Professor Thompson's initial doubts faded quickly as I dove into the assignments with unexpected focus and energy. It was more than just attending a class; it was an introduction to a new world of possibilities.

In class, I watched as Professor Thompson wrote equations on the board. I solved them faster than he could write and even found errors in the textbook, which I pointed out to him. When he reviewed my corrections, he chuckled and said, "You have a real knack for this, Ed. Thanks for catching those mistakes."

After class, he spoke with my mother. "Ed is really catching on. If you're bringing him with you, you might as well enroll him in the classes," he suggested.

My mother hesitated. "We can't afford it," she said, frustrated.

His expression softened. "Since he is still in high school, he can enroll for free. I'll also recommend him for expedited acceptance with the dean. He's got potential."

And that's how, in August 1973, during the height of the Watergate scandal, a year before Nixon's resignation, I started college at the age of fourteen.

Months later, I found myself taking calculus. After tackling a tough problem, I told my professor, "Numbers and formulas just make sense to me. They're like a puzzle that always has a solution."

My calculus professor smiled. "That's the attitude that will help you excel."

My older classmates, who mostly worked full days, demonstrated their commitment to improving their lives through education. They encouraged me and offered positive reinforcement. The professor fostered a supportive environment that enhanced the learning experience for everyone.

His support, and that of my classmates, was more than academic. For the first time in my life, people saw my potential without needing to know my pain.

That experience reinforced a lifelong truth: value the support of others.

We never truly rebuild alone. It's the people who believe in us when we can't yet believe in ourselves that make transformation possible. Mr. Thompson's encouragement became the foundation that helped me rise.

My mother's education paid off in more ways than one. Equipped with the skills and knowledge she gained in college, she secured a job as a tax preparer, assisting individuals and businesses with their tax returns.

"I never thought I'd get here," she said, smiling.

The new position provided her with a steady income and marked a significant turning point in our lives. Her twenty-five-year career as a tax preparer was a demonstration of her resilience and the transformative power of education.

By the end of ninth grade, I had already completed coursework in algebra, trigonometry, calculus, and college English and Spanish. My academic progress was accelerating at a pace that set me apart from my peers. Recognizing my advanced abilities, my mother requested that I skip the tenth grade. The school agreed, and I found myself propelled forward, academically ahead and at the same time, emotionally distanced from others my age. The rapid advancement left me feeling isolated, as I struggled to find common ground with my classmates.

The only constant support I had was Jay, my loyal friend since 1969. His unwavering presence provided a sense of stability and comfort during so many periods of significant change. Jay's friendship kept me steady when life felt confusing and hard. Together, we reached a major milestone when we graduated from high school in 1976, the same year America celebrated its bicentennial; a moment of personal achievement and transition for us.

Jay and I met right after my family moved to Miami. He lived just down the street and quickly became my closest friend and anchor. Our friendship formed at a time when I desperately needed stability. I remember one day, not long after we met, when Jay noticed my mood was darker than usual.

"Eddie, you're always busy with school and homework. I know things are tough, but I'm here for you," he said, his voice filled with genuine concern.

That simple statement of support meant more to me than he could ever know.

Jay was there through thick and thin, offering a sense of normalcy that was missing in my life. We rode bikes through the neighborhood, played games, and shared our dreams for the future; dreams that often felt distant were easier to imagine with Jay by my side. When I struggled with the isolation while enduring the abuse at home, Jay was the one who made sure I didn't feel completely alone. His support during those challenging times helped me navigate.

One afternoon, as we were riding our bikes through the neighborhood, Jay asked, "Eddie, you ever think about the future? What we'll be doing?"

I laughed, the wind in my hair. "All the time, Jay. Sometimes it's the only thing that keeps me going."

Jay's presence in my life was instrumental in helping me cope with the instability and fear that often consumed me. He was more than a friend; he was a lifeline. I can vividly recall another day when I was overwhelmed by the pressures of school and home. Jay saw the worry etched on my face and pulled me aside.

"Eddie, you're smart, and one test doesn't define you. Let's go for a ride and clear our heads," he suggested.

We spent the afternoon biking through the streets, talking about everything and nothing. By the time I got home, I felt ready to face whatever awaited me.

As our mothers' friendship also expanded, it provided another layer of support that we both needed. Every Wednesday, our families would go to a small diner for dinner. The food wasn't memorable, but the laughter and camaraderie we shared were.

I can still hear Jay's mom saying, "Even if the food isn't great, at least we have each other," her laughter filling the room and lightening the mood.

Those weekly dinners became a tradition that strengthened our bond and gave us something to look forward to amidst the challenges we faced at home. Our friendship wasn't just companionship; it was protection, empathy, and healing. Jay helped me see that love and loyalty could exist without conditions. This shaped one of the most important principles I've carried through life: cultivate meaningful relationships.

Whether it was the laughter at the diner, our long bike rides, or the unspoken understanding between us, Jay's friendship taught me that strong connections can ground you even when the world around you is spinning. That kind of relationship is not just nice to have, it's *essential.*

Education and friendship laid the foundation for everything that followed. My mother's persistent drive to rebuild our lives, paired with the unwavering support of friends like Jay, showed me that even in the darkest times, light could be found. As I moved forward, the lessons of perseverance, the power of relationships, and the belief in a better future became the pillars that sustained me. Those experiences were not just about surviving, they were about reclaiming a life that had been lost to chaos and pain, and beginning to build something new, something hopeful. The bonds we formed, the strength we discovered, and the education we pursued together were the first steps on the long road to healing.

Even as things improved, grades soared, friendships grew, and a glimmer of stability returned, there was a storm inside me I didn't know how to name. I was excelling in college courses as a teenager, praised for my intellect, and surrounded by encouragement; but none of that erased the shadows in my memory.

My father was no longer in the house, but he never really left. His absence was its own presence, echoing in the cracks of broken doors, the dents in the walls, and the quiet flinches in my body. The terror he caused had rooted itself in my nervous system. I woke each morning in a world where he no longer existed, but I still checked over my shoulder.

That made things complicated with my mother.

She had been brave. Unshakable, even. She was the one who picked up the pieces and rebuilt. She held us together with grit and phone surveys, sleepless nights, and tuition bills. I saw her try, and I helped her as best I could.

Underneath all the gratitude, something else stirred; I *blamed* her. I lashed out. I treated her with contempt in moments I couldn't explain. The rage I had swallowed for years had to go somewhere, and often, it went toward her. I was angry, distant, and at times, disgusted. Still, she never judged.

When I'd apologize, clumsy and ashamed, she'd just nod and say, "You have every right to feel what you feel, Eddie. After all you've been through, how could I not understand?"

Her empathy was unearned and she gave it anyway.

Yet, beneath that tenderness, something remained unresolved because I really did blame her. She was the adult. She was the one who could have gotten us out and she didn't.

Or, at least that's what I believed at the time.

Time moved forward, but I stayed stuck, somewhere between resentment and silence. I didn't know how to forgive her. I didn't know how to let go. We didn't talk about the past. We barely talked at all.

I thought I'd buried it for good, but the past always finds its way back, especially when you're not ready.

CHAPTER 11

LETTING GO OF FALSE PROMISES

In the midst of broken promises, find the strength to grow and learn, transforming pain into a powerful catalyst for growth.

Life has a way of testing the foundations we build. Two years had passed in silence, a respite from the turmoil that had once consumed us. Just when it seemed like we might finally be free from the past, it came rushing back. A voice from the other end of the line, a voice I hadn't heard in years, brought with it the weight of old wounds and the hope for something better. We didn't know it yet, but some promises would be too broken to mend. Some hopes would hurt more than the silence that came before them. The struggle between hope and reality would define the next phase of our lives, forcing us to confront the scars of our past.

My father's voice on the other end of the line was different, softer, almost pleading. "I'm sober now," he said, a note of desperation I hadn't heard before. "Please, come visit. I want to make things right."

Despite everything, his words stirred something in me, *hope*, perhaps, or maybe just a longing for the stability, love, and acceptance I had never experienced from him. We accepted the invitation, clinging to the belief that he had changed. When we landed in Atlanta, no one was there.

"Where is he?" Diane asked, her voice tinged with disappointment.

We waited, scanning the crowd as the airport buzzed with families reuniting, just not ours. Finally, our names came over the loudspeaker, directing us to the customer service desk.

The woman behind the counter handed me a phone. "It's for you," she said.

I took the receiver. "Hello?"

"Ed, it's Marta." Her voice crackled. "He's . . . not feeling well. You'll have to take a taxi. I'll give you the address."

"Why isn't he here? Is he okay?"

"Just get here," she said quickly, not answering.

So, we went. The taxi ride was long and filled with nervous silence. We arrived at a modest house, no hint of the chaos that lay within.

The following morning shattered our hopes. As we woke up, I heard muffled voices rising from their bedroom, murmurs of an argument that quickly escalated into shouts, followed by a loud thud.

"What was that?" my sister whispered, fear creeping into her voice.

My heart pounded in my chest as I recognized the sound of my father's anger. "Stay here," I told her, my voice shaking as I got up and crept toward the hallway.

Just as I reached the door, I heard my father bellow, "You think you can talk to me like that?" His voice was thick with the slur of alcohol, mingling with the stale smell of cigarettes that clung to the air.

"Jerry, stop!" his wife cried, her voice breaking. The sound of a scuffle followed, and then another thud as he pushed her against the wall.

It was a chilling déjà vu of the anger and violence we thought we had left behind. I walked toward the doorway, the shouting getting sharper, closer. My throat tightened. I knew that sound, that rhythm of violence. It was happening, *again*. I turned and hurried back to my sister.

"We have to go, now," I said, grabbing her hand.

As we made our way to the door, he appeared, blocking our way. His bloodshot eyes locked on mine, the same look I remembered, the one that always came before everything went wrong.

"Where do you think you're going?" he bellowed, his voice a thunderous roar that made my heart pound. He lunged before I could move, slamming me into the wall, his hands pressing hard against my chest, holding me there.

"Take your hands off me," I said, steady and low, locking eyes with him. I wasn't bluffing and he could see it. For a moment, he stood there, stunned by my resistance. His eyes widened, and for the first time, I saw a trace of uncertainty cross his face. The grip of his hands loosened, realizing that his control over us was slipping.

"You're not leaving," he growled, but there was a hesitation in his voice.

I took advantage of that moment. "Yes, we are," I said, my voice trembling and resolute. "And you're not going to stop us."

I wasted no time. I grabbed my sister's hand tighter and turned toward the door. "Let's go," I urged, leading her out. Together, we fled from the chaos, not looking back as we left behind the toxic environment that had haunted us for so long.

As we walked out of that house and away from the chaos, a heavy silence fell between us. My heart was still pounding. However, with every step, the fear began to dissipate, replaced by a growing sense of empowerment. For the first time, I had stood up to my father, for myself *and* for my sister. It wasn't just for my own safety; it was for hers too. The responsibility I felt for Diane gave me the strength I didn't know I had.

Even though we barely talked about it in the moment, having each other's silent support made the difference between freezing and moving forward. That's what it truly means to value the support of others, quiet presence can be the thing that carries you when nothing else will.

The weight of his influence had lessened, though I knew it hadn't completely disappeared. There was still a long road ahead. As we left the toxic remnants of our past behind, I felt a small spark of hope ignite within me. It was the beginning of something new, a tentative first step toward reclaiming my life.

It didn't undo the past, but it changed something. I had faced him and didn't back down. That moment showed me: survival wasn't enough. I could take back power, piece by piece. That night planted something I didn't have before: the belief that I could be more than what he tried to make me.

* * *

For more than a year, there was silence, yet again. The distance between us, both physical and emotional, felt safer, like a wall I had built to protect myself. Then, unexpectedly, he reached out, expressing a desire to mend our relationship once more. His voice on the other end of the line was tired, almost weary.

"Eddie, it's Dad," he began, his tone softer than I remembered. There was a fragility in his voice that I hadn't heard before. "I know it's been a long time. I want to see you and your sister. I promise I won't cause you any problems. I've changed. Please, just give me a chance. I'm still your father."

His voice lingered in my ear. The violence, the lies, the years of silence, all of it crashed into one stubborn question: *What if he meant it this time?*

"Why now?" I asked, my voice taut with the effort to keep steady. My emotions swirled beneath the surface, threatening to break through.

"I've had time to think," he said, his voice cracking slightly. "I want to make things right. Can we talk? Can we meet?"

I glanced at my sister, who was watching with wide eyes, silently waiting for my decision. Her expression mirrored the same uncertainty I felt, a mix of fear and cautious hope. Diane and I had been through too much together to ignore the weight of that moment. Our bond was forged not just through shared trauma, but through survival. Even without words, we understood each other. She was a constant, and in that moment, her quiet presence helped anchor me.

"Okay," I finally replied, the word slipping out before I could stop it. "We can meet, but it has to be in a public place." No longer just reacting, it was a deliberate choice, made with clarity. It marked a step toward who I was becoming: someone who refused to stay trapped in the cycle of his chaos.

"Of course, of course," he quickly agreed, almost as though he was afraid I'd change my mind. "I'll call you when I get to town."

"Okay," I said after a moment's hesitation, my heart pounding in my chest.

As I hung up the phone, a whirlwind of emotions surged through me. The silence had been shattered by his voice. *Perhaps, it would be different. Perhaps, after all the anger and broken promises, he really had changed,* I thought.

As the evening wore on, I found myself teetering on the edge of belief and doubt, waiting for the next step, the next call.

But just like that, hope collapsed.

CHAPTER 12

EMBRACING THE UNFINISHED

Even when life takes an unexpected turn, adapt, learn, and let every ending become a new beginning.

It's September 12, 2024.

Exactly forty-nine years prior, I waited by the phone, anxious, hopeful, and too young to understand the weight of that moment. It was the day my father was supposed to call and tell us where to meet. The day everything changed.

When the phone finally rang that evening, I picked it up expecting to hear his voice confirming our plans. Instead, a strange voice spoke, heavy with sorrow.

"Eddie, it's about your father," the voice said gently. "He's gone."

"What do you mean, *gone*?" I asked, my voice sharp with confusion.

There was a pause on the other end of the line, as if the person on the other side was struggling to find the right words. I stood there, gripping the phone tighter, my mind racing. *Had he disappeared? Had he run off, breaking his promise like he always did?* The idea of him vanishing felt oddly familiar. Except the tone in the voice was different, more *final.*

"No, Eddie," she said, each word heavy with a sorrow that began to creep into my bones. "He's *dead*."

The words hit like a punch to the gut, knocking the air from my lungs. *Dead?* My father was dead. It didn't make sense. Just like that, any hope for reconciliation vanished. All the thoughts, all the scenarios I had played out in my mind about seeing him again were crushed in an instant.

"What happened?" I asked, my voice barely a whisper, the room spinning around me.

"His gun went off while he was cleaning it," the voice said. That was all. No explanation. No questions. No closure.

Numbly, I hung up the phone and called my mom. She was out with Blanche, so I asked the restaurant to find her, insisting it was an emergency.

When they put her on the phone, my voice trembled as I said, "Mom, it's Dad. He's dead."

There was a stunned silence on the other end. "Oh," she whispered, her voice small and distant, as if the news had drained all the life out of her. "I'll be right home."

Blanche drove my mother back. Before they arrived, I called Jay. I didn't know who else to turn to. "My dad's dead," I said, my voice hollow and distant, still in shock.

Jay didn't hesitate. "I'm on my way," he replied, and true to his word, he was there in no time. In that moment, his words felt like the only solid thing in a world that was rapidly crumbling around me.

The hours that followed blurred into grief and disbelief. One thing was clear: I had to be the one to tell his parents. No one else would, so I did. Jay stayed with me, his presence steady as we walked around the block late into the night. I told him everything, what I couldn't say to anyone else. Confusion, anger, guilt, they all came rushing out.

"I can't believe he's gone," I said, my voice trembling with the weight of the reality settling in. "I don't know how to tell my grandparents. I haven't seen or spoken to them in nearly three years."

Jay nodded, his expression serious and kind. "I'll be with you, whatever you need. You can do this, Ed. They need to know, and it's better coming from you."

As the night wore on, the air helped to clear my mind, though the dread still lingered. Jay's support helped me find the strength I would need for the next day.

When my mom and Blanche arrived home, they were comforting, their words soft and steady. We sat together, talking through what had happened, the gravity of it all sinking in. Jay remained by my side, a calming presence amidst the chaos swirling in my mind. In that moment, Jay's friendship wasn't just comforting; it was life-sustaining. There are times when words don't fix anything, but the presence of someone who refuses to leave is everything. His support helped carry me through something I couldn't have faced alone.

Decades later, as I sat reflecting, I realized just how long I carried the weight of that moment, and the mask I'd worn to hide it. It took me nearly a lifetime to understand that we don't grow in spite of our pain, we grow because of it. I had to go through it to get to the other side. That moment, and the years of silence that followed, shaped my path. The grief was real, the trauma lasting, but what I chose to do with it became the beginning of a different life. Growth doesn't always look like triumph. Sometimes it means staying upright long enough to tell the truth.

My father was forty-nine years old when he died. He lived forty-nine years, and in a bitter twist of fate, it has taken me an equal lifetime for me to find the strength to remove the mask and speak of the pain, grief, and unresolved questions I've carried for so long.

The mask offered protection and demanded silence. It came from my father's abuse and a world that taught me to hide my emotions, to pretend everything was fine. The harm perpetuated itself in three ways: first from my father, then magnified by society that encouraged my silence and taught me being vulnerable is a weakness, and finally by me, who unknowingly carried it forward, inflicting pain and abuse on myself, all while hiding behind the mask meant to conceal my suffering.

The next morning, after a night filled with thoughts of the daunting task ahead and very little sleep, I knew what had to be done. Breaking the news to my grandparents was a responsibility I couldn't avoid, no matter how much I wished I could. It was a long thirty-minute drive to their apartment; a drive I didn't look forward to.

As I got closer, my stomach churned with a mix of dread and sadness. I wanted nothing more than to turn around and escape the burden of delivering the news. I knew there was no turning back. Jay's presence the night before had given me the strength I needed. As the morning sun rose and I found myself alone with my thoughts, the weight of what I had to do pressed down like a lead blanket.

When I arrived, I sat in the car for a moment, trying to steady my nerves. The apartment building loomed ahead, familiar and foreboding. I stepped out, feeling the pavement warm under my feet, and walked up to their door, each step more difficult than the last.

I knocked, and after what felt like an eternity, the door creaked open. My grandfather Les peeked out, his expression a mix of surprise and concern. I could tell he was happy to see me, but he had never wanted any part of the silence my father had created between us.

"Who is it, Les?" my grandmother's voice called out from inside the apartment. He was my grandmother's second husband, and the only grandfather I've ever known; a man of quiet strength and kindness.

"Eddie?" he said, opening the door a bit wider, his eyes lighting up with a cautious warmth. "What are you doing here?"

"Grandpa," I began, my voice trembling, "I need to talk to you and Grandma."

He didn't open the door any further, sensing that something was wrong. "Is everything alright?" he asked, surprised and concerned.

From the hallway, my grandmother's voice sounded again, this time sharper with suspicion. "*Who* is it, Les?"

"It's Eddie," he replied, trying to keep his voice steady.

My grandmother appeared in the hallway, her expression hardening as she saw me standing there. The years of tension between us, fueled by my father's anger, were visible in the way she looked at me.

"What do *you* want?" she asked, her voice tight, afraid of the consequences of talking to me.

I didn't know how to feel; my emotions were a tangled mess of confusion and devastation. I had loved and hated my father in equal measure, and now, with him gone, I was feeling the first hints of freedom from his grip. That freedom was bittersweet, laced with guilt and sorrow. How could I mourn the man who had caused so much pain, and whose approval I had always craved? The conflict was almost unbearable.

I took a deep breath, trying to steady my nerves. "Dad is dead," I said, barely able to get the words out. "He died last night."

My grandmother's face twisted with disbelief. "No, that's not possible," she said, her voice rising in pitch. "You're lying. He was supposed to be arriving later today. Why are you causing trouble, Eddie?"

"Grandma, I'm not lying," I said, my voice cracking under the weight of my grief and her disbelief. "He was cleaning his gun and it went off."

Her eyes narrowed, and she pointed a trembling finger at me. "No," she insisted, her voice filled with denial. "He's on the airplane right now. I don't believe you!"

My grandfather's eyes widened, and he reached out to grip my hand. "Oh, Eddie," he whispered, his voice thick with emotion. "What happened?"

Tears welled up in my eyes as I repeated, "It was an accident. He was cleaning his gun . . . it happened fast."

Behind my grandfather, my grandmother's face softened slightly. She still shook her head in disbelief. "No," she said, her voice faltering. "No, he can't be dead." She sank into a chair, her hands trembling. "Why are you here?" she asked, her voice cracking with emotion. "Why did you come here?"

I was not sure she had absorbed the news fully. "Because you needed to know," I replied, my voice steadying as I looked at both of them. "No matter what happened, you're still my grandparents. I couldn't let you find out any other way."

My grandfather squeezed my hand, tears streaming down his face. "Thank you, Eddie," he said, his voice choked with gratitude. "Thank you for coming."

My grandmother's eyes filled with tears, and she covered her face with her hands, sobbing uncontrollably, her body shaking with the force of her grief. The years of bitterness and anger melted away, replaced by shared disbelief and sorrow.

My grandfather nodded, his grip on my hand tightening. "We loved him too, Eddie," he said, his voice barely above a whisper. "We loved him too."

They feared him the same as we did. The fear was etched in their voices, in the way they spoke of him, and in the hesitance with which they had opened the door to me. All of that seemed to melt away, leaving behind only the raw, complicated truth of our emotions.

We sat together for the first time in years, not as estranged family, but as people stripped down to pain. The past still loomed, yet something shifted. Grief connected us, not resolution, and that was enough.

* * *

We were initially told that my father's death was an accident; a tragic mishap that no one could have foreseen. However, when we landed in Atlanta, the truth confronted us in stark, bold letters on the front page of the local newspaper.

The headline was accompanied by a stark picture of his gas station. The article described how my father, surrounded by three others who begged him to stop, spun the cylinder of a revolver, pressed it to his temple, and pulled the trigger. It was Russian roulette; a reckless, deliberate, and fatal ending. The report relayed the details with a chilling detachment, stripped of emotion.

Panic surged as we grasped the implications of the headline. My grandfather had been too ill to travel, so my grandmother flew with us. As we stood in the airport, the weight of the situation pressing down, I could see the pain etched on her face. Despite everything, despite the wedge she had once allowed my father to drive between us, my mother became the one who responded with the most compassion. In that moment of vulnerability, she stepped forward with a heart full of grace.

As we walked through the airport, my mother suddenly handed me her bags and rushed ahead. I watched her frantically buy every newspaper in sight, hands trembling as she paid. Without a word, she tossed them into a trash bin.

"Mom, what are you doing?" I asked, confused.

"Your grandmother doesn't need to see this, Eddie," she said quietly. "She's lost so much already."

I never forgot the image, my mother, protecting the woman who once helped break her. She didn't act out of forgiveness. She acted out of dignity. In that moment, she showed me what strength looks like: doing the right thing, even when no one deserves it.

Years later, Grandma Mary passed away still believing it was an accident. She had already endured the loss of both her sons and two husbands. She didn't need a final cruelty. My mother's kindness shielded her. That moment defined her strength more than any words could.

They called it Russian roulette, a reckless game of chance. More than twenty years later, Marta told me the truth. It wasn't impulsive. It was *intentional.*

Alone in his office, surrounded by silence, he made a choice. Whether to end his own pain or to punish those he left behind, no one can say for sure. What's clear is this: the act didn't come out of nowhere. Years of torment and despair had led him there.

He opened the drawer, pulled out the gun meant for protection, and turned it on himself. Did he hesitate? Think of us? Or was he too far gone? No one was there to stop him. A single shot echoed through the station. By the time they reached him, he was gone.

To protect his wife's chance at the insurance payout, they told the world it was Russian roulette. A lie built from desperation.

His final act wasn't a gamble, it was surrender.

* * *

For the first time in my life, I didn't fear waking up.

Didn't fear he'd take my life.

Didn't fear he'd ruin whatever part of me he could still reach.

It was unfamiliar, this thing people call "safety."

So unfamiliar, I almost missed it.

He was gone, and in that moment, I felt something I didn't recognize at first: freedom.

What remained was silence, questions, and wreckage. More than anything, I was left with the weight of truth, and the unbearable task of making sense of emotions no child should ever hold: grief, relief, and confusion.

I've since learned: my purpose isn't to explain his choices. It's to heal from mine.

Telling this story is part of that healing, not to relive the pain, but to transform it.

Staying purposeful means continuing to grow, even when the world tempts you to shut down.

Relevance isn't about visibility, it's about truth.

This story may live in the past, but its lessons still guide how I live today.

CHAPTER 13

GRIEVING YOUR WAY TO STRENGTH

Healing is a journey, not a destination—it's a path without a clear end, where each step forward nurtures growth and resilience.

I had often fantasized about truly confronting my father, about reclaiming the power he had stolen from me for so many years. I played out the scene countless times, a moment where I would finally stand tall, no longer the scared boy cowering in the corner—someone strong enough to face the man who had terrorized me for so long. I envisioned the intensity of it: fists clenched, eyes locked, with the raw force of my anger spilling out after years of repression. I wanted to make him feel the pain he had inflicted on me, the emotional scars, the fear that kept me up at night, the wounds that colored every aspect of my life.

I saw him crumble, confronted by a version of me he could no longer control, no longer belittle or destroy with his words or belt. In this imagined confrontation, I had the upper hand. He would see the consequences of his cruelty, the damage he'd caused, and the person I had become in spite of it. For once, I would be in control, and he would be forced to face the weight of his choices.

His death shattered the confrontation I had imagined for years. There would be no reckoning. No moment where I stood taller.

No release of rage. Instead, silence fell, and in it, something worse than anger: relief.

I didn't have to flinch anymore. I didn't have to listen for footsteps or measure the danger in his voice. The fear that had lived in me for so long disappeared overnight. What remained was a heaviness I didn't expect.

How do you grieve someone whose absence feels like freedom? How do you mourn a man who never gave you what you needed, yet left behind a void only he could fill?

That contradiction took root in me. I didn't know how to explain it. I didn't know what it made me. I only knew it was real.

At sixteen, while my classmates navigated the typical whirlwind of high school, social events, parties, sports, and the excitement of graduation, my reality felt far removed from theirs. The focus on grades and college preparation wasn't about standing out; it served as a lifeline, a way to escape the emotional turmoil of living with my father's abuse, and later, processing his death. While their lives brimmed with the promise of new beginnings, mine felt like it was slowly closing in.

I was no longer afraid, and that should have been enough. Instead, I was haunted by guilt; a twisted sense that my freedom had come at too high a price. Was it wrong to feel grateful he was gone? Could I miss the idea of a father and still feel relief that mine would never return?

When I returned to school, no one knew how to talk to me. They didn't ask where I'd been. One classmate finally did, and I replied flatly, "I buried my father."

The pity in her eyes made me want to disappear. I walked out without explanation and went home in silence. The house felt off, too quiet, too hollow. I wasn't grieving the man. I was furious. He got to vanish, leaving us with the wreckage. My mother was there, trying to offer comfort I couldn't begin to take. I didn't want comfort, I wanted answers, I wanted someone to blame. All I had was silence.

That spring, just months before graduation, I came undone.

One afternoon, I locked myself in the bathroom. I just needed the pain to end.

I sat on the cold tile floor, my back pressed hard against the door, sobbing uncontrollably.

My mother heard me and rushed to the door.

"Eddie? Open the door!"

Her voice trembled, sharp with fear.

She tried the handle, gently at first, then again, as if hoping it might just turn this time.

"Please, sweetheart . . . just open the door," she said, her voice cracking under the weight of panic. "Talk to me. Let me in."

The door had been broken so many times before, splintered during my father's violent outbursts, that she hoped it might give. That's why I was sitting against it, using my weight to keep it closed. Not to keep her out, but to keep everything else in. Why wouldn't the pain go away and leave me to move on?

"Please," she begged again, barely able to speak through her tears. "Please don't shut me out like this . . ."

When there was still no response, she turned and hurried down the hallway into the kitchen. The yellow phone hung on the wall, familiar, yet suddenly impossibly far away. Her hands trembled as she lifted the receiver. She dialed quickly, silently willing someone to answer.

When Blanche picked up, my mother's voice broke.

"Blanche . . . it's me. Eddie's locked himself in the bathroom. He's crying, and he won't come out. I've tried everything. I'm really scared. Could you please come over?"

There was only the briefest pause before Blanche responded.

"I'm coming. I'll be right there."

Blanche and Jay arrived quickly. Jay stayed in the living room with my mother and Diane, the three of them suspended in helpless silence, listening for any sign from me.

Blanche walked slowly down the hallway, pausing outside the bathroom door. She didn't knock hard. She didn't call my name over and over. She just placed her hand gently on the door and said, softly but clearly:

"Eddie, it's me. I'm here."

There was no fear in her voice, no judgment, no pressure. Just steady presence. She sat on the other side of the door and started to talk, not to fix me, but to *be* with me. Her voice was calm but full of care, like she was holding space wide enough for all the things I couldn't say.

"Eddie," she said, steady and clear, "this is not the answer. You don't get to give up—not like this. I'm here, and I'm staying, until you remember you still matter.

"You're hurting, I know," she continued, "but this pain doesn't get to decide your future. You've survived too much to let it end like this."

I didn't respond, but something inside me shifted. Her words weren't instructions, they were invitations. To breathe. To consider another way. To trust that someone could hold even the worst of what I was feeling.

The truth was, I felt unworthy. Not just broken, but worthless. I was angry, and terrified of what that anger meant. Afraid I would become him. That the violence I had endured might already be living inside me, waiting for a trigger. I couldn't separate my fear of him from my fear of myself.

I was ashamed of what I felt, ashamed of not being strong enough, ashamed of wanting to die.

Then, beneath all of that, the quietest question:

Why hadn't I died when he tried to kill me?

He was dead, and yet he was still hurting me. Still living inside me. Still shaping how I saw myself, how I suffered, how I stayed silent. I hated that. I hated him for it. I hated myself for letting it continue.

I didn't know how to carry all of that, and I didn't know who I was without the pain. The pain had become my compass, my armor, my identity. Without it, I didn't know what would be left.

I just wanted it to stop. I needed it to stop.

Somehow, in the middle of all that chaos, something in Blanche's voice reached through the fog. Her calm. Her steadiness. Her belief that I still mattered, even in that state.

Eventually, with shaking hands and a hollow chest, I stood up and opened the door.

Blanche didn't rush in. She stepped in gently, then slowly sank down beside me on the cold tile floor. She didn't try to fix anything. She didn't fill the silence. She just sat there with me, in the wreckage, in the rawness, in the truth.

She stayed and I cried.

I cried until my throat was sore and my body was tired. Until the sobs gave way to silence. Until I had nothing left.

In the living room, my mother, Jay, and Diane sat frozen in fear, hoping I would find a way back.

That day didn't bring resolution, but it cracked something open. The weight of the duality I'd carried, grief and relief, guilt and anger, was exposed. With it, I felt lighter. For the first time, I had let some of those feelings out. My father had drilled into me that it was forbidden: "*Real* men don't cry." "Don't tell anyone, or I'll kill you, your mother, and your sister."

All those threats, all that messaging that kept me silent for so long, finally fell away.

In that moment of desperation, I let someone in, just enough to breathe again. Just enough to imagine, that maybe for the first time, healing was even possible.

Looking back now, I realize that opening that door was more than a moment of surrender; it was the beginning of reclaiming my life. It didn't fix everything. It didn't erase the trauma or silence the shame overnight, but it was the first time I allowed myself to be seen in the middle of the storm. The first time I chose presence over disappearance. While healing would take years, and more doors would need to open along the way, that day marked a shift. I was no longer alone in the darkness. Someone had come in and sat with me.

* * *

While I was grappling with the paradox of grief and relief, my brother Phillip was walking through his own hell. The trauma from our early abuse led him into the hippie movement, where he immersed himself in drugs, searching for escape and meaning. Eventually, his quest for peace brought him to a Mennonite church in Altamont, Tennessee. The sect he joined was strict—focused on simplicity, resistance to modern life, and a devotion to humility and God. That conversion created a new kind of separation between Phillip and the rest of our family. Not just physical distance—spiritual distance. That kind of divide felt even lonelier.

His wedding in 1976, just five months after our father's death, marked a turning point. The ceremony was austere and cold. Men and women entered the church through separate doors. Our mother, Diane, and Grandma Mary were directed to enter through the basement—a small but telling symbol of how far we'd drifted. For Grandma Mary, the wedding offered hope. A chance to rebuild after our father's death. For me, it underscored just how far away Phillip had gone.

For the next twenty-six years, that divide defined our relationship. Phillip and his wife had nine children, but we rarely saw them. When we did meet, his attempts to convert us loomed over everything. The gap—spiritual, emotional, and physical—seemed too wide to bridge.

When Pris and I married in 1989, Phillip refused to come. His beliefs didn't recognize marriages after divorce, which was the case for both Pris and me. His absence on one of the most important days of my life reminded me that I hadn't lost him to death—I had lost him to faith. I never judged his choices, but I deeply resented how they closed the door to a real relationship.

Even after Phillip and his family eventually left the Mennonite church, it felt too late to undo the damage. After his children had grown, they began to reach out and build relationships with us. While those connections matter deeply to me, they often felt unfamiliar. Like meeting strangers who share your blood, but not your history. The lost years had taken their toll, and building something real would take time.

Phillip eventually shared his own version of the journey in his 2023 memoir, *Jesus Shines Through: A Lifelong Search Through Hippies, Communes, Rage, and Redemption*. In it, he chronicles his path from rebellion and rage to faith and healing. It's his truth and it helped me understand parts of him I never knew.

It's not that we haven't tried. We both have, but our journeys, and the distance between them, have made true reconciliation feel just out of reach. There's a constant sense of not being fully accepted. Maybe he feels the same from me. I've dreamed of having a deep friendship with my big brother. Maybe it's still possible, but time is running short.

This past year, Pris and I celebrated our thirty-fifth anniversary. We invited everyone. Our niece Anna and her husband, Ken, came all the way from Mississippi. Phil and Gina weren't able to attend. On the day of the celebration, we received flowers with a card from Phil. It read:

I'm sorry for all the years of not accepting.

That meant a lot to me.

Over the years, Phillip and I have tried to connect with each other. At times we've gotten along; other times we've clashed. Overall, we've accepted that we're on our own journeys and learned to respect our differences.

* * *

Like Phillip, my sister Diane took her own path, but hers led into a different kind of darkness. She married young, full of hope and perhaps seeking a stability that she had never known in our chaotic childhood home. She had two children, and for a while, it seemed like she might find the happiness and sense of family we had always longed for. Her marriage, like much of her life, was built on shaky ground. Her husband was unfaithful, repeatedly. His affairs were not just isolated incidents, but a pattern that stretched over years, eroding whatever love and trust had once existed between them.

As Diane's marriage deteriorated, so did her spirit. She remained in that dysfunctional relationship, trapped by the fear of being alone and the wounds from our childhood. I think she believed that if she held on long enough, things might change. Perhaps she thought she could endure the betrayals, just as our mother had endured our father's rage, clinging to the hope that love might somehow win in the end.

Over the years, we became estranged. At first, our contact was still regular, but it was clouded by her increasing reliance on us for financial help. Every phone call or visit eventually circled back to money, her requests for help, explanations for why she needed it, and promises that, "this time it would be *different*." At first, we gave what we could, hoping that it might be the lifeline she needed to turn things around. The pattern repeated itself over and over, and with each request came new excuses and, sometimes, outright lies. Diane became more and more deceptive in her attempts to get money from us, using guilt, manipulation, and stories that never quite added up.

Before long, the strain of those interactions began to wear on our relationship. Emotional distance widened with every unmet promise and every dollar that vanished into the void. We stopped giving, not out of indifference, but because helping no longer felt like enough. Something deeper was unfolding, something we couldn't yet name.

The space between us became insurmountable. Every attempt to reconnect only pushed us further apart.

What we didn't fully realize at the time was how Diane was struggling with the pain from the abuse she had endured and the weight of her life choices. While we were focused on the surface issues, the money, and the lies, Diane was battling something far more profound. In her suffering, she turned to drugs as an escape from the overwhelming pain that had followed her from childhood into her adult life. What started as an attempt to numb her emotional wounds spiraled into full-blown addiction. Meth became her refuge, a temporary reprieve from the chaos of her reality, but it quickly took over, consuming her life.

The addiction ravaged her body, tearing away at her health bit by bit. Her once vibrant spirit was dulled by the drugs, and the physical toll they took became impossible to ignore. Over the years, the damage to her lungs became severe, a stark reminder of the destructive path she had been on for so long. It reached a point where her body could no longer keep up with the abuse it had endured. She was placed on a respirator, her life hanging by a thread.

Diane passed away at just sixty-one years old. Her life was cut tragically short; a victim of circumstances that had been set in motion long before she ever took her first breath. I often wonder what her life could have been if things had been different; if she had found the support she needed before addiction took hold, if she had managed to break free from the toxic relationship that had sapped her spirit, or if the pain of our childhood hadn't followed her so relentlessly into adulthood.

Her death left a void, not just because she was gone, but because it felt like the ending of something already broken. I had let go years earlier, worn down by the lies, manipulation, and endless requests for money. We stopped trying, not from lack of love, but because nothing we gave ever actually helped. In the end, she carried her pain alone. I grieved for the sister she might have been if life had offered her something different.

Diane's death, like Phillip's spiritual withdrawal, had already happened long before the final moment. In both cases, I didn't lose them all at once, I lost them over time, through silence, distance, and choices that created chasms between us. Their absence reshaped how I think about family, not as something you're born into, but as something you build through love, truth, and mutual care. I've found family in people across the world, people who see me, support me, and choose me. That, to me, is what real family means.

* * *

Throughout it all, our mother remained a steadfast presence, her unconditional love never wavering, even as she watched the family splinter and drift in ways that no parent could have anticipated. She stood by each of us, despite the paths we chose, holding the pieces of our fractured family together the best she could. Even in moments when I felt like I was drowning, her presence reminded me that love didn't always have to be loud, it just had to be there.

As my siblings and I each dealt with our trauma in different ways, I remained caught in the middle, too young to understand how to escape but old enough to feel the weight of everything that was happening. While Phillip found solace in faith and Diane in escape, I still needed to find my own way. I didn't have the answers, but I kept listening, first to the silence, then to the lessons hidden inside the pain. Each step was its own education. At that point, I didn't know how much more would be asked of me or how many fires I would need to endure before discovering my own strength.

As much as I tried to make sense of my father's death, the emotional turmoil it left behind was something I couldn't have prepared for. I had spent so many years waiting for the day when I no longer had to live in fear of his voice, his fists, or the unpredictability of his rage. I imagined that when that day came, I would finally feel free.

Freedom, as it turns out, comes with its own weight; a different kind of heaviness that I wasn't ready for. Yes, his death brought relief, but also devastation. The relief felt like a betrayal, a cold reminder that I had been waiting for the end of my own father's life. How do you reconcile that? How do you grieve for someone who caused you so much pain, yet still long for the love they never gave?

The devastation was not just the loss of my father; it was the loss of any possibility that he might one day own what he had done. I had imagined he might've tried; maybe even apologized. That door slammed shut with his death, leaving behind silence where some kind of closure might have lived.

That silence settled into my life, always there, but never speaking. I kept moving forward. Some mornings I felt lighter. Other times I dragged the weight of the broken pieces he left behind. The contradiction remained: I missed what I never had. I felt relief that he was finally gone.

CHAPTER 14

FREEDOM THROUGH LEARNING

Reinventing oneself becomes a path to overcoming the past and forging a new identity, allowing us to transform scars into strength and build a future.

With my father gone, the reckoning never came. There was no closure, just the choice to build something new. If I couldn't face the past, maybe I could outgrow it.

In the fall of 1976, I began anew at the University of Florida, more than three hundred miles north of the place that had shaped and scarred my childhood. Jay was there too, my friend since I was nine, one of the few people who had walked with me before and after. He was the only one who knew my past, allowing me the freedom to reinvent myself and focus on becoming the person I aspired to be.

I joined the marching band as a trumpet player. Performing at Gator home games gave me structure, pride, and a sense of belonging I hadn't felt before. It was a way to be part of something bigger, and to disappear into the music when life felt too loud.

Despite earning an academic scholarship, the reality of college expenses, books, meals, and housing quickly set in. To cover my expenses, I worked various jobs, from bookkeeping at a travel agency to working at a library. These positions required attention to detail and taught me valuable skills.

As I juggled my school responsibilities with work, I learned to prioritize and manage my time efficiently. This balancing act was challenging, and it provided invaluable lessons in perseverance and self-discipline. After turning eighteen, I expanded my work experience by taking on jobs as a bartender and tax accountant. Working late nights at the bar and early mornings on tax forms demanded resilience and adaptability. Those positions were not only financially necessary; they were instrumental in developing skills that have served me well throughout my life. The juggling act between classes, work, and survival became my first real immersion in pursuing lifelong learning and adaptability, not just academically, but emotionally and practically.

At the University of Florida, I often contrasted the chaos of my childhood with the newfound stability I was finally experiencing. The university provided a structured environment where I could thrive academically and personally. Late-night study sessions in the library emerged as an escape where I could lose myself in books and knowledge, providing an escape from the painful memories of my past. The quiet of the library, the smell of old books, and the soft hum of turning pages created a sanctuary; a place where learning became my refuge from painful memories. In those moments, the stress and trauma that had once dominated my life seemed to fade into the background. The library became a haven of peace and possibility, a place where I could envision a future shaped by my own choices rather than my past circumstances.

The camaraderie in study groups and social activities enhanced my feelings of stability. Collaborating on assignments and sharing hopes and fears during late-night parties fostered connections. Those friendships filled a void I had felt for years. Growing up, I had often felt isolated and disconnected. There, I found a community that welcomed and supported me. The shared experiences of navigating college life created bonds that went beyond academics. In those bonds of shared late-night talks, laughter, and vulnerability, I began to cultivate meaningful relationships, ones that finally gave me a sense of belonging I hadn't known before.

Initially a premed major driven by the desire to help others, I soon realized that the extensive time commitment required for medical studies wouldn't enable me to escape poverty quickly enough to help support my family. I decided to switch my major to something that would allow me to graduate sooner and start working without accumulating much debt. I chose accounting because it promised a stable and well-paying career.

One of the impactful relationships I developed at the University of Florida was with Dr. Doug Snowball, my accounting professor. His passion for the subject and dedication to his students were truly inspiring. He was a mentor to me, offering guidance not only in academics but in life. His belief in my potential gave me the confidence to chase my goals with unwavering determination.

One afternoon after class, I approached Dr. Snowball for advice on my course schedule.

"Dr. Snowball, do you have a moment?" I asked hesitantly.

"Of course, Ed," he replied warmly. "What can I help you with?"

"I'm trying to figure out the best order to take my accounting classes. I'm a bit overwhelmed by all the options."

He nodded thoughtfully. "Let's take a look at your current schedule and your long-term goals."

I handed him my list of classes, and he scanned it quickly.

"Okay, I see you've got the basics down. Next semester, I recommend you take Intermediate Accounting I before tackling Intermediate Accounting II. It's crucial to build a solid foundation."

"That makes sense," I said, scribbling notes. "What about the electives?"

"For electives, consider Cost Accounting and Auditing. Cost Accounting will give insights into internal financial decision-making processes, and Auditing will help you understand external evaluations of financial statements," he advised, pointing to the courses on my list.

"Should I take them in any particular order?" I asked.

"Take Cost Accounting first," he suggested. "It will give you a solid understanding of how companies manage their internal finances. Then, Auditing will make more sense because you'll see how those internal processes are evaluated from an external perspective."

"Got it," I said, feeling more confident. "Thank you so much for your help, Dr. Snowball."

"Anytime, Ed," he replied warmly. Then, his expression softened as he asked, "How are you doing otherwise? Everything okay?"

I paused, not sharing much. Knowing that he cared was enough. "I'm managing," I said with a small smile. "Thanks for asking."

"Remember, it's not just about the classes you take, it's also about how you apply what you learn. Stay curious and don't be afraid to ask questions," he encouraged.

His guidance was valuable. I navigated my coursework strategically, allowing me to achieve academically and build a robust understanding of accounting principles. His belief in my potential, coupled with his genuine concern for my well-being, gave me the confidence to pursue my goals.

* * *

I met Rosalynn Carter once. She visited our high school and spoke to our psychology class. At the time, I had no idea who she was. After her talk, our teacher asked me to walk her to her car. As we made our way across the parking lot, she turned to me and said, "My husband is going to be the next president of the United States."

I wasn't into politics. I barely understood what a First Lady did, but I was captivated by the certainty in her voice. She didn't say it as a hope or a wish. She stated it as a fact. That moment planted something in me—a recognition that even ordinary days can brush up against history. That sometimes, people carry unseen momentum.

A few months later, in November of 1976, Jimmy Carter was elected president. That same night, Jay and I smoked marijuana together for the first time.

Jay handed me a joint, and despite my hesitation, I took a puff and inhaled. At first, nothing happened. Then a strange calm settled over me. The noise in my head quieted. Colors looked richer. The world felt wide and full of possibility.

For a brief moment, I experienced a version of life unburdened by fear. I hadn't yet found the words for trauma or survival, but in that haze, I felt something akin to freedom.

I used marijuana often in the years that followed, to explore and to escape. The high muted my memories and softened the edges of things I didn't want to feel. People called it "freedom." For me, it was a break from remembering. A way to breathe without choking on everything I hadn't said.

However, as the novelty wore off and the demands of school took precedence, I realized those moments of escape were unsustainable. Gradually, I found a balance, partying less and refocusing on my responsibilities.

My first year was a period of adjustment as I navigated the complexities of university life. However, it was the summer after my first year that proved to be transformative. Before I left for college, my mother had told me that I spent too much time with my head in books. She encouraged me to take time to discover myself and have fun while at college. I took the "have fun" part very seriously, and my grades reflected it. However, the social experiences were valuable. I made new friends and had a few relationships that built my confidence and helped me feel wanted.

That period of growth and self-discovery, coupled with the stability and support I found at the university, set the stage for a future where I could pursue my goals with confidence and determination.

That summer, I decided to visit my cousins in Tennessee. I was so excited as I made the drive alone from Gainesville to Nashville, eager to have my car to explore the beauty of Tennessee on my own terms. The drive was a significant experience, providing time to reflect and enjoy the open road.

Leaving Gainesville, I took I-75 North, passing through the lush, green landscapes of northern Florida. Crossing into Georgia, I noticed a shift in scenery. The highway took me through the heart of the state. In Valdosta, I stopped briefly to stretch my legs and grab a bite to eat. The small-town atmosphere was welcoming, a nice contrast to the hustle and bustle of university life.

When I arrived in Tennessee, the landscape transformed again, with the road winding through the scenic foothills of the Appalachian Mountains. Approaching Nashville, my excitement grew. The drive, though long, had provided a feeling of freedom and anticipation for the adventures that I hoped lay ahead.

Upon arriving in Nashville, I looked forward to spending time with my cousins. However, their busy lives often left them with little free time, which led me to spend more time with my Aunt Audre. She welcomed me warmly and became my guide to Tennessee's charm and history. Our time together allowed me to bond with her in a way I hadn't expected, making the trip even more memorable.

"Eddie, it's so good to have you here!" Aunt Audre exclaimed as I arrived. "I've planned some fun activities for us."

We played racquetball, went to dinner theater, and just enjoyed spending time together. One evening, after a game of racquetball, we sat down to catch our breath.

"You've got a mean serve, Aunt Audre," I said, laughing.

She chuckled. "You keep me on my toes, Eddie. So, tell me, how's school going?"

"It's tough," I admitted. "But I'm managing."

Her presence made me feel loved and accepted. The change of scenery and the warmth of family provided a much-needed respite from the pressures of university. More importantly, the fun and camaraderie with her shifted my perspective. She encouraged me to step out of my comfort zone, to engage more with my studies, and to form lasting relationships.

One evening over dinner, she looked at me with a gentle expression. "Eddie, how are you coping with your father being gone? I know it's been hard for you."

Something inside me broke. The floodgates opened, and everything I had kept bottled up came pouring out.

"It's been more than hard," I said, my voice trembling. "I haven't just been missing him. I've been dealing with the aftermath of his drinking, his beatings . . . all of it."

She looked at me, stunned. "What do you mean beatings? Eddie, I had no idea."

I nodded, feeling some relief and very vulnerable. "I couldn't talk about it before. I didn't think anyone would believe me."

"You don't have to go through this alone," she said softly, reaching out to hold my hand. "You're strong, Eddie. You always have been. But it's okay to lean on others for support." Her words touched me and I started to cry.

She listened as I recounted the night I came home from the hospital after the fire on her birthday, when we had the double celebration. My father, angry about my absence from the party, stormed into my room and slapped me hard. He demanded I return to the party and act like nothing was wrong, despite the pain and exhaustion I felt.

I also told her about Labor Day weekend in 1971, when my father, in a drunken rage, pinned my mother to the floor and pressed a switchblade into her chest . . . how he patched her up and then left her there on the floor to go to the bar. And how, when he came back, he terrorized us for two days making us think he had already killed everyone.

Then I told her something that I had never told anyone else, not even Jay. I recounted the times he would move the TV into his room, forcing us to go there if we wanted to watch anything. It felt like a subtle control; an invisible chain binding us to his presence. The TV was just a part of it. He would show his erections and insist that I touch it.

"One day you will have this too," he would say boldly. "When you're a real man." Admitting the memories out loud was like releasing a weight I had carried for too long, a step toward freeing myself from the shadows of the past.

Her voice filled with shock and anger. "Why didn't your mom stop him? How could she let this happen?"

"She was too beaten down by him to do anything," I explained, my voice shaking. "She couldn't protect herself, let alone me."

Aunt Audre's eyes flashed with anger. "I never would have put up with it," she said, her voice rising. "I would have fought back. Your father . . . he was a monster for what he did."

Her voice cracked with emotion, and she used expletives I had never heard from her before, berating him for all that he did. Her words were raw, slicing through the air with a combination of anger and pain.

"He had no right to do any of that to you," she whispered, her eyes burning with a fierce protectiveness. "You were just a child, and he took advantage of that."

I never admitted it; her words had fueled my anger toward my mother because I too could not believe she had put up with it all those years. I could never understand why she did not take us with her and leave.

She paused, taking a breath as if trying to steady herself. Then she turned to me, her expression softening, her resolve unwavering: "It's time for you to move past it, Eddie," she said firmly, squeezing my hand. "You deserve better. You deserve to be happy and far away from his shadow."

Her words echoed in my mind, a beacon of hope cutting through the darkness. It was a moment of clarity, a crucial point where I realized the power I had to reclaim my life and forge a pathway untainted by his memory.

We talked late into the night, her concern for me and her anger and disgust at my father evident. Her words were filled with compassion and rage, a powerful combination that made me feel cared for and supported. She expressed her horror at the things I had endured, her voice trembling with indignation.

"I can't believe he did that to you," she said, her eyes glistening with unshed tears. "It's unforgivable. No one should have to go through what you did."

Her hands were warm as they held mine, a physical anchor in the emotional storm. "You have to know, Eddie, that none of it was your fault. He was a monster, and you were just a child trying to survive."

The conversation was a cathartic release, each word peeling away layers of pain that had built up over the years. Her unwavering support and fierce anger on my behalf provided validation I had never experienced before. In those late hours, wrapped in the warmth of her concern, I saw a glimmer of hope for the future.

When my head finally hit the pillow, every part of me felt spent. The emotional toll of the night left me exhausted. A kind of relief, one I hadn't known in years, began to settle in. My secret had finally been spoken. The burden of carrying it alone lifted. As my eyes closed, a strange lightness spread through me, and a glimmer of peace reached into the corners of my mind.

That night marked more than just a release; it signaled the beginning of transformation. No longer merely just surviving, healing had begun. That was the moment growth took root; growth through everything I had endured. Speaking the unspeakable didn't erase the past, but it gave it shape, meaning, and finally, a way forward.

For the first time in my life, I felt truly safe. I slept better than I had in years, free from the haunting nightmares that had plagued my nights. In the silence of the early morning, I realized that it was the beginning of a new chapter.

As the summer came to an end and I was getting ready to leave, Aunt Audre begged me to stay.

"Eddie, please, can't you stay longer?" she pleaded, her eyes filled with concern and love.

To convince me, she even had her husband offer me a job at a McDonald's they owned.

"You could work at the restaurant," she suggested earnestly. "We would love to have you here."

Her plea tugged at my heartstrings, and the idea of staying with family who genuinely cared was tempting. The thought of being in a supportive environment, surrounded by people who wanted the best for me, was almost too good to pass up. However, I knew I had to get back to school.

"I have to get back, Aunt Audre," I replied, though her words touched a part of me. It was a bittersweet moment, realizing that while I had found a place where I was genuinely cared for, my journey required me to move forward.

Those moments with Aunt Audre were transformative, providing the stability, acceptance, unconditional love, and emotional support that I desperately needed. Her reassurance and the time spent with my cousins helped me open up. It was through her unconditional presence that I truly began to value the support of others, a lesson that would stay with me for the rest of my life.

Previously withdrawn and introspective due to past traumas, I formed even more lasting relationships and gained the confidence to pursue my goals.

Her belief in me, along with the encouragement from a few other key individuals, instilled a desire to help others in need. That newfound confidence and purpose fueled my academic pursuits, allowing me to excel in my studies.

"Aunt Audre," I said one day before leaving, "thank you for everything. You've made a huge difference in my life."

She hugged me tightly. "I'm proud of you, Eddie. Go out there and show the world what you're made of."

Her words echoing in my mind, I returned to college with renewed purpose and determination.

* * *

Life at the University of Florida was full: classes, late-night talks, music, and friendship. We cheered for the Gators whether we won or lost, not because of the game, but for the joy of showing up together. Concerts, parties, and spontaneous adventures filled the gaps between studying and work. For the first time, I felt surrounded by people who saw me as the person I was becoming, not who I had been.

Before every game, we would meet at someone's place for a pre-party several hours before it started. Then we would parade over to the stadium together, laughing and having fun the entire time. We lost most games, but it didn't matter whether we won or lost because we were there for each other and our friendship.

At the stadium, known as Florida Field or "The Swamp," people cheered for the Gators with excitement. The stadium, with its open-air design and seating capacity of around 62,800, was a sea of orange and blue. The beloved pregame cheerleader, Mr. Two Bits, would run from one section to the next, blowing his whistle and holding up signs animatedly while chanting:

"Two bits, four bits, six bits, a dollar. All for the Gators, stand up and holler!"

Everyone would jump up, laugh, and scream at the top of their lungs.

A highlight of the fall semester was the Gator Growl, the world's largest student-run pep rally, held annually during Homecoming Week. In 1976, Bob Hope headlined the event, bringing national attention to the university. His humorous and entertaining performance was a memorable experience for everyone present and helped solidify the university's reputation as a lively and spirited place. During that time, UF was considered one of the top party schools in the nation; a title that reflected the vibrant social scene and numerous events and festivities that took place on campus.

After every game or concert, we would go to an after party. For the first time, I felt safe; no longer in the house haunted by his rage. Campus life wasn't just fun; it was *healing*. That contrast alone was its own kind of awakening.

Beyond campus, the world was shifting. Conversations about justice and global unrest made their way into our lectures and late-night debates. The human rights movement inspired me. The hostage crisis in Iran reminded me how fragile freedom could be. Those events didn't just shape the world; they sharpened my purpose.

The emotional impact of finding stability and connection at UF was profound. I went from feeling isolated and burdened by my past to feeling supported and capable of achieving my goals. It was more than just an academic institution for me; it was where I grew as an individual, forging connections that have endured. The experiences and lessons learned during those formative years laid the foundation for my future endeavors, personally and professionally. The challenges I faced and the support I received shaped my character and helped me move forward from my past.

However, even during that moment of growth, the scars of my past were never far from my mind. While the emotional scars from my father's abuse were hidden, the physical scars from the fire were always there, etched into my skin for the world to see. Every time I went to the beach or took off my shirt, I was met with looks of discomfort or curiosity. Those reactions served as constant reminders that my past was not just a part of my history, it was imprinted on my body, shaping how others saw me and how I saw myself. Each glance intensified my self-consciousness, making me feel exposed, physically and emotionally.

Despite those challenges, my time at UF gave me something I had long sought: a sense of belonging. My community college credits and advanced placement exams allowed me to graduate early at the age of twenty in March of 1980, giving me a head start in my professional career. Early graduation was a tangible achievement, yet I often still felt unprepared for the challenges ahead.

The support network I built—friends, professors, and mentors—was crucial to my success. Those personal relationships offered guidance and encouragement, reminding me that I was capable of more than I believed. Even when doubt crept in, I reminded myself that to stay purposeful and relevant, I had to keep moving forward with intention, aligning my actions with a life of meaning, not just success.

Looking back, my years at UF were about more than just academic growth, they were a transformative experience. The lessons I learned, inside and outside of the classroom, would guide me for many years to come. Those years, set against the backdrop of the seventies, intertwined with historical events that shaped my worldview, instilling in me the power of resilience and determination. It was a reminder that personal growth often happens alongside broader societal changes.

My graduation was a moment of triumph. My roommate John and I celebrated our achievement by throwing a three-day party that was filled with joy, music, and the exuberance of newfound freedom. Friends and family gathered, and the air was electric with excitement. We blasted Pink Floyd's "We Don't Need No Education" from their album, *The Wall*, making it our anthem of rebellion and triumph. As we shouted the lyrics, our voices blended into a chorus of defiance and celebration. We had emerged from the educational system and into the world, free to define our own paths. The music became the soundtrack to our liberation, and for a moment, the weight of the past lifted.

Graduation felt like freedom. Music blared, people danced, and for a second, I believed I was free too. I laughed loud, smiled wide, and sported my mask well. Inside, nothing had healed. I had just gotten better at hiding the damage.

PART III

PURSUE LIFELONG LEARNING AND ADAPTABILITY

Staying relevant means staying curious, embracing new beginnings not as escapes, but as paths to healing. It's the courage that comes from wearing strength in uncertainty, hiding in plain sight while still doing the work, and thriving unseen. It means changing course without shame, choosing meaning over perfection, and learning to show up, for others, for yourself, and for the life still unfolding. Eventually, it's the strength that comes from letting go to move forward, wiser, humbler, and more whole than before.

CHAPTER 15

NEW BEGINNINGS

Resilience is the process of healing by embracing the struggles and using them as stepping stones toward personal growth.

The past often resurfaced with a vengeance, derailing the progress I had fought so hard to fake. I wore my mask well, convincing others, sometimes even myself, that I was fine. I threw myself into work, school, and life. I wasn't building a future; I was outrunning a past I hadn't yet faced.

My teenage years were marked by intense therapy sessions in which I finally had to stop running. Those sessions were grueling, leaving me emotionally drained, but they were necessary. Healing didn't come in revelations. It came in fragments, moments of cracking open, of speaking what had never been said.

During those times, my mother was doing her own surviving. Her depression made it hard for her to be present in the ways I needed. She showed up with empathy, even when she couldn't do more. Her love didn't fix things, but it gave me just enough to keep going.

I brought my trauma with me to college, packing it between textbooks and ambition. I buried it under a full schedule and a practiced smile. I called it independence—it wasn't. It was still hiding.

It wasn't until that summer with Aunt Audre that something real started to shift. She didn't push. She just made space, and in that space, I let my guard down. Her steady presence helped me begin to peel back the layers of protection I hadn't even realized I was wearing.

It showed me what it meant to grow through what you go through. Healing didn't mean forgetting, it meant facing what had once destroyed me and choosing to move forward with strength, clarity, and grace.

That wasn't the end of it.

The trauma had shaped the way I connected with others. I was quick to judge, always scanning for signs of betrayal or danger. I kept people at a distance, whether friends or something more. I had built an invisible fortress to survive childhood. As I got older, that same wall became the thing keeping me alone.

Still, that dream haunted me, always the same: alone in a funeral home, his eyes locking onto mine, his hands tightening around my throat. I would wake up, drenched in sweat, gasping for air, as if his grip extended beyond death itself. My roommate, concerned, would ask if I was okay. I couldn't explain it. I would turn over, pretending to sleep, hoping to escape the lingering terror that continued to choke me, even in the safety of my own bed, more than three hundred miles away from where it had all happened.

It wasn't until much later that I began to understand the importance of vulnerability and the strength it takes to let others in. As I slowly let go of the fear that had shaped so many of my interactions, I started to cultivate meaningful relationships; ones built on truth, empathy, and mutual trust. Each connection became a brick in the bridge back to me.

The journey of healing is ongoing, and while the past will always be a part of me, it no longer defines me. The walls I once built are slowly coming down, brick by brick, as I continue to embrace the power of connection and the freedom that comes with it.

After college, I immersed myself in the professional world, which again allowed me to keep my past buried inside. I was determined to build a successful career, and in many ways, that drive helped suppress the painful memories of my childhood. However, the more I tried to outrun my past, the more it seemed to catch up with me. It wasn't until I moved to New York and found myself alone much of the time that those buried emotions began to resurface.

* * *

My first professional position was as a district manager with H&R Block. I relocated to Tallahassee and was responsible for managing eighteen offices. During tax season, I oversaw more than two hundred employees, ensuring that each office operated smoothly and efficiently to handle the influx of clients. In the off-season, my responsibilities shifted to managing a smaller team of five, focusing on training, process improvements, and preparation for the next tax season.

At just twenty years old, I faced several unique challenges. I was too young to rent a car, and often relied on others for transportation. Additionally, I looked younger than I actually was, which made it difficult to establish credibility with clients and employees, many of whom were significantly older and more experienced. Building trust and authority in that environment required a delicate balance of demonstrating knowledge, competence, and empathy.

Reflecting on that period, I realize that I was unprepared for such significant responsibilities. The sheer scale of managing eighteen offices was daunting, especially as a recent graduate with limited professional experience. I had to quickly learn how to navigate complex tax regulations, manage diverse teams, and handle high-pressure situations. The job required meticulous attention to detail and an understanding of tax laws to ensure compliance and accuracy across all offices.

Despite the initial hurdles, the experience was formative. It taught me the importance of precision, accountability, and how to inspire and guide others. I learned how to make critical decisions under tight deadlines and manage high-pressure situations with composure. Those skills would prove invaluable throughout my career, shaping my approach to leadership and problem-solving.

One memorable instance from that time was when I had to step in and personally handle a particularly challenging client situation. A major error had occurred, leading to a significant tax discrepancy for a client. The client was understandably upset, and the staff were struggling to find a resolution. I took it upon myself to review the case, identify the mistake, and develop a corrective plan. By directly addressing the issue and working closely with the client to resolve it, I not only salvaged the client relationship, but reinforced the benefits of accountability and customer service within my team.

Those early experiences laid a foundation for my future career. The lessons learned in those formative years, about leadership, precision, and the impact of effective training, became core principles that guided me through subsequent transitions and achievements in my career.

* * *

Despite the success I found in my career, the emotional toll of my past remained. Inspired by the kindness of Mrs. Hanson, my first-grade teacher who stepped in when I was hospitalized, I decided to pursue my passion for teaching. In mid-1982, I left behind my stable career to become a math teacher, driven by a desire to inspire and ignite learning in young minds. My first teaching assignment was at a school just down the street from my high school alma mater, adding nostalgia to my early teaching career.

Ten years had passed since he left and seven since he died. The floor was still cement. The doors still broken. Even his death hadn't set me free.

I stood at the front of a classroom, helping others find their voice, but part of me was still twelve, still in that bedroom, still trapped in that house. I could still feel the blade; the chill of it against my throat. His voice low, almost casual. "Are you ready to die?"

In that moment, at twenty-two, I gave instructions with calm authority, but inside, every breath still felt held, still trapped in that house.

In my second year, I transitioned to Nova Southeastern University School. Around the same time, International Business Machines Corporation (IBM) released its first desktop computers and offered them to Florida schools at no cost, on one condition: a teacher had to be sent to their Boca Raton campus for training. As the newest and youngest member of the staff, the assignment landed squarely on my shoulders. "Voluntold," as they liked to say.

Embracing the opportunity, I quickly enrolled in Nova University's Technology Education master's program. The first year was a whirlwind of learning, where I often found myself barely keeping up with the tech-savvy students. The immersive experience proved invaluable. I integrated computer technology into the math curriculum, enhancing student engagement and learning outcomes.

During that time, I fully embraced what it meant to pursue lifelong learning and adaptability. It wasn't just about learning technology, it was about adapting, evolving, and applying new knowledge to help others grow as well.

One day, I saw a poster in the teachers' lounge advertising for a camp program called Computer Summers. I applied and got the position, which led to an incredible opportunity to spend my summers in Brant Lake, a picturesque area in upstate New York known for its natural beauty and tranquil environment. As someone from Florida, living in Brant Lake for the summer was an experience.

The difference between the humid, subtropical climate of Florida and the cooler, forested landscape of upstate New York was striking. At Brant Lake Camp, I taught kids computer skills while immersing myself in a completely different way of life. The serene mornings by the lake, the vibrant camp activities, and the close-knit community of campers and staff offered a refreshing and enriching environment. Over the next few summers, that experience honed my teaching skills and broadened my horizons, giving me an appreciation for diverse environments and lifestyles.

The person running Computer Summers, Dr. David Sachs, played an essential function in my career development. He was also engaged in training IBM employees on the first desktop computers, further connecting me to the burgeoning field of computer technology. After my first summer at the camp, I returned to regular teaching. David then offered the position of program manager on the IBM Computer Learning project, prompting me to move to New York.

I had adapted. I had learned how to perform, teach, and survive. What I hadn't yet learned was how to live without a script.

On paper, everything looked like progress: new titles, new cities, forward motion. Inside, I was still chasing something I couldn't name; still stitching myself together while pretending I was whole. The world saw resilience. I felt fatigue from wearing the mask so well, for so long, that I forgot what my own face looked like underneath.

CHAPTER 16

WEARING STRENGTH

The best revenge is living well, turning past pain into purpose, and finding light even in the darkest times.

Strength became my disguise, something I wore so convincingly that even I sometimes believed it. By day, I was the polished instructor: teaching, traveling, guiding others toward their goals. By night, I unraveled; alone in my apartment, chain-smoking in silence, the tears would come, unannounced, and unrelenting. It was the version of me no one saw; the one even I tried to avoid.

That was the truth I lived with, and it was getting harder to hide.

Working for IBM placed me at the forefront of the digital revolution. My professional life thrived. However, behind the scenes, I was crumbling.

Moving to Peekskill, New York, from South Florida plunged me into one of the darkest periods of my life. The natural beauty, rolling hills, and the Hudson River that surrounded me stood in stark contrast to the storm raging within. By day, I maintained a facade of normalcy. At night, I collapsed into the corner of my living room, rocking back and forth, lost in the shadows of everything I hadn't healed.

One evening, I sat curled in the corner of my living room, a cigarette burning low between my fingers, the ash long and fragile. The walls felt too close. My own breath sounded foreign. "What am I doing?" I whispered into the quiet. "How did it come to this?"

No answer came, just the hum of the refrigerator, the soft tick of the wall clock, and the ache in my chest growing louder by the second. That night, I felt *the edge*. My body knew despair before my mind could catch up.

The nightmare returned, the one that wouldn't let go. I could feel his hands again. Hear his breath. "Why won't you just leave me alone?" I screamed into the dark. The silence that followed felt like a trap; as if the walls themselves were closing in.

The physical pain I inflicted on myself became a substitute for the emotional anguish I couldn't bear. Bulimia became my outlet, a ritual of punishment and control. I'd eat in secret, fast and furious, chasing comfort. Then I'd purge, trying to erase the shame. It wasn't about food. It was about pain. About trying to empty myself of everything I couldn't name.

"This is the *last* time," I'd say. It never was. The relief was short, the emptiness louder than ever.

I became obsessed with my body, spending countless hours in the gym, sculpting a facade of strength and control. *Maybe if I can just look perfect on the outside, the inside will follow,* I thought, staring at my reflection. No matter how hard I pushed, the mirror always reflected the same hollow eyes and empty soul.

Although the physical abuse had ended a decade earlier, the emotional scars remained fresh. I couldn't escape the torment. My mind was a battlefield; memories wouldn't stay buried. Still, I found solace in my work. Teaching, writing courses, and showing others how to use computers gave me purpose. *At least here, I can be someone else,* I told myself, hiding behind the mask of a competent instructor.

I wore the mask well.

During a break, one participant once said, "You seem so put together."

I smiled politely, happy that I had achieved my goal—if only they knew.

Within the confines of my apartment, I withdrew myself, like a turtle backing into its shell. Summers in Upstate New York gave me a break from the isolation. At camp, there was always something to do or someone to talk to; I taught kids, made friends, and stayed busy enough to forget my past and the pain that still existed.

When the summers ended, the silence returned, as did the darkness.

I cut myself off from everyone including family, friends, and even Jay. I buried myself in my apartment, numb and alone.

In the arms of strangers, I searched for *something*; comfort or connection, maybe. Each encounter was a momentary escape. *This time, it will be different,* I told myself—but it never was.

The eating. The purging. The workouts. The hookups.

They were all a way to feel something, or nothing. One night, I finally said it out loud:

"I can't keep living like this."

The truth hit hard. It wasn't life. It was survival on a loop. Something had to change.

So, I made the call.

My initial therapist was kind and empathetic, and I was hopeful that his approach might help me untangle the knots of my past. He suggested I write letters to my parents, letters in which I could express all the things I never had the chance to say.

When I sat down to write, I found myself staring at a blank page, paralyzed by the words that refused to come. "Why can't I do this?" I whispered to myself in frustration. Every attempt felt forced. The words felt unreal, fake, as if I were trying to script a version of myself that didn't exist.

In therapy, I tried to explain this to him. "It's like I'm hitting a wall," I said, the frustration evident in my voice. "I can't find the words. They just don't feel right."

He nodded sympathetically, except his suggestions didn't seem to help. He recommended more letter writing, but the exercise only intensified my sense of failure. *Maybe therapy just isn't for me,* I thought, disheartened. I knew I couldn't give up. I needed someone who could push me beyond the surface, someone who could help navigate the dark corners of my mind where I had locked away the most painful memories.

Then I found *her*: a therapist whose strength matched my need. From our first session, I could tell she was different. I had almost given up on therapy altogether. I told myself it wasn't helping, that maybe I was broken beyond repair. Desperation kept me searching.

"So, why are you *here*?" she asked, her eyes steady and unflinching.

"I'm not sure anymore," I replied, the uncertainty heavy in my voice.

As soon as the words left my mouth, a memory flashed through my mind—one I had tried to bury, but always found a way to resurface. It was the sound of my father's voice, angry and disgusted:

"If you don't know, who does?"

The question had cut through me like a knife, leaving a scar that hadn't healed. I could still see his face and smell the alcohol on his breath. His words had made me feel small, insignificant, and powerless. Even then, sitting in the therapist's office, that same feeling of dread washed over me.

I swallowed hard, trying to push the memory back into the recesses of my mind, but it clung to me, refusing to let go.

"That brought something up, didn't it?" she asked, her tone softer, sensing the shift in my mood.

I hesitated before nodding. "My father . . . he used to say that to me. If I didn't have an answer, he would—he would lash out." I could feel my voice trembling, the old fear creeping back in.

"What did that do to you?" she pressed gently.

"It made me feel . . . like nothing I did was right," I admitted, the words feeling both liberating and terrifying to say out loud. "No matter how hard I tried, it was never enough. I felt . . . useless. And when I couldn't answer his questions, he'd get even angrier."

"That must have been incredibly hard to live with," she said, her voice filled with empathy. "But you're not in that situation anymore. You don't have to have all the answers right now. It's okay to not know. That's what we're here to figure out together."

For the first time, I felt a glimmer of hope. Maybe I didn't have to have all the answers. Maybe it was enough, for the time being, to simply start asking the right questions.

But she didn't let up. "You're here because you know everything is not fine," she said, cutting through my defenses with a single sentence.

Her words hit like a punch to the gut, and I knew she was right. I had spent so long building walls to protect myself that I had no idea who I was anymore. The mask I had crafted was beginning to crack, and the truth, my truth, was starting to seep through.

"We've got work to do," she said, her tone leaving no room for avoidance.

* * *

After one brutal week, I arrived tense, silent. She didn't press. Just said, "I want you to start journaling."

I groaned. "I've tried. It never works."

"This time it will," she said. "If you're honest."

I wasn't sure I could be—but I started. Late at night, I'd sit with a pen in one hand and a cigarette in the other. One night I whispered, "What am I doing?" and instead of letting the question vanish, I wrote it down.

In our next session, I told her. "I wrote it."

Her eyes didn't move. "Good. That's how you stop floating. That's how things land."

Something began to shift. Each entry pulled a bit of pain out of hiding. I stopped trying to sound strong. I wrote what I actually felt.

The nightmare came back—the one with his hands around my neck, ice-cold and unrelenting. I'd wake up choking, fists clenched. "It's always the same," I told her. "His eyes open. He grabs me. I can't breathe."

"And what do you do then?"

"I scream into the dark, 'Why won't you leave me alone?' But the silence just stares back."

"Then try to face it," she said. "That's the only way it loses power."

Piece by piece, I started reclaiming what I'd buried. It hurt, but it helped.

I handed her a journal entry once—bare, angry, unpolished. "This is hard."

She held my eyes a second longer than usual. "Hard means *real.*"

The eating, the purging, the endless workouts—they weren't just habits. They were armor.

"You're numbing," she said. "Let's stop numbing."

So, we peeled back the layers—slowly and unevenly, but honestly. I began to meet a version of myself I hadn't seen in years.

* * *

It had been almost a year since we last spoke. Our conversation was strained, filled with awkward silences and unspoken accusations. Finally, I blurted out, "Mom, I'm in therapy," my voice trembling with a mix of anger and desperation. "One of the things I'm trying to understand—to figure out—is why you didn't protect us."

There was silence on the other end of the line, and for a moment, I thought she might have hung up. Then, I heard her take a deep, shaky breath.

"I couldn't, Eddie," she finally said, her voice small and fragile. "We had nowhere to go. He convinced me that no one would want me, that if I ever tried to leave, he would kill you and your sister. I was trapped . . . I was terrified."

Her words hung in the air, each one sinking into my heart. For so long, I had held onto my anger. I had blamed her for everything: her inaction, her silence, her failure to protect us. But in that moment, I listened and actually heard the truth for the first time. She was a *victim* too, just as trapped and powerless as we were.

"But you were the adult," I said, my voice breaking. "You had the power. We were just kids."

"I know," she whispered, and I could hear the tears in her voice. "I know, Eddie. I live with that every day."

Then, we both cried, the years of pain and misunderstanding pouring out. Just as I was about to hang up, frustrated and overwhelmed, she said something that shifted everything for me.

"Eddie," she said, her voice trembling yet filled with a strength I hadn't heard before. "The best revenge is living well."

I didn't respond. Not right away. The words had hit something I didn't know I was waiting for. I had been chasing survival, and she had offered a different path: living.

Her words echoed into my soul, penetrating the armor I had spent years building.

The best revenge is living well, I repeated in my mind.

That single phrase reframed everything. For the first time, staying purposeful and relevant made sense, not for others, but for myself. Survival no longer defined the moment; life had begun to unfold with intention.

Something snapped inside me. The words I had clung to for so long, "I'm not crazy; he is," instantly lost their power. A new mantra took its place, one rooted in hope and resilience.

"The best revenge is living well."

The moment served as a reminder: my past didn't have to define me. Rising above it meant choosing to live on my own terms. The best revenge had nothing to do with avenging my father, it meant reclaiming myself, confronting the things I had allowed, and healing from the wounds I had inflicted on my own life.

This shift in perspective marked a significant leap forward. The change didn't happen overnight; the transition was slow, gradual, and fraught with setbacks. There were still days when the darkness pulled me under, when old fears and doubts crept back in. On those days, the weight of my life felt overwhelming, and it took every ounce of willpower to resist the pull of old habits and destructive thoughts; there were times I gave in.

"The best revenge is living well" became more than just words; it became a lifeline—something to hold onto when everything else felt unstable. Over time, it started to work. The mantra reminded me that my life was my own, that I had the power to shape it, and that I wasn't defined by what had been done to me or what I had done to myself.

I began to realize that living well wasn't just about surviving. It was about taking the steps, no matter how small, to build a life that was meaningful and had purpose. Purpose wasn't something I found once and held onto; it was something I had to shape daily. Setting even the smallest goal was an act of resilience. Each goal, each forward step, helped me stay connected to a deeper meaning. That was the heart of staying purposeful and relevant.

I set goals for myself, some small, some ambitious. Some days, just getting out of bed or smoking fewer cigarettes was enough. Other days, I pushed further, taking on challenges that once paralyzed me with fear.

I learned healing isn't linear. Setbacks were part of the process. When I stumbled, I no longer berated myself. I found strength in simply continuing, in refusing to let the past define me. As I kept fighting for the life I deserved, I began to get a glimpse of the person I was becoming. It wasn't easy, and it wasn't without pain.

The journey was about more than just overcoming my past. It became a mission to build a future that truly belonged to me. The goal wasn't to live well out of spite, but to live well because, for the first time, *I believed* I deserved good things.

Gradually, change took hold. The anger that once consumed me softened into quiet reflection. I reconnected with my mother. Our relationship wasn't perfect, but we had found our way back to conversation.

Somewhere in my reflections, I thought about Roy White. I couldn't shake the feeling that I had one more thing to finish. So, when I went to Chicago to teach some classes, I opened the Chicago phone book and started calling every Roy White listed. One after another, I asked the same question until I found him.

It was 1986. I was on a layover at O'Hare International Airport in Chicago, and he agreed to meet. He brought his wife and we had lunch together in the terminal. I thanked him for pulling me from the fire and for giving me a chance at a life I hadn't yet imagined. He had showed me I was worth saving.

I told him my father had died, though I didn't go into the details. I wasn't ready to share the full truth, and he didn't press. We spoke as strangers do when history connects them more than memory. I was in my twenties, he in his late thirties. We didn't really know each other, not then. Yet, something essential had passed between us all those years before.

I never saw him again. Years later, I continued to search but never found him. Still, I'm grateful I met him that day. Saying thank you was part of my healing.

All these years, I believed Roy had saved me on his own. Recently, while going through a box of my mother's things, I found an old newspaper clipping. It was difficult to read, so I scanned it and had it transcribed with an AI tool. That's when I learned something I never knew: there were actually two boys who saved me that day—Roy White and Donald Thiery. I have no memory of Donald at all; in our house, the only name ever mentioned was Roy's. I want to thank them both.

The pain and fear still surfaced, but no longer held the reins. That helpless child had grown into someone stronger. Someone more resilient. Living well wasn't about chasing happiness. It was about reclaiming my power, my identity, and my future. It meant turning pain into purpose and healing and building from it; learning how to stand back up, even when I stumbled again. It meant finally seeing myself as a survivor, as a creator of something new.

That, I realized, was the best revenge of all.

CHAPTER 17

HIDING IN PLAIN SIGHT

Success isn't just about reaching the destination; it's about navigating the journey—learning, adapting, and growing through every challenge along the way.

I thought I was done repeating the past. I had done the work, built something stable, and even found moments of peace.

Then I met *her*.

It started fast: short visits, long phone calls, the kind of chemistry that makes you believe this time might be different. She was magnetic, funny, impulsive; always chasing a high. It felt exciting, like something that could rescue me from the quiet ache I hadn't named. Part of me knew it was dangerous. I mistook volatility for passion. I wanted the story to be different, so I ignored the familiar warning signs. We met at a wedding. She lived in Orlando. I was based in New York. From the outside, it looked like a new chapter.

Inside, it was something else entirely.

I quit my job, packed up my life, and moved to Orlando to try and make it work. The partying never stopped. Neither did the drinking.

What started as hope felt like a reset. I didn't see the signs at first, or at least I didn't want to. Her drinking. Her mood swings.

The way I began shrinking in my own home. Six months in, it hit me: I had married someone just like my father. Six months later, the marriage ended in divorce.

I needed something solid, something that couldn't drink, leave, or unravel. So, I built it myself. I cashed out my 401(k), bought a dozen desktops, and poured myself into one of the few things I still trusted: education.

As a child, school had been my escape. As an adult, work became my anchor. It gave me structure, focus, and control. Like solving a problem set, it was something I could master.

Still, behind every professional milestone raged an inner battle. I wasn't just building a business; I was trying to outpace the damage. My father's voice—*useless, worthless*—echoed through everything. What helped me fight back were my mother's words: "The best revenge is living well." That simple mantra reminded me to keep moving forward. Work became my shield and, in time, it paid off.

* * *

The turning point came when I met Pris Nelson. She was the founder of her own company, Insource International, and was just as sharp, visionary, and mission driven as I was. We merged our companies to form Innovative Resources, expanding our reach and deepening our impact. What started as a collaboration would eventually become something far more personal, though neither of us saw it coming.

Pris believed in me in ways I hadn't yet learned to believe in myself. Once, after a client meeting I thought I had fumbled, she pulled me aside and said, "You see failure. I see passion and intelligence." No one had ever said anything like that to me; not without an agenda. It stopped me in my tracks. She even nominated me for the Entrepreneur of the Year Award sponsored by PricewaterhouseCoopers and the *Orlando Sentinel*.

I won.

It meant a lot, however, like school had been, business was still a way to stay busy enough not to feel.

On paper, I was winning. The business was growing. We had national clients, a talented team, and headlines that called me a pioneer. People shook my hand like I had the answers. I smiled in the photos. I said all the right things.

I felt I did nothing to deserve it.

There were days I stood at the front of the training room, teaching with perfect precision, but inside I was empty. Once, in the middle of a class, a student asked me how I stayed so calm under pressure. I opened my mouth to answer, but nothing came out. For a second, the room blurred. I didn't see their faces, I only saw *his*. The belt and the forced silence. I blinked hard, forced a smile, and made a joke about caffeine and deep breathing. The class laughed and the moment passed. Inside, something had cracked. That was the day I realized: even success can't silence a scream you've swallowed for too long.

Not sad. Not angry. Just *gone*. Like I was watching myself through someone else's eyes being applauded and admired.

I had built a business from nothing, but I couldn't feel proud, because the boy inside me still didn't believe he was real.

Looking back, each chapter prepared me for the next.

Whether managing tax offices, teaching high school, or training IBM employees, I kept showing up, curious, flexible, and determined to grow. It wasn't just about skill. It was about survival. It was about learning to adapt without losing who I was.

That's what this chapter was really about: pursuing lifelong learning and in doing so, starting to believe that the life unfolding ahead of me could really be mine.

The skills I built—leadership, technical fluency, and the ability to educate and inspire—shaped my professional identity. Founding

Hands On Computer Training and later merging with Pris's company to create Innovative Resources, crystallized my belief that learning should be accessible to everyone, not just those already ahead.

I wasn't just running a business; I was living my commitment to stay purposeful and relevant in a world that kept evolving.

Still, my father's voice lingered. *You're useless.*

Even at my best, those words echoed. Whenever self-doubt crept in, I'd reach for my mantra given to me by my mother, *the best revenge is living well.* It reminded me that I wasn't broken, I was becoming.

Every step forward required me to unlearn something, relearn something else, and try to stay open to who I was becoming. That was the real work.

Maybe, for the first time, I wasn't just hiding in plain sight. I was beginning to arrive.

CHAPTER 18

CHANGING COURSE

Our greatest strength as a couple lies in our ability to navigate conflict together, turning obstacles into opportunities for growth.

I didn't expect to fall in love, especially not in the middle of rebuilding my life.

When Pris and I met, I was still navigating the emotional wreckage of my past: a failed marriage, unhealed patterns, and the pressure of a growing business. She entered my life through a mutual friend who somehow sensed we needed each other, even before we did.

From the start, we were anything but easy. We came with our own histories, our own triggers, and very different ways of managing conflict. Blending our work lives with something more personal felt like walking a tightrope without a net.

Yet there was something in her, a steadiness, a drive, a refusal to give up, that made me want to stay, even when it got hard.

We didn't avoid the hard conversations. We learned how to have them.

That became our strength.

One of my new neighbors in the office suite was Sandi Thomas. Sandi was the kind of person who had a natural talent for connecting people. She quickly became a friend, and before long, she was introducing me to others in the community, helping me find my footing professionally and personally. It was through Sandi that I first got involved with the Association for Talent Development (ATD), and it was also through her that I met Pris.

When Pris first walked into the room, her warm smile and confident demeanor immediately caught my attention. We quickly found ourselves engrossed in conversation. Despite the initial attraction, we didn't get along well; in fact, we didn't like each other at all. Yet, Sandi was so sure we belonged together that she kept arranging opportunities for us to meet; even when we couldn't see the potential, she did. Whether it was casual lunches, professional events, or spontaneous gatherings, Sandi always found a way to bring us into the same room. At first, those encounters were more a test of patience than anything else; Pris and I were both dealing with our own issues and often clashed in our interactions. Sandi never wavered in her belief that we were meant for each other. She saw something in us that we were too stubborn to acknowledge.

Sandi persisted in bringing us together over the next two years, subtly nudging us closer with each meeting. She had a knack for creating situations where we couldn't help but interact, whether it was assigning us to the same project, or seating us next to each other at dinner. With time, our defenses began to lower. We started to see past our initial misgivings and appreciate each other's strengths, realizing that beneath the surface differences was a connection waiting to be uncovered.

The shift didn't come as a sudden epiphany, but as a gradual realization that grew stronger with each encounter. We moved from barely tolerating each other to becoming friends, and eventually, something much deeper. It was as if Sandi had been quietly guiding us along a path we hadn't even noticed, until one day, we found ourselves standing side by side, wondering why it had taken so long to arrive.

That encounter marked the beginning of a lifelong partnership, one that blossomed from a friendship into a loving relationship. Sandi's intuition and perseverance weren't just instrumental in bringing us together, they were the foundation upon which our relationship was built. Her belief in us, even when we couldn't see it ourselves, led to a connection that has profoundly shaped our lives. It reminded me that relationships, when nurtured with honesty, patience, and mutual respect, could truly be transformative. It was a powerful example of what it means to cultivate meaningful relationships, even when the path is anything but easy. We often look back and marvel at how things fell into place, all thanks to a friend who simply refused to give up on us.

* * *

Early on, our relationship was fraught with challenges. We experienced many ups and downs, navigating the complexities of emotional baggage from my traumatic childhood and each of us having a prior failed marriage. Pris had remarkable patience and understanding that slowly helped lower the defenses I had built to protect myself, allowing our relationship to grow and flourish. However, one significant challenge we faced was how differently we handled conflict. Over time, we learned to respect each other's ways of dealing with disagreements. Through patience and better communication, we found a balance that allowed us to work through conflicts in a way that strengthened our bond rather than tearing it apart.

On the night of November 9, 1989, Pris and I sat in front of the television, watching in awe as history unfolded before our eyes. The Berlin Wall, a symbol of division and oppression for nearly three decades, was about to fall. People from both East and West Berlin were climbing over the wall, hugging, and celebrating their newfound freedom. The atmosphere was electric, filled with tears of joy and disbelief. As we watched the scenes of jubilation, we experienced feelings of hope and possibility. The fall of the Berlin Wall symbolized a new beginning not only for Germany, but for the world. It was a moment that underscored the power of unity and the human spirit's resilience as we embarked on our own new beginning.

We got married the week after the fall of the Berlin Wall, and our wedding was a testament to our own collaborative spirit. Through bartering with clients, we managed to arrange a beautiful wedding and an unforgettable honeymoon. Our photographer was a friend we had helped with business consulting, our caterer offered services in exchange for training sessions, and even our honeymoon travel was bartered with Iceland Airways.

During our honeymoon, Pris and I reveled in the beauty of new places and the thrill of discovering the world together. From the streets of Paris to the geothermal pools of Iceland, it looked like the beginning of a fairytale. But even in moments of joy, I struggled.

In Paris, we wandered hand in hand, sharing laughter and wine on a street corner beneath the Eiffel Tower. Pris had surprised me with a bottle of wine and a loaf of bread to celebrate our new life together. The city glowed around us, and for a moment, I let myself believe in the promise of happiness. Yet still, something in me resisted.

I became tense and argued about little things: a delayed train, a shift in plans, the weight of the luggage. I disguised my unease as frustration, not yet realizing how I was still protecting myself from joy. Back then, I hadn't learned how to fully trust peace. Joy always felt temporary and conditional.

After Paris, we traveled to Manchester and Leeds to visit Pris's family. They welcomed me; we shared stories and meals. Even so, I didn't yet know how to accept their kindness without suspicion.

From right: Pris and I on our wedding night (November 18, 1989).

In London, we explored landmarks and caught a show in the West End. Everything looked perfect on the outside, yet inside, I was bracing for collapse, for the moment she might say she couldn't do it anymore. That's what trauma does: it conditions you to expect rupture, even in the middle of wonder. A part of me never stopped fearing that the people I loved would leave; that even joy came with an expiration date.

Our final stop was Reykjavík. We didn't see the Northern Lights, but the magic found us anyway. Floating in the milky waters of The Blue Lagoon, surrounded by steam and silence, I experienced a rare kind of calm. It passed quickly, though it left a trace, a reminder that healing sometimes shows up in brief, quiet moments, not grand declarations.

At twenty-nine, I held my first passport, and in ten days, it had four stamps. It was a glimpse of a life I wasn't sure I had permission to enjoy. Not yet.

Nine months after our wedding, we adopted our daughter, MacKenzie. The journey to parenthood was filled with anticipation and hope. Once we decided to grow our family, we reached out to every local resource we could find. That's when we met an attorney whose story moved us; he had fifteen children, thirteen of which were adopted. His compassion and experience helped guide us through the complexities of the process, offering reassurance at every step.

The day we received the call that MacKenzie had been born the night before felt like the culmination of everything we had hoped for. Pris even predicted her birthday, which was three weeks sooner than she was due.

Later that day, on July seventeenth, when she was still less than twenty-four hours old, she was place in my arms for the first time. The moment I held her for the first time, love flooded through me—gratitude followed close behind, then fear. Fear of failing her. Fear of repeating a legacy I had worked so hard to escape. I knew the sound of slammed doors, the sting of silence, the weight of being unseen. Holding her, I felt the full force of responsibility rise in me. I had no map, only memory—and a promise: she would grow up free of harm, seen, safe, and loved without conditions.

MacKenzie's arrival marked the beginning of a joyful but complicated chapter. When Pris and I married, she had a twelve-year-old daughter from a previous marriage. While her parenting experience was invaluable, it also highlighted the gap between us. She had twelve years of experience; I was just stepping into the role. Balancing our marriage while learning to parent required constant growth, and plenty of mistakes.

At the same time, we had merged our businesses to form Innovative Resources. Juggling entrepreneurship with new parenthood demanded full-time collaboration, trust, and more than a little forgiveness. Our differing parenting styles, layered with professional ambitions, often collided. It became clear that both our personal and professional lives would require intentional effort, mutual respect, and compromise.

After MacKenzie was born, Pris suggested counseling to help us work through mounting arguments. She knew early intervention mattered, especially with the weight of a newborn and the complexities of a blended family. Having a teenager and an infant in the same home created emotional whiplash; their needs were so different, and the dynamic required constant adjustment.

Parenting forced us to look inward. Pris brought insight from experience. What I carried was fear—fear of doing it wrong, of becoming the kind of father I had worked so hard to escape. Terrified of repeating the very patterns I had vowed to break.

Almost twenty years had passed since my father had left, and I had just become a husband, father, and founder. From the outside, everything appeared solid. On the inside, the house still held me, not through violence, but through fear. Fear of failure. Of falling short. Of not knowing what would come next.

I moved from room to room, holding MacKenzie, steadying Pris, and leading our business, all while looking over my shoulder for something I couldn't name.

The floor was still cement. The doors still broken.

Only now, I was the one trying to hold them shut.

The fear of failing as a parent weighed on me. Sometimes it showed up as frustration, other times as distance. I escalated conflicts I didn't want, driven by a fear that Pris might leave. I didn't have the language for it then. I was living under the influence of a lifelong fear of abandonment.

Any disagreement, even over something trivial, could detonate. I wasn't reacting to the moment. I was reacting to ghosts. Pris could pause or turn inward to reflect, and I would panic, fearing that distance meant abandonment. The reaction wasn't really to her; it was to every silence I had ever endured.

Counseling helped begin the unraveling, but it wasn't quick. Fear had been present for so long that it became hard to know who I was without it. Every time it felt like progress had been made, a trigger would pull everything right back.

Over time, I started to see the fear for what it was: a powerful force, not an unchangeable truth. That insight gave me room to respond, not just react. I learned to approach conflict with compassion, for Pris, and for myself. I started to believe that connection didn't always have to hurt.

Pris stood by me through it all. When I stumbled, she helped me rise, sometimes with grace, sometimes with grit, but always with love. She taught me that healing wasn't about never falling again. It was about standing back up with more courage and clarity each time.

Letting others in stopped serving as a survival tactic; it became a way of living. I wasn't just enduring anymore. I was evolving as a partner, father, friend, and man, learning, finally, to live without fear.

* * *

The boundaries between our personal and professional lives blurred completely when we merged our businesses. Innovative Resources was an act of trust and vision, but the weight of running a company together while raising a family eventually became too much.

After starting the business seven years earlier and three since we had merged, we made the difficult but necessary decision to end the business so we could focus fully on our family. It was one of the hardest decisions we made, but one of the best. Pris returned to school to pursue a master's in counseling, eventually becoming a psychotherapist. I helped launch a curriculum development company. We both continued to grow, not by climbing ladders, but by choosing paths aligned with who we were becoming.

Rather than cling to an old idea of success, we redefined it on our terms. Staying purposeful and relevant didn't mean staying in the same place, it meant staying true to our values, even when they changed.

Pris has been my partner in every sense: business advisor, coach, confidant, cotraveler. Together, we've lived in and traveled for work or play, to more than seventy-five countries, growing through shared experiences. Her patience helped untangle my past; her perseverance helped us find common ground.

From early trials to global adventures, from raising kids to building companies, from breakdowns to breakthroughs—we grew, side by side. We didn't merge into one. We each held on to who we were. She was fully her. I was fully me. And between us, something new formed—something that belonged to both of us. You could say we were three: me, her, and us. We became partners, not by dissolving into each other, but by standing alongside each other—stronger together because we stayed whole.

That's what lifelong love and learning really look like.

There was still no happily ever after. Life doesn't work that way—for any of us. It's more like thriving and surviving simultaneously.

Sometimes, just when you think you've arrived, life hands you a mirror to show you who still needs to be seen. And that was about to happen—again. Only this time, through someone else's silence, and the courage it would take to help her find her voice . . . while rediscovering my own.

CHAPTER 19

LEARNING TO SHOW UP

Healing begins when we confront our biases, embrace vulnerability, and pursue lifelong learning, allowing our shared humanity to guide us toward understanding and connection.

After Innovative Resources, I helped launch Courseware Development Group in 1992; a new venture, a new city, and a new phase of learning (professionally and personally). On the outside, it looked like a new opportunity. On the inside, I was still trying to prove I deserved the life I had built. I hadn't yet realized that moving forward professionally didn't mean I was moving forward emotionally. We had just moved to Tampa when we met Vina.

She had recently arrived from Thailand and was attending the University of South Florida. Quiet and reserved, Vina joined the company as an intern. Like many navigating a new culture, she struggled to speak up, and was often overlooked and underestimated. Her voice was soft, her presence gentle, and colleagues took advantage of that. What she lacked in confidence, though, she made up for in potential. I just had to figure out how to help her see it too.

Recognizing her potential, I tried to encourage Vina to stand up for herself. My efforts were initially met with resistance. She was trapped in a cycle of self-doubt, feeling invisible and unable to assert herself. My persistence in pushing her to break free from that cycle eventually led to a significant confrontation, where she finally expressed her frustrations. That confrontation cracked something open in her. She spoke through tears, of being invisible, of never feeling good enough, of carrying shame for things that weren't her fault. It was raw, and it was real. From that day forward, something shifted. Her voice didn't just get louder, it got clearer. She started asking questions in meetings. She corrected a senior colleague without flinching. People began to see her as someone with something to say.

As she began to assert herself more confidently at work, it became clear that she was no longer the shy intern who had once been overlooked. Unfortunately, Courseware Development Group was not well funded and soon ran out of money. In 1994, we decided to leave Florida and move to Cary, North Carolina, a suburban town centrally located in the Research Triangle, known for its family-friendly atmosphere, excellent schools, and abundant green spaces.

I had spent so long helping others find their voice that I hadn't realized mine was changing too. With every move, every lesson, I wasn't just showing up for others, I was learning to show up for myself. Not as the fixer. Not as the overachiever. Just as me.

Joining Seer Technologies in North Carolina was my first real experience leading on a global scale. Seer was known for its cutting-edge tools like the High Productivity System (HPS), originally developed by First Boston Corporation and funded by IBM. My time at Seer was shaped by the mentorship of three remarkable individuals, especially Frank, my manager, who introduced me to the SWAN principle: Smart, Winner, Positive Attitude, and Nice; a guideline that has since shaped my approach to hiring and team building. He once pulled me aside after a tense leadership meeting.

I had spoken sharply, defensively, and impatiently, so he waited until we were alone.

"You've got the fire," he said, "but if it burns too hot, no one will stand close enough to feel it." It wasn't criticism, it was care. That moment stayed with me. He was teaching me that leadership wasn't about being the smartest in the room, it was about making space for others to shine.

When we moved to North Carolina, Vina was one of the first people I asked to join my team. She moved to an apartment near us, and we continued to support each other personally and professionally. Over the years, Vina became like family, always there to help out as MacKenzie grew; even today she and her family are a central part of our lives. Her journey, and the bond we built, reminded me of another core principle: valuing the support of others. Her growth paralleled mine, and in each other's presence, we found the strength and resilience we couldn't have mustered alone.

Pris and I had been married for five years at the time, navigating the complexities of raising a sixteen-year-old, Jennifer, and a four-year-old, MacKenzie, who was just starting preschool. Moving our home to a beautiful, quiet neighborhood allowed us to settle into the rhythms of small-town life. Over the four years we spent in Cary, we experienced a few major milestones: Jennifer graduated from high school and started college and Pris successfully opened and expanded her psychotherapy practice.

* * *

In 1996, two years after our move, Grandma Mary reached out to me. She was in her late eighties and could no longer take care of herself. Time had taken its toll, leaving her frail and dependent on others for even the simplest tasks. She had lost all of her children and her two husbands. The people she had once relied on, the ones who had shaped her life, were all gone. She was the last of her generation, left alone, and my heart broke for her.

Her request to come be near us carried the weight of years of regret and loneliness. After my father's death, she had clung to me, as a way to hold onto the last connection who was willing to be in touch with her; the last bit of family who remained. For more than three years before his death, my father had severed the bond between us and my grandparents. He manipulated them into his vendetta against us, warning them that they would be dead to him if they continued to see us.

I still remember those times when I would pick up the phone, hoping to hear their voices again, only to be met with the hollow click of the receiver as Grandma Mary chose silence over connection. It wasn't that she didn't recognize me; it was that she was choosing not to speak to me, her love overshadowed by the control my father still exerted even from a distance.

Years later, her once formidable presence was diminished by age and loss. I didn't know how to feel. Part of me wanted to protect her, but another part of me still held onto the pain of her silence. How could I trust the version of her who needed me, when she had once turned us away?

We moved her to a senior home nearby, a modest place filled with the quiet murmur of others who, like her, were in the twilight of their lives. We spent almost every weekend with her, helping with every detail of her life, from managing her medications to ensuring she went out or came to our house for her favorite meals. Each visit was a chance for her to express the love she had once withheld, a love that seemed endless, as if she were making up for lost time.

When she passed a few years later, I sat beside her as she took her final breath. In that moment, emotions I thought had long since settled came rushing back. Losing Grandma Mary unearthed so much from the past: memories of my father, the ache of our estranged years, and the silence that once filled the space where love should have lived.

Her death marked more than the end of a life. It closed a chapter heavy with unresolved feelings and the weight of a complicated history. Yet again, I found myself growing through what I had gone through, facing old wounds through a new lens of compassion and clarity.

In the days following her death, I struggled internally, the old wounds reopening despite time having passed. The peace and stability we had found in Cary felt tenuous, as if the ghosts of the past were threatening to pull me back into the darkness I had fought so hard to escape. I found myself slipping into old patterns: overworking, withdrawing, avoiding the stillness. Grief wasn't new, but the grief was layered. I wasn't just mourning her death; I was mourning the childhood I wished I would've had with her. I grieved the silence between us almost as much as the final goodbye.

Despite the internal turmoil, life in Cary continued to offer the stability and peace we all desperately needed. It was a time of healing, of building new memories, and of cherishing the moments we had with each other. The process wasn't without its difficulties. Gradually, I found ways to push the pain of those memories down into the depths of their hiding places.

* * *

Back at Seer, my professional growth continued to be shaped by influential colleagues. Susan, my friend and office confidante, helped me navigate frustrations, and advised me to decide "which hill I was willing to die on that day." Her counsel taught me to prioritize effectively, a skill I've shared throughout my career. She also cautioned, "When you go in the room with a skunk, everyone comes out smelling like the skunk," a memorable lesson in hiring and interactions that I've widely imparted. The SWAN principle and Susan's wisdom have guided many, helping to build high-performance, relationship-centered teams around the world.

Lisa, who joined Seer two years later, consistently made interactions positive and memorable. Her attention to detail and creativity in relationship building profoundly impacted my approach, showing that meaningful connections are possible with everyone, including subordinates. Lisa had an innate ability to make people feel valued and understood, often going out of her way to remember small details about their lives and interests. Her thoughtful gestures and personalized communication style fostered a sense of belonging and loyalty among the team.

One particular instance that stood out was when Lisa organized a surprise celebration for a colleague's milestone achievement. She meticulously planned every aspect, from the decor to the heartfelt speeches, making it an unforgettable experience for everyone involved. That event highlighted her organizational skills and her genuine care for the well-being and happiness of her colleagues. Her actions demonstrated the importance of recognizing and celebrating individual contributions, which, in turn, boosted morale and productivity within the team.

Lisa's influence extended beyond professional interactions; she often facilitated team-building activities that encouraged open communication and collaboration. She exemplified the power of cultivating meaningful relationships. It wasn't about transactional communication, it was about human connection, and she modeled that every day. Her ability to create an inclusive environment where everyone felt heard and appreciated inspired me to adopt similar practices in my leadership style.

The influences of colleagues laid a strong foundation for my leadership principles. My manager's strategic thinking, Susan's empathetic approach, and the relational creativity of others collectively shaped my understanding of what it means to be an effective and compassionate leader. Those experiences at Seer were instrumental in preparing me for the next phase of my career at Booz Allen Hamilton, and equipped me with the skills and mindset needed to navigate complex challenges and lead with integrity. They also reinforced one of the guiding principles I've come to live by: the importance of pursuing lifelong learning and adaptability. Every challenge sharpened my capacity to learn, unlearn, and grow.

* * *

In 1998, I joined Booz Allen Hamilton, a management and technology consulting firm headquartered in Northern Virginia. That transition marked a significant step. I relocated several months before Pris and MacKenzie, allowing her to finish the school year without interruption. During that period, I lived in a temporary apartment in Northern Virginia, eagerly anticipating when we would all be together again. Pris and MacKenzie visited during the interim, and our weekends were spent searching for the perfect home.

One memorable trip stands out. Just before heading to the airport, we stopped at a small shop where I bought two small metal hearts, one for myself and one for MacKenzie. At the airport, as we waited, MacKenzie looked up at me and said, "Daddy, can we trade hearts?"

Puzzled, I asked, "Why do you want to trade hearts, MacKenzie? They're exactly the same."

With a wisdom far beyond her years, she insisted, "It's different if we trade. Now yours will have my love, and mine will have yours."

Her words touched me deeply. "That's a great idea," I said, my voice thick with emotion. "Now we will always have a part of each other."

We traded hearts, and as I held the small metal heart, I looked at MacKenzie with admiration. Her intuition and ability to convey profound sentiments always amazed me. Those identical hearts became symbols of our bond, a tangible reminder of our connection, no matter where we were. That period of transitions tested our family bonds while marking the start of a rewarding time in my life. That heart still sits on my desk, even today.

As the head of Learning and Organization Development at Booz Allen, I was proud to lead the creation of the Center for Performance Excellence, which garnered many prestigious accolades. Those included top rankings in *Training* magazine's "Top 125," Association for Talent Development's BEST Awards, more than forty best practice awards, and top honors from *Working Mother* magazine and *Diversity Magazine* for our outstanding learning and development practices. The awards recognized our comprehensive approach, which encompassed professional and leadership development, technical skills training, and personal growth initiatives. More than just professional achievements, my work allowed me to stay purposeful and relevant, aligning my passion for education and equity with the ever-changing needs of a modern workforce.

Despite those achievements, I often struggled with imposter syndrome; the persistent belief that I was undeserving of those successes and that I could at any moment, be exposed as a fraud. Even with all the awards and recognition, I often felt like a fraud, like I had fooled everyone into thinking I belonged. I could lead teams, build programs, win accolades—but I couldn't speak the truth that haunted me. I was still hiding the most formative part of my story: the abuse I endured and the silence that followed.

The silence about my past was a mask that I continued to wear.

On September 11, 2001, the energy of our executive retreat in Princeton, New Jersey, was palpable, as leaders from around the world gathered together. We were all excited about the five days ahead during which we would be sharing insights, discussing strategies, and fostering connections. The atmosphere was one of anticipation and camaraderie as we dove into the sessions that would shape our work and collaboration for the months to come.

We were on a break, gathered in the conference center's break area, where televisions were broadcasting the news. Initially, we watched, not fully realizing what was happening. The early news reports were uncertain, with anchors suggesting that a small plane had accidentally crashed into the North Tower of the World Trade Center. The tone was cautious, with reporters trying to piece together limited information while the live images of the burning tower played on the screen.

As we continued watching, the situation escalated rapidly. We saw live as the second plane, a large commercial jet, crashed into the South Tower. The reporters' voices, once measured, grew increasingly alarmed. The realization dawned that it was not an accident—it was a coordinated attack. The newsroom became frantic as the scale of the tragedy began to unfold before the eyes of the world.

The atmosphere in the room where we stood intensified and became filled with disbelief. The news anchors, who had likely prepared for any number of breaking stories, seemed to struggle to find the words to describe the horror that was unfolding. They were watching the same images we were, of thick, black smoke billowing from both towers, people hanging out of windows, desperately waving for help that would not come.

Then, the unimaginable happened. The South Tower began to collapse. At first, the reporters seemed unable to comprehend what they were seeing. As the tower crumbled into a cloud of dust and debris, there was a moment of stunned silence on air, broken only by the shocked reactions of the reporters and the gasps of those watching.

Not long after, the North Tower fell, and the reporters began speaking in tones of disbelief and despair. Words like "devastation," "apocalyptic," and "unthinkable" were used as they tried to describe the sheer magnitude of the destruction. The collapse of the second tower cemented the sense of loss and tragedy. I stood frozen. It wasn't just the world that felt broken. It was something inside me, cracking again under the weight of helplessness. I had spent a lifetime trying to control chaos, and there it was, unfolding on live television—unstoppable, incomprehensible.

In that break area, as we stood glued to the screen, the sense of shock deepened into something more profound: an awareness that the world had changed in those brief, terrible moments. The news anchors' attempts to report on the events were tinged with the same emotions we all felt: fear, grief, and a dawning realization that nothing would ever be the same.

The shock quickly turned into anxiety as I realized I had no way of contacting Pris. The phone lines were down, and I couldn't reach her to find out what was happening. I rushed to my hotel room, hoping the hotel phone might work. The lines were down there too. In a moment of desperation, I sent an email, uncertain if it would get through amidst the chaos. To my immense relief, Pris responded with a brief message, letting me know that everyone was safe. Knowing that they were okay even as the world seemed to be falling apart provided some comfort. In return, I let her know a few of us would be coming back as soon as we could.

Three of us decided to drive back to Northern Virginia in our rental car. The drive was haunting. We talked and listened to the news, trying to make sense of what was happening. The roads, usually bustling with activity, were eerily empty. The regular sounds of planes overhead were absent, as all flights had been grounded. The silence was oppressive, amplifying the surreal and unsettling nature of the day. When we arrived at Washington Dulles International Airport to return the rental car, the total stillness of the usually busy hub underscored the magnitude of what had occurred, making the reality of the events sink in even deeper.

That day, Pris and I promised never to end a day angry, knowing we never wanted anyone in our family to go to bed without feeling loved. While that commitment was aspirational and much easier said than done, we realized the fragility of life and the importance of cherishing those we care about should never be taken for granted.

That realization stayed with me. It softened something. In the months that followed, I found myself more open, more willing to listen for wisdom in unexpected places.

* * *

In the spring of 2002, I attended a leadership conference where the keynote speaker was Holocaust survivor Gerda Weissman Klein. She endured six years of Nazi brutality, forced labor camps, starvation, and a 350-mile death march through snow-covered terrain in the final months of the war. Out of four thousand women, only a few hundred survived. Gerda was one of them. When she spoke, it wasn't with anger. It was with quiet, determined strength. She said something that hit me harder than I expected:

"Ninety percent of what you worry about will probably never happen. And the other ten percent, you can't stop. So why worry?"

She wasn't offering a slogan. She was offering lived truth.

Gerda signed a copy of her memoir, *All But My Life*, for us. She was gracious, warm, and fully present. It was a brief exchange, yet one I've never forgotten. Her words had landed in me while she spoke. Meeting her in person made the moment unforgettable.

That experience shifted something in me, and it embodied three of the principles I live by. First, we grow through what we go through when we allow our pain to shape us rather than define us. Second, the support we need often comes from unexpected places, sometimes from a stranger who, without knowing us, guides us. Third, healing calls us to keep learning and adapting, to stay open to lessons, no matter where or from whom they come.

Years later, I saw her again on television receiving the Presidential Medal of Freedom. She stood with the same grounded grace and said:

"If the darkness seems so total . . . remember, never ever give up."

Gerda passed away in 2022 at the age of ninety-seven. Yet her voice still echoes in the work I do. To this day, when I'm coaching or mentoring someone carrying more worry than they need to, I share her story, and that quote. One conversation. One book. A lifetime of impact.

* * *

The Healing the Heart of Diversity program, developed by multiple innovators including Pat Harbour, was crafted to transform the culture within organizations by fostering meaningful dialogue and an understanding of diversity. It was designed to challenge participants to confront their biases, both surface level and hidden, and encourage the creation of more inclusive and compassionate environments.

During one of the three-day retreats, the program included an activity in which our facilitators asked participants to group themselves based on affinity. As the Women of Color, Men of Color, White women, and White men gathered into their respective groups, I found myself standing alone, uncertain of where I belonged. The facilitator's words echoed in my ears. However, my mind was elsewhere—suddenly thrust back into a whirlwind of memories.

For me, the experience was profoundly transformative, albeit in a way that was both scary and uncomfortable. My affinity was not with the group I was expected to join: White men. The realization stemmed from the lasting impact of my father, a White man, whose domination, violence, anger, and repression had instilled in me a deep-seated fear. In my eyes, all men were oppressors, and I feared that by joining them, my secret shame would be revealed. That fear and discomfort were rooted in the trauma of my past, making it difficult to find common ground with those who represented the very forces that had caused me so much pain.

As I stood there, seven-year-old me came rushing back, paralyzed in the hallway, my father's booming voice echoing through the house: "Get out of my sight before I really lose my temper!" I saw my mother crumble to the floor, her body collapsing under the weight of his fury. The living room returned in full: the sound of his belt slicing through the air, the sting of the buckle against my bare skin. Bent over, naked and trembling, I endured the relentless blows as his voice dripped with venom: "You're useless! Why can't you do anything right?"

The mantra I whispered to myself, "I'm not crazy; he is," echoed louder and louder, trying to drown out the pain, the fear, the endless cycle of abuse. Each blow, each command, each belittling word repeated itself in my mind, a never-ending loop of despair and helplessness.

The facilitator's voice broke through the haze, pulling me back to the present. "Please go and stand with your affinity group," she repeated.

I couldn't move. "I have none," I whispered, the words catching in my throat.

I started to shake. Tears streamed down my face, the years of suppressed pain overwhelming me. The facilitator's eyes widened with concern as she gently asked, "Are you okay? What's happening?"

Like a massive waterfall, it all came pouring out from the depths of my soul. "I can't . . . I can't belong to any of these groups," I choked out. "My father . . . he was supposed to be my protector, but instead, he was a monster. I can't stand with them . . . I can't stand with anyone." My voice quivered as I shared the unbearable memories that had haunted me for so long.

The room fell silent as others quickly realized there was a depth I had not shown before, a despair equal to, if not deeper than, their own. I could feel their eyes on me. I couldn't just stop. "He beat me . . . he beat me until I bled, until I couldn't cry anymore. And when he was done, he left me alone with my thoughts, with the fear that it would happen again. And it did. Over and over." My voice cracked, the flood of emotions leaving me raw and exposed.

This marked a significant revelation; the first time I had openly confronted the truth: no real sense of identity existed within any of those groups. By my forties, the abuse had been over for more than twenty-five years. A life had been built that, on the surface, appeared solid. Married for over a decade. Two children. A career well underway. Professional success had been reached, and the love for my family ran deep.

Yet, the echoes of the past still lingered. All of the achievements, pain, and confusion from those early years remained just beneath the surface, leaving a sense of disconnection and uncertainty about where I truly belonged.

For too long, I had been forced to suppress my pain, a burden that began with my father's abuse, that was compounded by society encouraging my silence, and then perpetuated by the pain I unwittingly continued to inflict upon myself.

When I shared the reasons behind my inability to identify with any one group, it was as though a dam had broken. The response was overwhelmingly supportive. Each group surrounded me with love and understanding, creating a safe space to explore the complex emotions that I had kept buried for so long.

It was during those moments of intense struggle that Pat Moore, another one of the program's creators, and a Black woman, shared a story about growing up during the late sixties in a segregated community. She recounted a day when she and a friend, engrossed in conversation, boarded a bus and took a seat without thinking. The bus driver, a White man, harshly instructed her to move to the back of the bus; a command that felt like a slap in the face. That single experience profoundly shaped her perception of herself and White men for years to come. When she shared her vulnerability and the lasting impact of that moment, it was deeply moving. She amplified my own feelings of displacement and raised questions about identity that I hadn't fully faced until then.

The day culminated in a profound exploration of "White guilt," a concept that struck a chord with my ongoing struggles around identity. White guilt, for me, became an unsettling mix of remorse and discomfort, rooted in the awareness of privileges I hadn't fully acknowledged and the injustices faced by People of Color throughout history. The guilt was like a weight on my shoulders, but at the same time, it pushed me toward growth and a deeper understanding of myself.

Logically, I knew that process was necessary as our society moved toward acceptance of diversity and healing from the past. Emotionally, though, I found myself wrestling with questions. Upon reflection, I wondered why I couldn't be seen simply as a human, instead of being defined by societal categories. My yearning to be recognized beyond labels and to connect on a human level was an underlying struggle, amplifying the internal conflict I felt during the program.

Returning from the three-day retreat, (one in a series of four held at the Fetzer Institute in Michigan), left me profoundly changed. Through tears and emotion, I tried to share with Pris what had unfolded, but words couldn't convey the effect the experience had on me. Something had shifted. A path forward had begun to emerge: toward becoming a better person, a better husband, a better father, and a more compassionate leader.

The experience was a turning point that continues to shape my approach to diversity, inclusion, and the broader conversation about how we connect with others in meaningful and compassionate ways. It helped me understand that the stories we carry—about ourselves, and about each other—are often shaped by a single moment. Those stories can evolve.

For most, the Healing the Heart of Diversity program was about understanding the world. For me, it was about reclaiming myself. The program gave me tools. It gave me permission; to feel, to speak, to belong.

Healing the Heart of Diversity began with healing the fracture in my own. For the first time, I wasn't just learning to show up. I was learning to stay.

Just when I thought I had found my footing—just when I believed I had done the work—grief came for me again. But not as a storm; as a whisper that was familiar, slow, and unrelenting. It would ask me to face the one relationship I still couldn't fully name, even in silence.

CHAPTER 20

LETTING GO

Some women survive the unthinkable and still find a way to show up gently, to love unconditionally, and to rise. My mother was one of them.

In January 2003, my mother had a stroke. I was working late when Pris called with the news. I knew it then: it was the beginning of the end. I wasn't ready to lose her, and especially face the part of me still tethered to her survival. Her decline would force me to confront grief, memories, and the truth I still hadn't fully told to anyone including myself.

We had reconciled. In her final years, we shared a close, quiet relationship. For the last six weeks of her life, Pris and I took turns staying with her at home, each of us carrying the silent weight of what was coming. Over time, my mother and Pris had formed a bond that went beyond in-laws. It became a true mother-daughter relationship. Even though my mother lived just two miles away, they spoke multiple times a day. I never knew what they talked about. There were no grand declarations, no dramatic goodbyes—just presence, care, and a kind of stillness that only emerges when time is running out.

We leaned on each other.

I began to understand something I hadn't been able to name before: sometimes, the support of others is the only way through.

They say that when you are dying, your life flashes before your eyes like a movie, a final, poignant tribute to the journey taken. For my mother, that was no mere saying; it became her reality. Over the course of several days, with her eyes often closed, she relived the moments of her life. Each breath seemed to carry her further back into her past, revisiting the moments that had defined her life.

She was still able to function with assistance, a blessing that allowed her to stay at home, surrounded by the familiar comforts of the life she had built. We were there with her, guiding her through daily routines, helping her eat and move about. Though she struggled to remember recent events, her body carried on, driven by a resilience that both inspired and broke our hearts.

One evening, as I sat beside her in the quiet of the apartment, she called out, her voice trembling with emotion, "I loved him. I loved him." Her words filled the room, laden with a depth of feeling that pierced my heart.

"Who did you love, Mom?" I asked gently, though a part of me already knew the answer.

"Your father," she replied softly, her voice resolute. Her eyes remained closed, as if the mere act of opening them would pull her away from the memories she was so immersed in. Even in her final moments, she clung to the memory of the man who had been both her partner and her tormentor. In some twisted way, he had been her love. Her words cut through me, confusing, painful, and strangely human. How could she still love him after everything? Part of me wanted to scream, but part of me understood. Trauma bonds are complicated. So is grief. I realized then: forgiveness doesn't mean forgetting and love doesn't always make sense.

My mother, who had lost so much, had not lost the memory of the man she had lived with for so long. Their complicated, tumultuous relationship was the one thing that remained untouchable, even by the cruel hands of time and illness.

"No, Eddie," she whispered. The time for sleep had come, so I said, "Good night."

She responded, "Sleep tight."

Instinctively, I added, "Wake up bright."

She softly finished, "To do what's right, before the night."

Tears welled in my eyes as I knew those might be our final words.

The mantra, "Good night, sleep tight, wake up bright, to do what's right before the night" became more than a nightly ritual; it symbolized the bond we shared and the connection she had with her mother. It was one of those rare, meaningful threads that tied generations together, and reminded me of the power of even the simplest rituals. Even after her passing, these words still echo in my heart as a reminder of her love and wisdom.

We had the words, "Good night, sleep tight, wake up bright, to do what's right before the night" etched into several rocks. One sits at our house. I gave one to my sister and one to my brother, ensuring that her presence would remain with us always.

Then, the day before she passed, she began to fade. Her strength, which had carried her through those difficult weeks, ebbed away, leaving her more fragile than ever. I lay beside her in bed, holding her close. "Mom," I asked quietly, "are you afraid?"

* * *

Over the next year, I was caught in a whirlwind of emotions. I struggled at home and at work and found myself arguing with everyone about everything. My mental state deteriorated rapidly as depression swallowed me whole. The bulimia resurfaced, and I spent countless hours in the gym, desperately trying to sweat away the pain. I buried myself in excessive work, hoping to numb the anguish. Her death ripped open old wounds, resurrecting memories of my father's abuse and the relentless self-abuse that followed.

More than thirty years had passed since he left, and still, the feeling of being trapped in that house remained. No longer did the weight come from his fists, belt, or blade, but from grief; from the chaos inside me. From the fear that I might break everything I loved.

I had survived him, built a life, become a husband, father, and leader and yet, when my mother died, something in me collapsed. As if the foundation I had built my life on was still laid on cement floors, still framed by broken doors.

I didn't know what would happen next. I only knew, I still wasn't free. Not yet.

The nightmare returned, bringing back the terror of my father's grip, even in death. I found myself back in the funeral home, leaning over his casket. His eyes snapped open, his hands lunged at my throat. I would wake up in a panic, drenched in sweat. Would his control over me ever truly end? It wasn't just a dream; it was a message. That even dead, he lived in me, in my muscles, my fears, my reflexes. I had escaped the man, but not the imprint and part of me was terrified that I never would.

Not even the transformative experiences from the Healing the Heart of Diversity retreats, nor hours of grief therapy, could numb the pain. Despite my efforts, the memories haunted me. Even so, those experiences gave me tools, ways to reflect, adapt, and stay open to learning, even in the depths of grief.

As I continued to struggle, an opportunity arose in September 2003. I was invited to give the keynote speech at a graduation for Northern Virginia Family Service's Training Futures program. During my time at Booz Allen, we supported this workforce development initiative, which trained more than five thousand individuals from 2000 to 2005, achieving an 80 percent placement rate. Graduates saw an average of an 87 percent increase in compensation, and their tenure was 70 percent higher than others.

Standing before those graduates, I realized that the journey through pain had also forged a strength I never knew I possessed. In that moment, I wasn't just honoring their resilience, I was quietly honoring my own. I had grown through what I had gone through, even when I didn't realize it. I could inspire others, but still couldn't find the words to comfort myself. Grief doesn't care how articulate you are. It seeps through the cracks no one sees, especially the ones you hide best.

* * *

When I stood before the graduates, here's what I told them:

Ladies and Gentlemen, I'm both honored and humbled to be your speaker this morning. Booz Allen Hamilton has been a sponsor for the Training Futures program for several years now. We're very proud to say that six previous graduates from Training Futures now work for Booz Allen.

I'm especially proud of NaTasha Crawford because she works on my team. NaTasha came to Training Futures, a twenty-two-year-old single mother of two whose last job had her flipping burgers. NaTasha lived in government-subsidized housing in Falls Church when she began with Booz Allen after graduating. Four years later, NaTasha has earned three promotions and just last month, she and her two children moved into their very own newly built home.

Programs like Training Futures make a difference today for people like NaTasha, and for people like you. That impact reaches far beyond NaTasha and the present day. It reaches into the future.

This morning, I'd like to talk about that future—about the "Next Generation." I'd like to talk about the next generation by telling you a story from the past. I know a story from the past is an odd way to go about talking about the next generation, but I'm hoping you'll understand by the time I'm done.

A man and a woman meet, they fall in love, and get married. Two years later they have their first child. They open a mom-and-pop grocery store and all appears to be normal.

Except this man is very unhappy, tormented you might even say. He drinks to ease his pain. He gambles to pass the time. Eventually they lose the store because they owe too many people too much money. And, so they move on.

He goes to work for a major airline. She learns to type and goes to work in a typing pool. He still drinks. He still gambles. Only now to share his misery he verbally and physically abuses his wife and he cheats on her.

He wants more children. She is afraid to have more children who might be subjected to his abuse so takes precautions not to get pregnant, never letting him know. Almost ten years pass. They have another child, a girl, and then two years later, a boy.

Life, for the man and woman, settles down, taking on a rhythm as they raise their family. But he is still not content with his life. He likes the fast world of wine, woman, song, and gambling, and is constantly tempted back to it.

He continues to have affairs. She continues to pretend everything is fine. Until, one day he goes to work after having too much to drink and loses his job.

He decides to move the family to Florida for a new start. He is unable to hold down a job. Alcohol, and now pain pills, exaggerate his anger. He hates his life. He is unable to find happiness in anything he does. So, he takes his pain out on his wife and his children.

Yet, to the outside world, this family seems quite normal.

No one speaks about the violence.

No one speaks about the indiscretions.

No one speaks about the fear.

He spends his days drinking from the bottle of whiskey that sits next to his bed. He spends nights with body-wrenching hangovers. She spends her days taking care of the family, making small amounts of money by conducting telephone surveys and swallowing the little pride she has left as she stands in line for welfare and food stamps. She and her youngest children spend their nights nursing his hangovers.

One day, he meets a man at a bar. They become friends. He goes to work with his new friend in a gas station. For a while, again, life seems normal. Until he decides he is in love with his new best friend's wife.

So, he leaves his wife. This woman who has been with him for twenty-five years that he has convinced would be nobody without him. Off he goes with his new wife, moving to Georgia, leaving his family behind with no money and a mountain of bills to pay. Eventually his new life with his new wife deteriorates and he puts an end to the misery and pain by committing suicide.

Meanwhile, back in Florida, she still has two children at home with physical and emotional wounds from many years of abuse. For years, he told her that she would be "a nobody" without him.

Now, she has no confidence in herself. She can barely take care of herself, let alone help her children. Yet somewhere, inside, she finds the strength to pull herself up, to reach out and find help.

She seeks guidance and counseling for her family and makes attempts to make up for the years of horror. She realizes she needs to do something to support her family so she enrolls at the community college. She spends her days taking care of the family and conducting telephone surveys. She spends her nights attending school and studying. She learns to prepare income taxes and she works hard and learns her new craft well.

She loves her children, the best she can. She tries to provide the trust, encouragement, and freedoms they were never before allowed. She loves her children unconditionally. She encourages them to look forward and not back. She tells them to build lives for themselves and to not remain imprisoned by the past, something we all know is easier said than done.

When she retires at seventy-two, she moves to be near her youngest son and his family. Five years later, she has a stroke. During her short illness, he writes almost daily in a journal.

Take her home; nothing more to do, let go.

Nonsense, he would know if she were leaving, he would feel the severing of their souls. They should not give up so easily.

A week passes. She sleeps. She wakes. She barely knows him.

Is this it? Was he wrong?

How do you say goodbye to the one who inspired your life? To the one who brought you through the darkest of nights and loved you unconditionally?

Daily they meet, few words spoken. They lay together, holding hands.

She opens her eyes; she smiles, they hug. A childhood prayer she whispers, "Goodnight, sleep tight, wake up bright, to do what's right, before the night."

He smiles when she says that. It was worth the wait.

The sun rises, piercing through the clouds; its light shining through.

Her breath faint, her journey nearing; surrounded by family, sweet music fills the room. The angels arrive. A final breath and her soul soars to heaven.

The next day, surrounded by her children, thirteen grandchildren, and one great-grandchild, she is laid to rest.

Ladies and gentlemen, you know the courage it took for this woman to reach out for help because each of you reached out for help when you began your journey with Training Futures. That was your first courageous step.

Your second courageous and well-earned step you are accomplishing today by graduating from Training Futures.

Your third step is finding a job and keeping it. Yes, there is always another step to take. And sometimes you'll not feel like you're getting very far.

As the woman I told you about today learned, it truly takes a lifetime. Your lives will not be perfect because of Training Futures and your accomplishments here. I'm pretty sure they will be better. And as you live your lives, I hope you'll think of the story I've shared with you, of a woman who, after being abused and beaten down for many years, reached out for help, picked herself up, and built a new life for her and her family. And along the way inspired a child to be so much more than she could have ever dreamed.

Several years ago, Laura Nyro wrote a song that was sung by a group called Blood, Sweat & Tears. The song ends with these words: "And when I die, and when I'm gone there'll be, one child born, in this world to carry on."

Ladies and gentlemen, I am that child. This woman was my mother. I am the next generation; I am the future I told you about earlier. And, I'm here today, representing the next generation who are your sons, your daughters, and all the children who you, in your lifetime, will influence.

For your future and for the future of your next generation, I'm here to wish you all the best on your journey. And to say thank you for taking that journey.

The speech ended with an extended standing ovation. It felt good to have honored my mother with her story and I had hoped it would help with my healing process. It didn't. I continued to binge and purge, work out at the gym, work excessively, have the recurring nightmare, and go to therapy, all the while pretending that everything was fine.

* * *

Everyone needs an Aunt Audre—a beacon of wisdom and love—who reminds us to move forward, encouraging us to embrace life beyond the shadows of our past.

Losing Aunt Audre was another crushing blow during an already difficult time. She was suffering from cancer, and in July of 2004, she passed away. The week before she left us, she called me into her room. Despite the toll the illness had taken on her frail body, her spirit remained unyielding, and her eyes still sparkled with the familiar warmth and wisdom that had been a constant in my life.

By then, I was already frayed, barely holding it together after months of pretending I was fine. Her room was dim and quiet. She had always seen me clearly. She even saw through my pain. I didn't want to say goodbye; I wasn't sure I could.

As I sat beside her, memories of the countless times she had been there for me flooded my mind. The family gatherings at her home, where she always made sure I felt welcome and included. She had an uncanny ability to know when I needed to talk and when I simply needed someone to sit with me in silence. Her wisdom had guided me through the darkest periods of my life, teaching me that it was okay to hope and to live beyond the pain.

She reminded me of Lucille Ball playing Auntie Mame in the 1974 film, *Mame*—quick-witted, theatrical, and full of life and mischief. Lucy had red hair, and Aunt Audre had the same striking shade for most of her life. Even after it turned white, every time I thought about Lucy, I thought about her.

Rooms lit up when she entered because of her dazzling smile, fierce love, and unforgettable style. Her fashion sense matched her personality: flowing scarves, oversized sunglasses, dramatic jewelry, and fearless colors that always turned heads. Every visit to her home felt like stepping into a celebration of life. Even in difficulty, she found a way to bring laughter and joy. Her courage, style, and unshakable belief in being yourself became part of me long before I understood how much I needed them.

Aunt Audre, sensing my thoughts, gently squeezed my hand. "Eddie," she said, her voice soft yet unwavering, "you need to move forward with your life. I see the pain in your eyes. You can't let the shadows of your past shape the path of your future. You deserve to be happy. Promise me."

I tried to lie, to hide my pain, but there was no use. Our connection was so deep that she could see through my façade into my soul.

"I promise," I said, and in that moment, I truly meant it. I wanted to honor her; to do my best to live the life she wished for me. It was one of those moments where I could feel myself beginning to grow, not in spite of the pain, but because of it. Something cracked open, not all at once, not dramatically, but just enough. At that moment, it was enough to let her words in. Enough to let go of just a little shame. Enough to imagine that maybe I didn't have to keep carrying it all.

On July 4, before the fireworks lit up the sky in celebration of freedom, Aunt Audre took her final breath. Alongside the sorrow, I felt a strange sense of liberation; a quiet release from the chains of the past that had bound me for so long. As America celebrated its independence, we spent the day planning her funeral. Her words lingered as a final gift; a reminder of the strength she had always helped me find within myself.

That wise woman had once again guided and cajoled me forward. Her words weren't just comfort; they were a call. A promise. They would push to keep showing up for others and for myself.

In our final conversation, she passed something on to me: strength, vision, and permission. I missed her terribly, but her voice stayed with me. It stirred something inside.

I continued therapy. The self-abuse stopped. The nightmare that had haunted me for years finally ended. Not all at once. Not neatly—just enough to know I was moving forward.

Healing wasn't a straight line. It was unlearning, relearning, and learning again. That was her final lesson, and maybe, the most important one of all.

A few weeks later, I walked the path behind our home, the one that wound through the trees and opened up near the lake. The summer air was thick with heat, the kind that slows everything down and makes space for stillness. I carried one of the small rocks in my pocket. When I reached the lake, I sat on a bench and held the rock in my hand for a long time.

"Thank you," I whispered. Then I walked to the edge of the water and placed it beneath the shade of a tree. The light rippled across the surface. For the first time in months, I exhaled fully. I stood there for a while, listening, letting the silence hold me. Letting myself feel it all.

I wasn't healed; not fully. I was finally willing to believe I could be. Just as I began to find my footing, life nudged me forward again, halfway across the world, into something new. Something that would test everything I thought I knew about healing, love, and showing up.

PART IV
CULTIVATE MEANINGFUL RELATIONSHIPS

Choosing connection as the path to healing begins with transformation through shared experiences, where trust grows through vulnerability. It continues with facing the mirror, confronting who we are and how we relate to others. From there, we move from silence to strength, learning that saying goodbye can be an act of love, and that showing up authentically is where true resilience lives, not in perfection, but in presence.

CHAPTER 21

TRANSFORMATION THROUGH SHARED EXPERIENCES

Embracing a new culture opens our hearts and minds, reminding us that the journey of adaptation and learning enriches our lives and the lives of those we touch along the way.

In early 2005, a recruiter reached out about a role with a company in India. I wasn't looking to leave Booz Allen and took the first meeting as a courtesy. The conversations kept coming, and so did the offers. They weren't just offering a job. They were offering something I hadn't yet experienced: the chance to lead on a truly global scale.

Still, I said no, many times.

They didn't accept it. Eventually, the company's founder flew from India to meet with us in person. That meeting changed everything.

Inspired by his vision, Pris and I decided to move across the world, to a country we'd never set foot in, for roles that would stretch us in every direction. I was appointed senior vice president and chief learning officer for Satyam Computer Services. Pris became Head of Executive Coaching and Development for the company's senior leaders. Our teenage daughter, MacKenzie, came with us.

We sold nearly everything: our home, our cars, our certainty. What we kept was boxed, shipped across oceans, and arrived in Hyderabad nine weeks later.

This wasn't just a relocation; it was a complete reset.

It would change all three of us, individually, and as a whole.

It was a culture shock to step off the airplane in November of that year and find ourselves in a completely different world. We moved into a home in a local Hyderabad neighborhood and began to settle into life in a new country. Hyderabad, known as the "City of Pearls," has a rich history, culture, and diversity. It is a bustling metropolis that blends its ancient heritage with modernity. The city was a sensory overload at first: the masses of people, the animals roaming the streets, the vibrant markets, the constant symphony of honking traffic. It was the complete opposite of the orderly life we had known in the United States.

Our two-year-old dog, Jasper, a schnoodle (half poodle, half schnauzer), joined us on our adventure. Jasper was fascinated by the new surroundings, especially the animals and the people. He often rode in the car with our driver, John Kennedy, his nose pressed against the window as he took in the sights and smells of the city. Whether it was cows leisurely walking down the road, goats grazing by the roadside, street vendors selling their colorful wares, or the beggars tapping on the car window, everything caught Jasper's attention. His excitement and curiosity added a layer of fun and discovery to our experience.

The streets of Hyderabad were a symphony of sounds and colors. The air was filled with the aroma of spices, mingling with the scent of street food being cooked on every corner. The bustling markets, or bazaars, were alive with activity: vendors called out to potential customers, and the vibrant display of goods ranged from fresh produce to intricate jewelry. It was a feast for the senses—the vivid colors of saris and spices, the rich sounds of bargaining in multiple languages, and the constant experience of navigating through crowded spaces.

Living in a local neighborhood gave us an authentic taste of daily life in Hyderabad. Most of our neighbors were welcoming, even inviting us to share in their festivals and traditions. There was always something happening, whether it was a religious celebration, a wedding procession, or simply a gathering of families in the evening.

However, the adjustment wasn't without its struggles. Indian society, particularly in 2005, was far more conservative and rooted in tradition than we were used to. That was evident in various aspects of daily life, from gender roles to social interactions. The caste system, although officially abolished, still lingered in subtle forms, influencing social dynamics and business practices. Navigating those cultural norms added a layer of complexity to our experience, as we had to be mindful of traditions and customs that were vastly different from what we were accustomed to in the United States.

Adjusting to a new culture and environment was challenging and enriching. It demanded one of our guiding principles: the pursuit of lifelong learning and adaptability. We immersed ourselves in Indian culture, guided by a culture expert, Pragnya Seth, who was instrumental in helping us navigate those early days.

Reflecting on those initial weeks, everything was different. For the first time, I experienced what it meant to be a true minority as the only American in the room. However, it's important to note that my experience was layered. While I was a minority in terms of nationality, I still carried a certain level of privilege due to my status as both an American and a man in India. Despite some brushing off my perspectives, claiming I didn't understand their culture, there was an underlying respect afforded to me because of those factors. That duality—being both an outsider and yet still holding a position of higher status—was a unique and sometimes challenging experience to navigate.

What I hadn't expected was the unraveling that came almost immediately. Just days after arriving, I fell violently ill with what the locals called "Delhi belly," but it felt more like full-body betrayal. Feverish, dehydrated, and disoriented, I lay in bed wondering what we had done. The heat was suffocating, the sounds unrelenting, and my mind started spinning with doubt. I remember whispering to Pris, "What if we made a mistake?" She squeezed my hand but said nothing. I knew she was wondering the same thing.

I closed my eyes, the hum of the air conditioner blending with the honking and shouting outside—life in full volume, pressing in. It wasn't just illness, it was disorientation, and maybe, that was the point.

I hadn't gone there to feel safe. I had gone there to change. That thought settled quietly. No comfort, no clarity, just a shift. Maybe transformation begins not when things get easier, but when you stop trying to make them make sense.

When I explained my experiences to our culture coach, Pragnya Seth, she nodded and said, "It's a common feeling for newcomers. My responsibility is to help you understand the social norms, customs, and traditions that might not be immediately obvious."

Her guidance was invaluable, and her strategy was a game changer during our time in India. Pragnya, who also worked for Satyam, was a local guide through a cultural labyrinth.

From the outset, Pragnya provided us with detailed insights into the cultural nuances that influence business interactions in India. Specifically, her tips on understanding the local languages were incredibly helpful and made us feel more confident and integrated into the community. Curious as to how we should go about bargaining, we asked her.

Pragnya smiled then explained, "Local markets can be quite vibrant. Knowing the bargaining etiquette can make a big difference. First, always start by asking for the price. The initial price quoted is often higher than what the seller expects to receive. You should respond with a counteroffer that is significantly lower, yet still reasonable. This starts the negotiation process. It's important to stay polite and friendly throughout. Use phrases like 'Can you give me a better price?' or 'What is your best price?'"

She continued, "Make sure to show interest but not desperation. If the price doesn't come down enough, you can show hesitation or start to walk away. Often, the seller will call you back with a better offer. Also, try to buy multiple items from the same vendor, which can help in getting a better overall deal."

Her advice was practical and made the experience enjoyable.

Pragnya's role as our culture coach was pivotal, and her presence as a friend and guide enriched our experience in India, reminding us how essential it is to value the support of others in unfamiliar territory. Her expertise not only facilitated our professional success; it ensured that we adapted smoothly to our new environment.

The city is also renowned for its culinary delights. Hyderabadi cuisine, especially its biryani, is world-famous. We had the opportunity to savor traditional dishes, guided by Pragnya, who introduced us to local eateries and explained the origins and ingredients of various meals. Also, while living in Hyderabad, we participated in traditional festivals, explored historical monuments, and interacted with the local community. Festivals like Diwali and Eid were celebrated with grandeur and enthusiasm.

Pris described our time in Hyderabad as a period of profound personal growth and adaptation. She feels that the city's vibrant energy, coupled with the warmth of its people, made our stay an unforgettable period in our lives. The experiences we had and the lessons we learned during our time there left an indelible mark on our family. It shaped our perspectives and elevated our lives in ways we could never have imagined.

And although that is all true, it hadn't started out that way. MacKenzie had always been resilient, but India tested her in ways we couldn't have predicted. At fifteen, she was pulled from everything she knew—her friends, her routines, her sense of home—and dropped into a world that was completely foreign. Her new school was filled with unfamiliar faces, unfamiliar rhythms, and expectations that didn't match the life she had left behind. Even though the school was international, the kids already had tight social circles. She felt like an outsider among outsiders.

MacKenzie's early days in India were marked by homesickness and frustration. She ached to return to the life she once knew, even begging us to let her attend boarding school back in the States. One night, while I was in New York for meetings, my phone buzzed with a message from MacKenzie:

Daddy, you promised to find a boarding school for me. I can't do this anymore. Please. I just want to come home.

I froze. The words hit like a punch to the chest. I had uprooted her for what I believed was a once-in-a-lifetime opportunity, but in that moment, all I could see was her pain. I stared at the screen, helpless.

My heart sank. I texted her back, offering comfort: *I know this is really hard for you.*

You don't understand. I feel so alone here, she replied almost instantly.

But, two days later, another message came in: *I think I'm going to stay.*

That was all she said, but everything had changed. Her words were cautious, almost tentative, like someone dipping a toe into unfamiliar water. I didn't know what had shifted, but I could feel it. There was a softness I hadn't heard in weeks. A quiet willingness to try again.

I called Pris that night, morning for her in India, and said, half joking, half hoping, "What's his name?"

She laughed softly, the kind of laugh that carries both relief and recognition. "He's her math tutor."

It wasn't just a boy; it was a bridge. A moment of connection in a world that had felt unreachable to her. It was enough to begin softening the edges of her loneliness.

Living in India ultimately transformed MacKenzie's worldview. Immersed in such a different way of life, she developed a strong sense of empathy and cultural awareness that shaped her future. She later became a massage therapist and master certified herbalist, integrating what she'd learned abroad with her formal training. Her knowledge of traditional Indian healing practices enhanced her approach, allowing her to offer a powerful and unique path to wellness for those in her care.

It was from a rich cultural tapestry that one of the most life-changing relationships of our time in India blossomed, with Devi, a bright and determined twelve-year-old who was already in ninth grade when we met her. Her quiet strength, fierce dedication to her studies, and kindness left a lasting impression on us. She and MacKenzie quickly became friends, and what began as simple acts of connection soon grew into a lifelong bond. Devi's journey, from studying by streetlight outside a one-room home to becoming a Microsoft engineer, is a testament to what's possible when someone is seen, supported, and given the chance to rise. My coauthored book with Devi, *Worlds Apart*, published by OM Books International, chronicles our journey over twenty years in a dual narrative.

MacKenzie's shift, from struggling to adapt to thriving in a vibrant new culture, mirrored the spirit of growth we witnessed all around us. And in friendships like the one she formed with Devi, we saw how shared humanity can transcend differences in language, background, and circumstance. Looking back, MacKenzie's transformation, and ours, was proof that we really can grow through what we go through, especially when we open our hearts to the unfamiliar.

* * *

Pris faced her own reckoning with bias—and it nearly ended our time in India.

In 2005, Indian society was still deeply rooted in tradition. Gender roles were rigid. The caste system, though officially abolished, remained present in daily interactions. Social cues were nuanced, and power structures operated through hierarchy and deference. Navigating it all required patience and humility. For Pris, it demanded even more: clarity, restraint, and steel.

Early on, we were invited to the home of Satyam's managing director. The men stayed in the living room talking business. The wives moved into the kitchen. Pris, an executive, stayed beside me.

When the host came around to refill everyone's coffee, he skipped her.

"I'll have some more," she said calmly.

He froze. "Why don't you go join the wives in the kitchen?"

She didn't respond, just looked at me; I knew. We left minutes later.

The silence in the car was louder than any argument. Back home, it broke.

"He erased me. Then told me where I belonged."

I tried to explain it as a cultural difference, a misunderstanding.

"Don't excuse it," she snapped. "Respect is universal. You've never had to shrink to stay in the room." She was furious, hurt, and concise.

I said, "You have the opportunity to bring about a shift—to create great change."

"I've already been in that position," she said. "And I refuse to go back to how women were treated in the States in the sixties and seventies."

We barely spoke for weeks. The air between us was thick with pain, principle, and uncertainty.

Then slowly, without fanfare, she made her choice.

She stayed. Not for them. Not for me. For *herself*. On her own terms. And she led with grace, strategy, and a quiet power that spoke loudly.

She brought about massive change, strategically and relentlessly. She changed the game.

Pris stood her ground and earned respect—for herself, for the women beside her, and those who would follow. Her presence changed the room. Her impact helped shift the culture.

Our tenure at Satyam was marked by numerous achievements that had a lasting impact on the company and its employees. A significant accomplishment was designing and building a state-of-the-art leadership school that served the top leaders of a fifty-thousand-person company. That facility became a cornerstone for leadership development, growing global leaders, and reaffirming our commitment to staying purposeful and relevant through work that truly mattered.

Early on, I reached back out to Booz Allen and recruited a few trusted team members to join me in India. One of them was Josh

Craver. He quickly proved himself—smart, steady, and driven. Before long, he was stepping into leadership roles with confidence and heart. During our time in India, we really got to know each other and he became one of the few who knew me without the mask.

We built a world-class team, developed new talent management capabilities, and created a new leader onboarding process that significantly reduced turnover and led to substantial return on investments (ROI) resulting in major growth for the company. In 2007, our efforts in talent development were recognized globally, earning Satyam Computer Services the prestigious American Society for Talent Development (ASTD) BEST Award, which recognized it as the first non-US learning and development company to rank number one. And in 2009, Satyam Computer Services was the first company outside the States to achieve a top-ten ranking in *Training* magazine's Top 125. The company also received many best practice awards reinforcing that they had achieved a reputation as the premier organization for talent development.

* * *

CHADUVU IS A TOOL, UPADESAM IS THE PATH

By Sunita Lanka, colleague, friend, and family member

"Chaduvu Is a Tool, Upadesam Is the Path" is inspired by the Telugu saying: "Education is a tool, but guidance is the path." That is what I think about when I remember all that my relationship has and is.

I first met Ed in 2006, during one of the most emotionally difficult periods of my life. My *anna*, my elder brother, had passed away unexpectedly. In Telugu culture, an anna is more than just a sibling. He is a protector, a guide, and someone who anchors the family with quiet strength. His loss left me heartbroken. One of the last places he had traveled before he passed was Dubai, and I carried a quiet connection to that place in my heart.

Soon after I joined Satyam, an opportunity came up to support a leadership program in Dubai. Ed and Pris had chosen me for the role. They may not have known the full story at the time, but they somehow understood that the assignment would carry deep personal meaning. Their presence, and the way they gave me space to simply *be*, was something I had never experienced in a workplace. It helped me heal in ways I hadn't yet understood.

Before Satyam, I had worked for more than ten years at Bayer CropScience as an executive assistant. I went in confident, believing I was prepared. But later working with Ed quickly showed me how much more I could become. He gave me room to grow into myself. He trusted me, challenged me, and stretched my thinking beyond tasks and into leadership. Under his mentorship, I stepped into the role of global business and program manager—and for the first time, I began to see myself not just as a capable professional, but as someone who could lead on a global stage.

There's a Telugu saying: *chaduvu oka saadhanam, upadesam oka maargam*, education is a tool, but guidance is the path. Ed has been that guide in my life.

In 2008, Ed and Pris witnessed my marriage to Natraj. They didn't attend as guests, they came as family. During the most sacred part of the ceremony, Ed and Pris performed the *Kanyadanam*, a ritual in which the bride's parents, or those held in the highest love and respect, give her away. In our culture, it is not just symbolic, it is sacred. For them to take that place was deeply emotional for me and my entire family. It was a living expression of love, trust, and chosen family.

Later that year, when our first son Shreyas was born, something beautiful happened. After my mother and my husband, the next two people to hold him were Ed and Pris. They came to the hospital not as visitors, but as family. They held Shreyas with the same tenderness and awe that we did. That moment lives in my heart as one of quiet grace, my son entering the world already wrapped in the arms of those who would love and guide him for a lifetime.

In late 2009, Ed left Satyam and then joined HCL Technologies. We stayed connected. When he later invited me to join him at HCL, I didn't hesitate. I resigned and followed, knowing that wherever Ed was, I would grow. His leadership was always grounded in trust, relationship, and clarity of purpose.

When I lost my *nanna*, my father, in 2012, it shattered me. He had always been the cornerstone of my world. His quiet strength, steady hand, and unconditional love had shaped so much of who I was.

The first person I called was Ed. Even though it was the middle of the night for him, he answered. Through tears, I shared the news. He didn't say much—he just listened. That moment created a quiet shift in me. Without fully realizing it, I began to fill the space my father had held—with Ed. Not as a replacement, but as a continuation of love, strength, and grounding.

A few years after Shreyas, our second son, Anirudh, was born. Ed and Pris were among the first to know, and they came to meet him when he was just a few months old. From the beginning, both of our sons have been surrounded by their love and wisdom.

Soon after, our sons began calling Ed *Tata*, a Telugu word that traditionally means grandfather and carries far more than biological meaning. Tata is a title of deep respect and affection, reserved for elders who embody wisdom, warmth, and a protective presence. It reflects a bond of trust and reverence. That is exactly who Ed became for our children. And of course, Pris became "Pris Aunty," a beloved figure whose grace and care were always present.

Through the years, they have remained close to every milestone—sending encouraging messages during school exams and blessings during Diwali, and celebrating birthdays, professional moments, and quiet wins. Their care has always been consistent. Their presence has never faded.

In 2021, I was working at HCL when Ed called again. He had joined SprintRay and asked if I would help establish the India operations. I had been waiting for that call. I had told myself long before: *When Ed calls, I will go.* And I did. I resigned and joined SprintRay without hesitation. It wasn't just about the job—it was about continuing the journey we had started years earlier. One built on trust, belief, and shared purpose.

Our younger son, Ani (as Ed calls him), has become a passionate badminton player. Tata has been his biggest cheerleader—celebrating every win, encouraging him through challenges, and showing up in spirit at every tournament. To inspire him further, Tata gifted Ani a keepsake for the upcoming 2028 Summer Olympics in Los Angeles: a LA28 pin to remind him to dream big, play with heart, and believe in what's possible.

In 2025, I traveled to America—along with others who had worked with Ed and Pris for nearly two decades ago. We had come from different corners of the world, united not just by shared memories, but by something far deeper. We came as a team—colleagues, mentees, and friends who had been shaped by their leadership and love. We came to honor them. What we held was not just a reunion but a sacred ceremony: their thirty-fifth anniversary recommitment.

In our culture, marriage is more than a milestone, it is a spiritual bond. To recommit, years later, is to say "I still choose you," even with all that life has brought. Ed and Pris stood before us, as husband and wife, and as partners who had walked through life with so many. Watching them honor their bond with such intention was moving. It reminded us that love renews itself with time and truth.

That trip also gave me time to reflect on MacKenzie's journey. I first met her when she was a teenager, full of promise and loud life. Over the years, I have watched her grow into a thoughtful healer who is a creative and grounded young woman. Seeing her stand beside Ed and Pris that day, so poised, so present, was very emotional. She, too, is part of the legacy they've built. A legacy of love, resilience, and chosen family.

In San Clemente, CA (2024).
From left: Sunita and Pris; Mackenzie and Sunita.

Natraj and I often speak of how blessed we are to have Ed and Pris—Tata and Pris Aunty—in our lives. They are not just family to us. They are *kutumbam*, a Telugu word that means family not only by blood, but by heart.

For nearly two decades, Ed and Pris have walked with me through every major chapter of my life. From professional growth to personal milestones, from grief to celebration, they have been present in ways few people ever are. Their mentorship gave me strength. Their belief gave me courage. Their consistency gave me a deep and lasting sense of belonging.

In Telugu, we speak of *sneham*, deep friendship, and *kutumbam*, true family. Ed and Pris have become both in my life. They are part of my story, part of my children's story, and forever part of my heart.

* * *

The theme of supportive relationships carried through into other areas of my life in India. One of our colleagues introduced us to an orphanage that quickly became a significant part of our lives. The orphanage, overcrowded and under-resourced, housed 135 children in four small rooms with three toilets and no hot water. The conditions were heart-wrenching, with limited access to necessities and personal space. Each child had all their worldly possession contained in the one small metal box that was assigned to them.

Some children were there alone, and some were there with their brothers and sisters. For example, Ganesh was there with his three younger sisters, Shailaja, Poojita, and Maheshwari. Maheshwari, who was only five years old, had a presence that was strikingly different than the lively atmosphere; she was so shy and sad that it felt like the weight of the world sat on her small shoulders. Whenever I approached her, her big, sorrowful eyes would widen in fear, and she would turn and run away, seeking refuge in the shadows.

She never smiled, her little face always drawn and serious, and she never spoke to me, only whispered into one of the older girls' ears.

Our dog Jasper was with us every time we visited the orphanage, and most of the kids loved playing with him. Jasper had a knack for bringing joy and laughter, his wagging tail and playful antics a source of endless entertainment. I had hoped that Maheshwari would take to him, that his gentle nature and infectious enthusiasm might help draw her out of her shell, except it didn't. She remained distant, her small frame tensed whenever Jasper was near, her eyes reflecting a mixture of fear and curiosity.

I was determined to reach her, to break through the wall of silence and sadness that surrounded her. One day, as we arrived, Maheshwari mustered the courage to come a little closer to me, her tiny steps hesitant and unsure. As soon as she realized she was too close, her fear took over, and she turned to run away. My heart ached to see her retreat, and in a moment of inspiration, I called after her, shouting, "*Yuvarāṇi Maheshwari!*" *Yuvarāṇi* means "princess" in Sanskrit.

The reaction was instantaneous. All the children cheered, their voices ringing with joy and excitement, and then, in unison, they started calling her "Yuvarāṇi Maheshwari." They were surprised and delighted that I spoke in one of their native languages. The title, filled with affection and respect, hung in the air like a magical spell. Maheshwari stopped and turned to look at me, her eyes wide with surprise. Slowly, as if the sun was rising inside her, her lips curled up, and I saw the biggest smile light up her face and body. She jumped up and down joyously, her earlier shyness melting away in the warmth of the moment.

Even with the language barrier, we were communicating. She walked with newfound confidence and took my hand in her small hand, her touch gentle. I felt true joy, having broken through her barriers and reached her heart. It was a powerful reminder of the impact of love and kindness and the extraordinary resilience of a child's spirit.

The children taught us their songs, one of which involved everyone standing in a circle. Someone would sing out "Watermelon," and everyone would repeat it, making a big circle with their hands in the air to form the shape of a giant watermelon. For "Papaya," we would make the shape of a curvaceous papaya, and for "*Chīkū, Chīkū, Chīkū*" (a type of tropical fruit), we would turn to the left and then to the right, pretending to pinch each other's cheeks. Then we would dance around, singing, "Fruit Salad, Fruit Salad." They sang it every time, over and over, everyone laughing the whole time.

As I spent time with the children, sharing laughter and joy, I noticed the familiar look in their eyes: the mask, the silence of what had or was still happening to them. It shook me to my core, evoking memories of my own childhood. I was reminded of the countless moments when I wore the same mask, hiding the pain and fear that lurked beneath the surface. I could see the echoes of my younger self in their haunted expressions, the same dread that accompanied my every step at home, where each day was a test of survival. Those flashbacks were impossible to ignore: the fear of bringing home a bad grade, knowing it would trigger my father's uncontrollable rage; the pain of being slapped, shoved, and belittled until I believed his venomous words that I was worthless.

Those memories fueled my desire to spend as much time as possible with the kids, to offer them the comfort and care that I had so desperately needed. Pris, sensing my connection with the children, supported me without ever needing to say a word. Together with MacKenzie, who shared our instinctive compassion, we embarked on a mission to bring a sense of normalcy and safety to their lives.

On Fridays, we would pick up five boys or five girls and take them home, where they would find a brief refuge from their harsh realities. We took five more home on most Saturdays. They would take hot baths, enjoy a home-cooked meal, and then we would let them stay up late to watch cartoons; simple pleasures that were monumental in the context of their lives. The next day, we took them for medical and dental check-ups, with local doctors generously donating their time to assist.

Those outings included trips to the movies, local markets, and treats at nearby restaurants, offering the children glimpses of a world outside the orphanage walls. We kept a meticulous list to ensure that all the kids had the chance to come with us, to experience love and care that many had never known before. Our interactions were filled with joy and laughter, bridging cultural and language gaps, proof of the power of cultivating meaningful relationships, especially with those who simply need to be seen.

In those moments, a profound connection formed with those kids, and the parallels to my own past came rushing in; the times when I had desperately needed someone to see through the mask and offer a helping hand. As I watched them smile and laugh, even if only for a little while, I hoped they could sense that a way out existed, and that they weren't alone.

The chance to make a difference in their lives went beyond mission, it became a way to heal old wounds, to rewrite the story of my childhood by becoming the protector and advocate I had once needed.

* * *

Prashanth was just nine when we met him at the orphanage in Hyderabad. His fingers were fused from an untreated electrical burn he'd suffered as a toddler. When we asked what happened, he explained through our driver, John, "I picked up a plug on the floor . . . it threw me five feet away."

The moment was personal for me; I, too, had been badly burned as a child. Hoping to build trust, I lifted my shirt and showed him my scars. He reached out gently to touch them. That quiet moment of connection changed everything. When Doctors Without Borders came to town, we took him for an evaluation. The doctor believed they could restore movement in his fingers. After the surgery, he stayed with us, as the orphanage wasn't sanitary. Though he spoke little English, he pointed to his bandaged hand one night and simply said, "Fingers."

I knelt beside him. "We will take care of you." He nodded, tears in his eyes.

When it was time to return him to the orphanage, the director shockingly demanded money. "You have spoiled the child," he said.

We refused. As we drove away with Prashanth, I reached back and said, "It's okay. We're family now."

MacKenzie turned to him and said, "You're my brother." He smiled shyly and said, "Yes, Sister." A few weeks later, on the way to a birthday party, Prashanth told John, "My auntie lives next door." We were stunned; he wasn't an orphan after all. His mother had sent him to the orphanage hoping he'd get an education. When they reunited, he translated our story for her in English. She listened, then cried, thanking us. With her blessing, we continued to support him, visiting often and taking him on travels across India, from Bangalore to a Tibetan village to the streets of Delhi, each journey helping him rediscover his voice and potential.

Years later, as a husband and father, Prashanth shared the truth of how he ended up in the orphanage: "I was roaming like an idiot on the streets of my hometown . . . my stepfather beat me for bunking school. My mother was scared for me, so she sent me to Hyderabad."

His honesty brought our story full circle. What began as a scarred child's silent plea for help became a lifelong bond rooted in

Left photo: me, Prashanth age ten, and Pris.
Right photo: me, Prashanth age twenty, and Pris.

healing, trust, and shared humanity. Prashanth's story reminds us that resilience is not only about surviving, but about what blooms when someone chooses to see your worth, over and over again.

What bloomed was extraordinary. From barely speaking a word of English to becoming fluent and academically strong, Prashanth transformed before our eyes. He grew from a boy weighed down by trauma into a man filled with purpose. Today, he continues to work hard and dream big, not just for himself but for his family. We remain closely connected, cheering on every milestone in his life. Our journey with him is a testament to what love, presence, and belief can do, not only for a child's future, but for our own. It's one of the clearest examples of why cultivating meaningful relationships remains at the heart of everything I do.

* * *

Satyam faced a significant challenge with the Ramalinga Raju scandal in 2009. The founder admitted to a massive accounting fraud, which shook the foundations of the company and the industry. Leading the company through that crisis was one of the more monumental moments in our careers. Pris and I focused on maintaining morale and continuing the development of our employees, which was crucial in navigating these turbulent times. The scandal eventually led to Satyam's acquisition by Tech Mahindra, marking a new period in the company's history.

During that time, Pris and I coauthored the book *Riding the Tiger: Leading Through Learning in Turbulent Times,* a way of staying purposeful and relevant by sharing what we learned with others navigating difficult transitions. The book served as a valuable resource for leaders facing similar crises, emphasizing resilience and continuous learning.

After leaving Satyam in 2010, we continued to go back to India to consult with other companies including HCL Technologies, Apollo Tyres, PwC, and Infosys, and to meet up with our friends for many celebratory reunions. By the time we returned to the States in 2012, we had made lasting friends all over India and have since returned many times to visit. There, we were reminded of the resilience of the human spirit and the incredible transformations that occur when people come together for each other.

* * *

Our travels around the world, including our time in India, taught us several key lessons. First and foremost, is the power of resilience. No matter how dire the circumstances, the human spirit can endure and overcome immense adversity. Our experiences taught us that perseverance and a willingness to confront and work through pain can lead to profound personal growth and transformation. Resilience was particularly evident during our time in Hyderabad, where we adapted to a new culture, faced the challenges of relocation, and built a new life from scratch.

While I am not advocating that everyone uproot and completely change their environment, it did help me on my path from pain to purpose. In India, I was free to be my authentic self and didn't worry about being judged. I felt free as if I truly belonged there.

The freedom to explore my identity in a new environment, away from the constraints of my past, was a significant part of my healing journey. The move allowed me to reflect on my past and begin to understand its impact even more. Like so many survivors, I had hidden my pain behind a mask of normalcy. Surrounded by new people and experiences in India, I felt a sense of liberation that allowed me to start dismantling the walls I had built around myself and to embrace who I was meant to be. It was a crucial step in my ongoing mission to break the silence and transform that pain into a powerful force for change.

Secondly, the importance of education cannot be overstated. It offered a path to stability and success, allowing us to build a better life for our family. The experiences in Hyderabad, including the educational opportunities for MacKenzie, reinforced the profound impact of learning. Living in a new country exposed us to different perspectives and ways of thinking, broadening our horizons and deepening our appreciation for knowledge.

Relationships had always shaped our lives. The love and support of family, friends, and mentors gave us the emotional foundation to grow. In India, that truth became even more evident. Pragnya, our culture coach, became more than a guide; she became a friend, a lifeline in an unfamiliar world.

Through giving back, especially our time with the orphanage, we were reminded that connection is more than shared history. It's shared presence, compassion, and the willingness to show up.

Those moments changed us. They softened us. They made us more human.

Forty years had passed since he left, and still, the house lived inside me. We had returned from India. I had led teams through crisis, authored and cowritten books, and spoken on global stages, yet I was still listening for his footsteps. Still unsure if the walls would hold. The floor was no longer cement, but it still trembled. The doors were broken, but light was peeking through the cracks.

India didn't free me. It taught me to stay open to relationships, healing, and myself.

CHAPTER 22

FACING THE MIRROR WITH HELP FROM OTHERS

Healing begins when we release the weight of the past, allowing ourselves to move forward with a lighter heart and renewed purpose.

For years, even as I navigated therapy, gave back to others, and found professional success, I still carried the weight. The past had shaped me in ways I couldn't fully name. Every step forward seemed to echo with his footsteps behind me. My life became a long walk toward the light, always building, always striving, trying to create a future free from the shadows I once called home. Healing doesn't always come in a straight line. Sometimes, it comes through people who know how to sit with you in the dark.

After the scandal that rocked Satyam, we moved back to Southern California in 2009 and settled down the street from my cousin, Elana, and her husband, Howard. We continued to go back and forth to India, spending close to half our time working with companies including another year full time in northern India where I worked with a major tech organization.

While living in Southern California, Elana and Pris shared a bond that was more than familial; it was grounding. In the emotional chaos that followed our initial return from India, Elana showed up with home-cooked meals, heart-to-hearts, and the kind of honesty that only decades of trust can bring.

Howard was unlike anyone I had ever known. By day, he was a psychiatrist helping people confront their shadows. By night, he became the "Comic Shrink," using humor as healing. He believed we grow through what we go through—and he embodied it. He was also the author of *The Healing Field: A Young Psychiatrist's Battle with His Anorexic Patient, Her Hunger Strike, and Their Journey through the Dark Night of the Soul,* a powerful book that explores how emotional pain manifests in the body and how healing requires presence, compassion, and a willingness to face inner truth. His philosophy combined Eastern insight, Western psychiatry, and years of lived wisdom. The core of his message: healing begins with seeing, not suppressing.

One day, not long after we returned, Howard and I went body surfing off the coast of Encinitas. As we floated between waves, I opened up about how everything from India had stirred up my old trauma, especially the guilt and powerlessness. I told him I felt stuck, useless and broken. I hesitated, unsure if I could say what I was really feeling. Just a few years earlier, I wouldn't have. I would have buried it—cracked a joke, changed the subject, or drowned the ache in work. Vulnerability wasn't safe, only silence was. But there I was, in the ocean, opening up to someone who wouldn't look away. That alone marked how far I had come.

"Eddie," he said, letting the silence hold space before his words, "you're in what we call 'reaction mode.' Your emotions are shaping your reality right now, and that reality feels heavier than it needs to."

I wanted to believe him. "I don't know how to get out of it," I said. "It's like I'm trapped inside it."

"That's exactly where Emotional Martial Arts (EMA) comes in," he explained. "You start by becoming the Non-Judgmental

Observer. Step outside the story. Watch what's happening in you without trying to fix or label it."

I didn't fully understand it then, but something in his steady, kind, and certain tone made me believe I could try.

"Start with awareness," Howard replied. "Just notice what's there—no need to fix it or solve it. As you do that, you can begin to recognize the emotions hiding beneath the surface. Is it fear? Guilt? Shame? These are the 'Committee Members' we talk about—your inner child, adolescent, and adult, each carrying different burdens. Identify them, validate them, and then release the judgment. This is what we call RVR: Recognize, Validate, and Release."

We floated in silence for a moment, the sound of the waves around us.

In the water that day, Howard didn't try to fix me, he just stayed beside me, holding space for the truth I wasn't ready to face alone. He knew that sometimes, healing happens not through advice, but through unwavering presence. His support reminded me what it means to truly value the presence of another.

"It's about breaking out of the prison of your story," Howard continued. "These emotions, Eddie, they're old patterns—reactions to wounds from the past. But they don't have to control your present. By practicing this awareness, by stepping into your Non-Judgmental Observer, you can create a space for healing. It's not about forcing change; it's about allowing it to happen naturally, as you evolve."

We spent hours in and out of the water that day, with Howard helping me to understand those principles. It was a revelation to see how my feelings of worthlessness and fear were tied to old wounds influencing my reactions in ways I hadn't realized.

That day turned into many more opportunities to spend hours with Howard, attending his workshops, listening, learning, and applying the techniques he shared. Each session increased my understanding of how to navigate my emotions and integrate healing into my daily life. Everyone takes a different path to healing the traumas we go through, and mine has been a long, winding road. Over the years, I had invested thousands of hours in individual and group therapy, attending retreats, and exploring various methods to process and rebuild my life. EMA added a profound new dimension.

I wished I had learned about it earlier and understood it sooner. EMA provided a quantum leap in my path from abuse to abundance. It gave me practical tools that complemented and enhanced the work I had already done, allowing me to connect the dots in ways I hadn't been able to before. Through this process, I found a greater sense of peace and the strength to continue healing. The clarity and empowerment I gained from EMA not only helped me navigate my emotions more effectively, it also gave me the courage to reclaim my voice and share my story with others, transforming my pain into a source of purpose and strength.

In their own ways, Howard and Elana have lived the very principles I would come to hold dear: growing through adversity, embracing support, learning endlessly, nurturing love, and living with purpose. Being around them was like watching the principles come to life.

* * *

In late 2009, Pris and I founded Nelson Cohen Global Consulting. It was not just another business venture; it was an opportunity to use the wisdom and insights we had gained from our experiences to help others grow. Our time in India was a significant part of our lives. Beyond the achievements at Satyam and the other organizations we worked with, it was the vibrant culture of Hyderabad and the relationships we built that truly enriched us.

Our time spent with the kids at the orphanage, where we provided educational support and mentorship, left an indelible mark on our hearts. Those moments broadened our understanding of community and the importance of giving back.

Over the years, our firm influenced leaders globally, helping them transform their organizations. However, it was the personal connections we forged and the opportunity to return to India that I cherished the most. Each visit to Hyderabad reminded us of the bonds we had formed and the growth we had experienced. The true reward of our work was witnessing the development of those we coached and seeing the ripple effect of positive change in their lives. Receiving India's Learning Luminary Lifetime Achievement Award was

From left: Satish, myself, and Kishore at Disneyland in California (2014).

not just a professional milestone; it was a testament to the relationships and experiences that had shaped our journey.

We had many opportunities to host close friends from India. Kishore and Satish were two of them, and over time, they became like sons to us.

During one of my trips back to India, I traveled with Prashanth, who was about fourteen at the time, from Hyderabad to Bengaluru to visit friends. It was his first time flying, and his wonder made the world feel new again. From there, we headed north and stayed at a coffee plantation nestled in the hills, where the air smelled of wet leaves. Life moved differently there—slower, quieter, reverent.

It was there I reconnected with Acharya Venkat. Once a trusted colleague at Satyam, now a spiritual teacher, he had traded boardrooms for stillness. He spoke with more silence than words and carried a presence that didn't require belief—only openness.

One afternoon, as the wind brushed against the plantation walls and rain tapped at the shutters, he invited me to sit with him in my sleeping room off the main house. I sat on the bed and he sat on a chair next to me. He asked me to close my eyes and guided me inward.

"There is a staircase," he said. "Ten steps down. At the bottom, go a thousand times deeper. Then ten thousand."

He counted slowly, and with each number I felt myself sink—not into sleep, but into a softer, slower awareness.

Ten.

Nine.

Eight . . .

By the time we reached one, I was already somewhere else. Then his voice came again:

"Now go a thousand times deeper . . . ten thousand deeper."

And I did; what came wasn't imagined—it arrived in full detail.

I found myself on a city street in the early nineteen hundreds. An Indian boy stood nearby, his eyes wide and alert. I saw myself frozen in place as a vintage motorcar barreled toward me—a bright yellow car, heavy and fast. Without hesitation, the boy ran forward and shoved me out of the way. I survived. He did not.

I felt the loss and I felt the sacrifice.

Then everything shifted again. I was in a place called Salem.

Not Salem, Massachusetts—Salem, India. Many, many years earlier. No vehicles, no sound of machines, just the rhythm of footsteps on stone and the scent of cooking fires rising with the heat. I saw the roads and buildings. I didn't feel like a visitor. I felt like I had come home. I wasn't in India as a guest. I was Indian.

When the session ended, we sat in stillness. Acharya didn't speak. He didn't ask me to share. He simply sat across from me—calm, steady, and grounded, and I found myself speaking freely.

I told him everything.

The boy, the street, the flash of yellow.

The weight of what was given.

And then Salem—ancient, wordless, known. I mentioned how I had never even heard of Salem, India, and how stunned I was when he gently confirmed, "It's real. It's in Tamil Nadu." (A state in South India). Then I said something I hadn't planned to say:

"I wonder if this is why Prashanth and I met."

We spoke of him—not as the boy in the vision, not literally—but as someone whose presence in my life may be tied to something larger—something older. Perhaps in this lifetime, I was repaying a debt I never consciously remembered but had always carried.

I admitted that I didn't know if what I saw were true past lives, or images my mind created to help me make sense of something I hadn't yet understood.

Acharya didn't challenge or explain. He only said, "What you saw is yours. Whether memory or message, it arrived because you were ready."

I didn't leave that room with certainty. I left feeling different and sometimes, that's what healing is.

After our initial return in 2012, we continued to return to India for periods of time, working with clients all the way until March of 2020, when the pandemic hit.

* * *

After Howard passed, Elana chose to carry her soulmate's work forward—and I agreed to help. We launched a series of virtual workshops during COVID-19, blending his teachings with her evolving vision. I didn't know then how much it would give me in return. Working alongside Elana gave me my voice back. It gave me the courage to speak about what had happened—and to begin living in truth instead of reaction.

Elana, with her presence and fierce clarity, brought EMA to life. Her mastery of those practices changed the way I related to myself. Twice a week, we met—once to build the content, once for her to coach me through the practices. She introduced me to the "Black Belt Tools." Each one was a doorway inward.

I learned to locate the five hiding places: story, emotion, body, behavior, and past. Those places had always held my pain—tucked away in silence, covered by strength. With Elana's guidance, I began to name the triggers as they surfaced, track the reactions in my body, and soften into awareness instead of shutting down. I wasn't just building tools. I was reclaiming pieces of myself I hadn't even known were missing.

My return to India (2020).

Together, we wove the tools into the workshops we offered—places where people, like me, could show up raw and real. Whether the wound was grief, betrayal, or deep shame, the work created space to feel and move through freely. It wasn't therapy; it was presence—and it worked.

Those practices became a way of life—awareness, release, and compassion. They taught me how to stay with myself. How to live fully in the now. How to use my own story not as a weight, but as a bridge—to others, to healing, and to purpose.

The legacy Howard began, Elana continued, and I became a part of, changed me. And through the ripple of that work, I have seen others shift too. I've watched people crack open and choose aliveness. I've watched myself do the same.

For most of my life, silence was my armor and my jailer. Through EMA, I began to dismantle that silence. The walls came down. A voice emerged. I began to speak what had once been unspeakable—and in doing so, I stepped out of survival and into truth.

* * *

Rebuilding my life through education was the first step in breaking free from the past. The support of teachers like Mrs. Hanson, who saw my potential when I barely could, laid the foundation for my future. Education became my sanctuary, a place where I could rebuild my shattered life and find solace in the pursuit of knowledge.

However, education alone wasn't enough. Relationships played a crucial role in my transformation. My partnership with Pris has been the cornerstone of my personal and professional success. Her unwavering support, belief in me, and love were instrumental in my journey from darkness to light. Together, we have navigated the complexities of life, transforming our own lives and the lives of those we have touched along the way.

Beyond professional milestones, my journey has always been about personal growth and healing. Pris and I have faced numerous challenges together, from managing our own businesses to raising a family and navigating different cultures. Merging our professional lives taught us intense collaboration and mutual support, which strengthened our partnership over time.

For a long time, I carried the weight of childhood trauma and the fallout from broken relationships. I buried the pain so deeply that it showed up in other ways—mistrust, isolation, the constant need to protect myself. I thought the walls I had built were keeping me safe. Really, they just kept me stuck.

Things began to shift when Pris came into my life. She didn't try to fix me. She stayed. She believed in me, even when I didn't. Her love wasn't loud, but it was steady. Little by little, those walls started to come down.

We've walked through a lot together—raising kids, living abroad, building a life full of color and culture. With her, I've learned that hard things don't have to harden you. That healing happens in relationship. That love—real love—can meet you where you are and still invite you forward.

Being with Pris didn't just help me heal. It gave me a new way to live—with an open heart and a life that feels more whole than I ever imagined.

* * *

Jay has been my best friend since 1969, and there were many times in my life when he was my only friend and confidant. From our early years in Miami, Jay was a constant presence, offering stability during some of the most turbulent times of my life. Amid the chaos at home, where I often felt isolated and disconnected, Jay provided a sense of normalcy and unwavering support. Whether we were riding bikes through the neighborhood or simply talking about our future dreams, his friendship was a lifeline, reminding me that I wasn't alone.

When my father died, it was Jay who stood by my side, helping me find the courage to face the difficult task of informing my grandparents. His support during that time, and throughout my life, was invaluable, particularly as I navigated the complex emotions of loss and uncertainty. Jay's influence on my life has been immeasurable; his friendship a constant source of resilience and comfort, providing a steadfast thread woven through the fabric of my existence.

As our bond deepened over the years, it wasn't just Jay and I who grew closer—our families did too. Our mothers became close friends, their relationship mirroring ours and providing a foundation of stability that has echoed through the years. Our daughters, born just three weeks apart, have grown up witnessing the strength of our connection. In many respects, it feels like we all coparented to raise our children; after all, it takes a village. We were there for Heather and Jay's sons, Danny and Josh, as they were growing up, just as Jay's family had been for my family.

The bond we share continues to be a source of strength and resilience, the enduring power of true friendship through life's many trials and triumphs stretching over four generations. It's a legacy of love, loyalty, and unwavering support that has shaped both of our lives and the lives of our children. Jay's friendship, from the moment we met as kids, has been my anchor, a constant reminder that no matter how difficult life gets, true friendship can carry you through.

* * *

We reconnected with Vina, who had long been part of our lives. Having moved to the West Coast, she had become an acupuncturist and started a family with her husband, Ernest. We were overjoyed to meet their daughter, Talia. After her birth, Vina struggled. We later learned she had Hashimoto's disease, an autoimmune disorder that was attacking her thyroid.

We flew to Oregon to be with them. She sat alone in the guest room, barely able to move.

"Vina, you need to get out of this room," I urged. Pris knelt and took her hand. "Let's go for a walk."

"I can't," she whispered.

Still great friends after fifty-four years. From left: me and Jay

"We're not taking no for an answer," Pris said gently but firmly. Together, we helped her to the end of the block. The air revived her just a bit. The next day, we walked a little farther. By week's end, she was walking the neighborhood. Each step was a win, and we saw her spirit returning.

As Vina grew stronger, we shared more memories—including a magical trip to Disneyland for Talia's fifth birthday. We wore shirts with characters from *Mulan*, and Talia dressed as the warrior herself. We went on many rides, watched a few shows, and let joy carry us through the day.

In 2016, we moved to Seattle for a role at Amazon. Vina's family followed when Ernest got a new job. For Talia's eighth birthday, we threw a *Wizard of Oz*-themed party in our building's panoramic top-floor space. She was Dorothy, Jasper was Toto, and we all played our parts in costume—laughter and joy threaded through every detail.

It brought back memories of the *Alice in Wonderland*-themed party we threw for MacKenzie's fifth birthday. She was Alice, I, the Mad Hatter, and my mom, the Queen of Hearts. Mom went around tapping shoulders with her wand, and shouting, "Off with your head!" The spirit of those gatherings—joy, creativity, connection—linked generations.

Eventually, we returned to California, settling near Vina's family. Her acupuncture brought me comfort in difficult times. In 2021, we moved back to Southern California. Fate brought them close again when Talia was accepted into a performing arts school nearby.

Throughout my journey, friends like Vina have been vital. Their love and presence have steadied me, lifted me, and reminded me that healing comes not just from within, but from the people who walk beside us.

* * *

Meanwhile, Josh Carver was building a remarkable legacy of his own. From the moment he joined my team straight out of college—introduced to me by his mother, a leader at Training Futures—I saw something rare in him. He was bright, capable, and hungry for impact. Not driven by ego or ambition, but by a deep desire to make things better—for people, teams, and organizations. He listened more than he spoke, absorbed feedback like oxygen, and leaned into every challenge as if it had something to teach him.

After our time at Booz Allen, including the formative chapter we shared in India, Josh's journey unfolded across the globe—South America, North America, and South Asia—each stop refining his perspective and expanding his range. He didn't just adapt

Still friends and colleagues after more than twenty-five years.
From left: Me and Josh

to new cultures, he integrated them, building a leadership philosophy rooted in empathy, clarity, and global awareness.

When Western Union named him chief learning officer, he became one of the youngest CLOs in the field. It was a milestone moment—for him, certainly, but also for me. Watching someone I had mentored step into that kind of responsibility—and do it with such integrity—was profoundly moving. Our relationship evolved again: I became a consultant working for Josh. The shift was seamless. There was no awkwardness, only trust and mutual respect. We had always been aligned in values; now we were aligned in purpose.

Together, we led the development of Western Union University, a global learning platform designed to empower employees at every level. In 2017, Under Josh's leadership, the company soared to the number one spot in the ATD's (Association for Talent Development) BEST Awards and earned a joint ATD Excellence in Practice Award for its leadership development process. The accolades, while meaningful, weren't the end goal. Josh was hungry for impact—and he delivered it by making learning a catalyst for performance, not just a function of human resources.

When he later launched Craver Consulting Services, Josh stepped even further into his calling—advising executives, coaching leaders, and helping organizations navigate complexity through clarity. He became a trusted voice in the intersection of leadership, learning, and artificial intelligence. Yet, through every evolution, he remained grounded. The same bright, capable, and impact-driven person I first met decades ago.

More than twenty-five years later, we're still working together. We're still growing, still laughing, and still learning. That's the beauty of true mentorship—it never ends; it transforms.

* * *

I wasn't always the father I wanted to be. I was still healing—sometimes overwhelmed by memories I hadn't yet named. There were years when being present was more aspiration than reality, like when I sat across from MacKenzie physically there, but emotionally far away. I wanted so badly to be a safe place for her. Sometimes I was. Sometimes I wasn't.

Still, we stayed.

I think back to that moment just before we moved to Virginia—how we each picked out a small metal heart at a little shop near the airport. As we stepped outside, she turned to me and asked, "Daddy, can we trade?"

We did. I still carry the one she chose. That quiet moment—so simple, so clear—has stayed with me ever since.

Years later in India, she showed me what resilience looks like. The loneliness of adolescence. The unfamiliar streets. She navigated it all with a quiet strength. Watching her grow during those years, I realized she wasn't just surviving; she was *becoming*. Even then, I saw the seeds of the healer she would one day become.

We've had our conflicts. We still do. We don't always agree. We don't always get it right and still, we stay.

When I had my cervical spine surgery and everything in me felt broken—my body, my mind, my will—it was MacKenzie who showed up. She drove down from Northern California and cared for me. She made meals and she placed ice on my wounds. She sat with me in silence. She didn't try to fix anything. She simply stayed.

She still calls me "Daddy," and I like it. There's something about that word that softens the years, as if somewhere inside us, we're both still holding those hearts.

She is almost thirty-six. A woman with her own wisdom. A healer in her own right. In her presence, I somehow feel safe, a feeling I had never known as a child. I no longer fear becoming my father. I became someone else entirely. Not perfect. Just present and that is enough.

* * *

Over the past thirty-five years, Pris and I have grown both individually and as a couple, weathering the storms of life and celebrating its joys together. Her resilience, adaptability, and passion for life continue to inspire me every day. Whether it was navigating the challenges of raising a family, managing our businesses, or supporting each other through personal struggles, Pris has been my steadfast partner. Her recent reinvention, obtaining certification in interior design and opening her own business, Home Designs Therapy, exemplifies her ability to evolve and thrive. This venture not only highlights her creative talents but reflects her dedication to pursuing her passions with unwavering determination. Watching her balance professional excellence with personal passion is a testament to her strength and serves as a constant reminder of the power of a supportive partner in achieving one's dreams.

Her courage to reinvent herself has reinforced the importance of resilience and adaptability in our lives. It's a reminder that growth doesn't stop, no matter where we are in life, and that we can always pursue our passions, no matter how daunting the challenge. Her success with Home Designs Therapy has inspired me to continue pushing the boundaries of my own growth, personally and professionally. Together, we have cultivated an environment where each of us can pursue our individual dreams while simultaneously building a shared vision for our future.

I am often reminded of the darker times, the childhood filled with fear, the trauma that haunted me, and the walls I built to protect myself. Those were the years where I felt disconnected, from others and from myself. The weight of those experiences made it difficult to see a future that was different from my past. Through education, nurturing relationships, and the enduring power of resilience, light eventually broke through. Pris played a significant role in helping me break down those walls. Her unwavering support, her belief in my potential even when I doubted it, and her love have influenced my healing.

The path from pain to purpose has never been a straight line. Pris and I faced countless challenges, individually and together. Except, through it all, we kept learning how to stay connected. How to listen. How to grow, not just side by side, but inward, toward ourselves.

Healing, I've learned, is a process that never truly ends. It's not a finish line you cross. It's something you return to, again and again, with more truth, more tools, and, if you're lucky, more love.

By the time that chapter closed, I had gained clarity, insight, and strength. EMA gave me the language. Relationships from around the world gave me the courage. Still, the scars remained. I had come a long way. However, the weight of the past hadn't fully released and I was beginning to understand: it lived deeper than I had known.

CHAPTER 23

SAYING GOODBYE

Healing begins the moment we stop carrying what was never ours to hold.

Trauma lives in the body. That's what no one tells you at first. You carry it in your shoulders, your gut, and your breath. It hides in the tension you normalize, in habits that look like coping, and in the silence you mistake for strength. Mine showed up quietly: a constant hum of anxiety, low-grade depression, the joy-dulling fog that hovered even in life's brightest moments. Never loud enough to stop me, but always loud enough to follow me. Despite years of therapy, meditation, journaling, and spiritual work, I couldn't shake it entirely.

Eventually, I understood: healing wasn't just mental. It was physical. Emotional. Cellular. EMA gave me the tools—Recognize. Validate. Release. They helped. They carried me, but the trauma didn't just live in my memory; it had settled into my body.

By my mid-sixties in 2024, I couldn't carry it any longer. The cost was too high. Decades of unspoken pain had left a trail: anxiety, depression, and irritable bowel syndrome (IBS). In 2015, I was diagnosed after being sick for more than three years, with sarcoidosis, a chronic, system inflammatory disease with no cure. In

2020 and then again in 2021, I suffered heart attacks. The science confirmed what I was living: unresolved trauma. And it doesn't just weigh on the mind; it wears down the body.

This is why I speak. This is why I write. My silence nearly broke me. It doesn't have to break you. What saved me wasn't one moment or method—it was the slow weaving together of many: the wisdom I gathered in India, the deep and enduring relationships that held me steady, retreats like Healing the Heart of Diversity, and the years of therapy that helped me find language for what had once felt unspeakable. Along the way, I learned EMA—the practice developed by my cousin-in-law Howard and carried forward by Elana. They taught me how to meet pain with presence, how to feel fully without becoming consumed. Each step brought me back to myself.

After trying everything, I still felt like something was unfinished; like something was trapped. That's when my long-time friend, Josh, suggested ketamine therapy. At first, I was hesitant, but the idea of a treatment that could reach what nothing else had touched was too compelling to ignore.

I threw myself into research, reading articles, watching videos, and learning as much as I could about the treatment. I also connected with others who had undergone ketamine therapy, listening to their stories of transformation and relief. Their experiences, combined with what I had learned, gave me the confidence to take the next step. The possibility of finally lifting the weight I had carried for so long was too important to ignore.

Each session, administered by Dr. Justin Yanuck, a very compassionate and knowledgeable medical professional on ketamine therapy, took place in his clinic. I was unprepared for the depth of the experience during the first session. As the treatment took hold, I felt a profound peace surrounding me, unlike anything I had ever known. As it progressed, I sensed the presence of others:

my father, mother, sister, and brother. They were there with me, not just in spirit, but in a tangible way. Their presence was subtle and not overwhelming as I thought it might be. I realized that I had been carrying them all these years, each tied to traumas and unresolved emotions that I had never fully released.

Toward the end of the session, something extraordinary happened: I felt the presence of my father, mother, sister, and brother growing more intense. It felt like they were physically with me. Slowly, one by one, each of them started to rise within me. They lifted from the depths of my soul, where they had been embedded for so many years.

First, my father, with all his anger and pain, began to ascend. I could feel the weight of his body, heavy and oppressive, as if it had been physically pressing down on me for all those years. His influence, the memories of his harsh words, and the fear he instilled were being pulled upward. As he floated away, the years of tension in my body unraveled, releasing me from the grip of his shadow.

Next came my mother, carrying with her the sadness and unresolved emotions I had held onto for so long. As she lifted out of me, I could feel the sorrow and the loss that had permeated my life start to dissolve. The burdens I had carried on her behalf began to evaporate, leaving me with a feeling of peace I hadn't known before.

My sister and brother followed, their presence lighter yet still significant. The subtle traces of guilt, regret, and unfinished business I had carried for them were drawn out of me. Each of them had been a part of the puzzle that made up my inner pain, but, piece by piece, they were being removed, and floating away gently.

As their spirits rose out of me, I could see them ascending higher and higher until they were no longer visible, taking with them the years of persistent pain and trauma that had been lodged in my being. It was surreal, an almost ethereal experience. I felt lighter and freer than I had in years.

More than fifty years had passed since he left and all that time, I had been trapped in that house without realizing it. The floor had been cement, the doors broken, and the silence, total. Even when the house changed its shape, becoming a classroom, a marriage, a boardroom, a stage, a home in another country, it was still there.

Until that moment.

I was inside the house, unchanged, familiar, haunting. No corner was forgotten, no memory silent. Then, like a mirage, it began to fade. The floor slipped away, the doors dissolved, and I stepped through the emptiness.

When I awoke, still dazed from the experience, I pulled Pris close, tears streaming down my face, and whispered, "I am free. They're gone." The relief felt was overwhelming. I explained to her what had happened, how I had been released. I cried in her arms for what felt like an eternity, releasing years of pent-up emotion. The doctor and nurse, who had been present throughout the session, stood nearby, visibly moved by the profoundness of my experience. Dr. Yanuck and his nurse's quiet respect for what had just transpired was evident, a silent acknowledgment of the personal transformation they had just witnessed.

That session marked more than a release, it was a transformation that reflected what I had come to understand all along: healing is not linear, but it is possible when you grow through what you go through. I found myself on a silent pilgrimage of the soul. In the quiet moments of each session, my soul embarked on a journey that transcended the physical realm. The mantra *I am enough, I have always been enough*, began to echo through the void of my consciousness.

As I kept going, something in me began to lift. The weight I had carried for so long started to ease. I no longer just talked about love—I started to believe I could receive it. I started to feel what it meant to give it, freely.

There was a strength inside me I hadn't seen before. A part of me that felt open, spacious, and alive. My connections—with others, with myself—felt softer, more real. They weren't bound by fear. They moved like water. They held light.

In those moments, I saw that my body was temporary, but my spirit wasn't. I belonged to something bigger. Healing didn't come all at once. It moved in quiet waves, like a dance I'd always been part of without knowing it.

Some days brought joy. Some brought fear. I often stood right on the edge between the two. Even there, especially there, I found a strength I hadn't known. I still carried scars; still felt the weight of all I had endured. And I had also touched something infinite in myself—something loving, steady, and whole. That gave me peace.

* * *

As I continued on my path of healing, EMA had already helped me understand that true freedom is not merely the absence of a burden, it is the conscious choice to continually Recognize, Validate, and Release them.

Ketamine treatments allowed me to delve deeper into the recesses of my mind, where unresolved emotions had long resided. Each session seemed to lift these burdens further, bringing a sense of relief that was physical, spiritual, emotional, and transformative. It was the moment I felt unshackled from the chains of my past.

However, I want to make it explicitly clear that I am not advocating for ketamine or any other specific methods I used. I am simply sharing my personal perspective on what worked, and what did not work, for me. Everyone's journey is unique, and it's crucial for each person to explore and find the options that best suit their own needs and circumstances.

Healing is not a one-size-fits-all process. What works for one person might not with another, and that's okay. It's about finding what helps you move forward. For some, it might be traditional therapy, for others, it could be alternative treatments, or perhaps a combination of many different approaches. The key is to remain open and to give yourself permission to explore different paths.

Healing, as I have often said, is a continuous process, a lifelong commitment to nurturing oneself and embracing the present. The shadows of the past may still linger, but they no longer dictate my future. Each step I've taken, from therapy to meditation to exploring new treatments, has been part of my unique journey, one that has led me to a place of greater peace and self-understanding.

Abundance doesn't always feel abundant.

It doesn't always look like joy, energy, or ease. Sometimes it shows up in the form of resilience—in the ability to keep going when things fall apart. As I wrote this chapter, I was in bed in Portugal, recovering from COVID-19. It was supposed to be a full family vacation—laughter, connection, and new memories. Instead, I was fighting fever, fatigue, and isolation. I was in a country where I didn't speak the language. I couldn't explore or engage. I felt helpless and alone.

And still—this is part of it too. Abundance lives in the way I now care for myself with tenderness, not judgment. It lives in knowing I can feel fear and not be swallowed by it. It lives in the tools I've gathered, the presence I bring, even to moments I didn't choose.

Healing didn't promise me freedom from pain. It gave me the capacity to meet it differently. That's the quiet truth: even when life feels empty, it can still be full.

From right: Pris, MacKenzie, and myself on vacation in Porto, Portugal (2024).

At one point in my life, that situation would've wrecked me: being sick, isolated, missing out, unable to communicate easily. I would've spiraled into fear, anger, and regret. It would have consumed me and infected everyone around me.

Now, even in discomfort, even in uncertainty, I don't collapse.

As I released the weight of my past, I began to feel something different: clarity. Each step forward became a step toward life, not away from pain, but toward possibility.

The lessons I've learned, the relationships I've nurtured, the courage to confront what once felt unbearable, those things have paved the way for a new chapter. One not just about surviving, but about thriving. One where I can support others as they step into their own healing.

This is where the story turns. Where pain becomes purpose, where abundance becomes an opportunity.

PART V
STAY PURPOSEFUL & RELEVANT

Purpose is not a title or a trophy. It's a return to what matters most. We stay relevant not by being louder, but by being honest—and by living the five principles to show up authentically. We lead not through expertise alone, but through alignment, humility, and presence. It begins with silence. It ends here, not as a final word, but as the moment your voice becomes a bridge for others still searching for theirs. This is where you begin—again, and again—not because you have to, but because you're ready. This is what's next for you and me: to keep living with truth, courage, and heart. Purpose doesn't end with survival; it begins each time you choose to live out loud.

CHAPTER 24

FIVE PRINCIPLES TO SHOW UP AUTHENTICALLY

Resilience isn't built in theory. It's forged in lived experience—when you carry forward what cracked you open, and let it make you whole.

By now, my story has unfolded—grief and grit, ruptures and reconciliations, joy that lifted me, and abundance that sustained me—all woven through. If you've walked through it, you know: this was never just one story. It was a mosaic of stories filled with survival and opportunities; of learning to live out loud.

Let's go back to where this began—my birthday, a moment of joy and reflection, followed by a spiral I never saw coming just a few months later. I became what I had spent a lifetime avoiding: an accidental addict, just trying to heal, and suddenly fighting to feel like myself again.

Those moments didn't define me. They reminded me of what I return to every day.

It's not just where we fall. It's where we soar. It's where we rest in simplicity, where we hold small wins and quiet losses. It's not a destination; it's a way of being.

Healing, growth, and leadership rarely follow a straight line. They move in seasons, between clarity and confusion, collapse and return and in that movement, certain truths begin to form.

These principles which have been a vital part of my life that I introduced at the start of my story, are not only for surviving storms; they are just as powerful for navigating what comes after and everything in between:

1. Grow Through What You Go Through
2. Value the Support of Others
3. Pursue Lifelong Learning and Adaptability
4. Cultivate Meaningful Relationships
5. Stay Purposeful & Relevant

They hold dual truths: yin and yang. Darkness and light. Loss and possibility. Not everything can be fixed; however, almost everything can be faced, and that's where authenticity and growth begin.

Growth is often associated with hardship, and that's true. However, growth also comes through success, through breakthroughs, relationships, milestones, and moments of joy.

These aren't steps to follow or checklists to complete; they are invitations to reflect and reconnect. To lead and live with greater presence and depth. At their heart, these principles offer a way to hold the full spectrum of experience. Not just the broken pieces, but also the bright ones. Not just the wounds, but the wisdom. Not just the pain, but the possibility.

Each principle offers a path forward, one that honors both the shadow and the light.

* * *

Growth isn't linear—and it's never just light. It spirals through darkness and clarity, failure and becoming, retreat, and renewal. Sometimes it emerges through crisis, when everything falls apart. Other times it comes quietly, as we stretch into success and realize we're capable of more.

Growth doesn't mean bouncing back. It means breaking open and expanding.

I grew up in a home where silence was survival. Where bruises outnumbered hugs. Where speaking up came with consequences. Pain shaped me before language did.

Yet in the midst of that pain, I learned: growth often begins in the fire. Not all growth feels like progress. Sometimes it feels like escape. Sometimes like surrender. Over the years, growth showed up in strange ways: through illness, leadership, fatherhood, and therapy, but mostly, though staying present. Through letting go of the need to fix or prove.

Growth doesn't happen because we conquer. It happens when we integrate, when we stop hiding and start living from wholeness. It's not just what follows trauma, it's what follows truth. To grow through what you go through is to carry tension and still move forward. Not with perfection, but with presence.

* * *

Support isn't weakness—it's what makes us human. It flows in both directions: giving and receiving, solitude and solidarity, independence and interdependence. It matters not only in moments of collapse, but also in moments of celebration, when the instinct is to isolate, but the opportunity is to connect.

Many of us were taught not to ask for help. To stay quiet. To minimize our needs. We confused strength with silence and self-worth with self-reliance. True support doesn't diminish us, it dignifies us. It says: "You matter. You're not alone."

Support doesn't always arrive with fanfare. Sometimes it's a steady hand, a quiet question, a presence that doesn't flinch. It's someone who sees behind the mask and stays anyway.

To grow, we must be willing to receive support. To heal, we must also learn to give it. In leadership. In friendship. In family. Support becomes transformational when it's mutual, when we show up for each other not because we have to, but because we *choose* to.

No one rises alone and when you do rise, the people who stood beside you, seen or unseen, are part of your strength.

* * *

Lifelong learning begins with humility. It's not about knowing more, it's about staying curious. Adaptability isn't about abandoning who you are, it's about refining how you move through a world that keeps changing.

Learning invites us to grow—not just upward, but inward. It's in the moments we listen instead of defending, unlearn instead of repeat, and ask instead of assuming. It's the willingness to be a beginner again, even when we're experienced; especially then.

True adaptability isn't reactive. It's attuned. It means noticing when old strategies no longer serve and having the courage to shift. It means embracing discomfort as part of growth.

This kind of learning happens in classrooms, but also in conversations, stillness, challenges, relationships that stretch us, and roles that ask more than we thought we could give. It happens when we stop leading with answers and start leading with presence.

Today, the world is moving faster than ever. Technologies shift, cultures evolve, expectations rise. What remains constant is this: those who stay teachable stay relevant. Lifelong learning isn't a checklist. It's a mindset and adaptability that isn't about keeping up. It's about showing up awake, willing, and ready to grow.

* * *

Relationships aren't just what we build—they're what build us. The deepest ones don't just comfort us; they stretch us. They mirror who we're becoming and reveal who we're still afraid to be. Real connection isn't effortless. It requires honesty, presence, and repair. It asks us to risk being seen, to speak even when silence feels safer, to stay even when leaving would be easier.

Many of us carry wounds from early relationships. When love wasn't safe. When being seen meant being hurt. Over time, we build walls and call them strength. However, healing invites us to soften, not to become unguarded, but to become authentic.

The most meaningful relationships, personal or professional, don't demand perfection. They ask for truth. They offer safety without rescuing, challenge without judgment, space without distance.

In leadership, partnership, and friendship, what matters isn't performance, it's presence. It's the courage to show up, to listen deeply, and to stay in the room when things get hard.

In the end, we become who we are in a relationship, not just with others, but with our own unfolding story. When those relationships are mutual, grounded, and real, they don't just help us belong; they help us become.

* * *

Purpose isn't a destination. Relevance isn't a title. Both are practices, rooted in reflection, shaped by alignment, and sustained by growth.

For too long, many of us chase achievement as proof that we matter. We measure our worth by what we produce, collect, or control. True purpose doesn't come from performance. It comes from clarity, knowing what matters, and letting that guide how we show up.

Relevance isn't about staying ahead. It's about staying attuned. Listening to what's emerging, within us and around us, and having the courage to respond, even when it means letting go of what once worked.

Sometimes purpose looks like momentum. Other times, like stillness. Sometimes relevance means stepping up; other times, stepping back. Either way, it requires honesty. The truth is: we don't stay relevant by doing more. We stay relevant by being real. We stay purposeful not by proving ourselves, but by living in alignment with what's ours to do.

These five principles aren't mine alone. You'll see them in your story too, if you listen closely. They aren't perfect, they're honest. They've held me up when nothing else did and if they help you find your footing, even for a moment, then this telling was worth it.

* * *

These aren't theories. They're lived truths—scarred, shining, and hard won. Forged in fire. Affirmed in grace. Each one holds power on its own. Together, they form a foundation for living and leading with integrity, depth, and compassion.

You don't have to master them all at once. You might already be living one. You might be rediscovering another after a long detour. Each one stands alone. Each one strengthens the others.

Sometimes, growth begins before you know what you're growing into. Sometimes, support finds you when you didn't know you needed it. Sometimes, learning means letting go of what used to work. Sometimes, relationships remind you of who you are when you've forgotten. Sometimes, purpose whispers at the edges of change, asking you to listen again.

Start with one. Let the others rise when they're ready. Wherever you begin, start from within.

Reflect

- Grow Through What You Go Through

  What pain, or success, reshaped you? Have you claimed the meaning in it?

- Value the Support of Others

  Who showed up for you? Who needs you to show up now?
- Pursue Lifelong Learning and Adaptability

  Where are you resisting change? What are you being called to learn or release?
- Cultivate Meaningful Relationships

  Which relationships are life-giving? Which ones need repair, or release?
- Stay Purposeful & Relevant

  What matters most in this season? Are your choices aligned with it?

Growth isn't about bouncing back. It's about breaking open and becoming whole.

This story was never just mine. It echoes the quiet courage carried by so many, silently, bravely, and imperfectly. If these words met you somewhere real, I hope they reminded you of this:

You are not alone. Growth is possible. Healing won't erase the past, but it can reshape the future. Leadership, at its most powerful, begins not with expertise, but with truth. These five principles were not just learned, they were lived. Through fire and forgiveness, through failure and finding my way back. Knowing them marks is the beginning. The world is still filled with silence, shame, and stories untold. Now, the work begins, to rise with truth. To respond with purpose, because some truths must be spoken. It's time to break the silence and become the voice we once needed.

CHAPTER 25

WHERE YOU BEGIN

Silence is the enemy of progress—by speaking out, we unleash change and pave the way for a brighter, more just future.

This is the chapter I never imagined writing. For years, silence felt like the only safe place. Except, silence didn't protect me, it preserved pain. Now as I speak, the scars remain, visible and invisible. They are not shame. They are proof of that truth now lives in the open.

My message is clear: WE WILL BE SILENT NO MORE.

As I reflect on the experiences that have shaped me, I realize that certain mantras have been my anchor. These simple phrases, repeated over and over, have guided me through both the good times and the darkest of times:

"Good night, sleep tight, wake up bright, to do what's right, before the night."

A crucial part of my values, this mantra serves as a moral compass that encourages optimism and integrity each day. Passed down from my grandmother to my mother and then to her children, it reminds me to start each morning with a clear mind and a positive attitude, ready to face challenges while staying grounded in the importance of doing what's right. When you need direction, this timeless nursery rhyme can be a powerful mantra to guide you. Embrace its wisdom as a daily reminder to approach life with clarity, integrity, and purpose, ensuring that each day is lived with intention and meaning.

"I'm not crazy; he is!"

This mantra was essential for my survival during the abusive years with my father. It reminded me that the chaos and cruelty I experienced were reflections of his issues, not mine. When you find yourself questioning your sanity or self-worth due to someone else's actions or words, remind yourself that their behavior reflects them, not you. Repeating this mantra can help you maintain your grip on reality and stay grounded in your truth, even when the world around you feels overwhelming.

"The best revenge is living well."

As I moved forward, this mantra became my guiding light. It represented a shift from living in the shadow of pain and anger to focusing on hope and resilience. I realized that the best way to triumph over my past was to build a fulfilling and meaningful life. If you're struggling with anger or a desire for revenge, consider channeling that energy into creating a life filled with purpose and satisfaction. This mantra can help you focus on your own growth and happiness, rather than being consumed by negative emotions. It's about choosing to rise above and live a life that makes you proud, rather than being defined by your past.

"I am enough, I have always been enough."

This more recent mantra emerged as I released the burdens of my past, including my family's unresolved traumas. Embracing this mantra reminded me that I've always been worthy of love, acceptance, and happiness, even when I doubted it. When feelings of inadequacy or self-doubt creep in, repeat this mantra to yourself. It serves as a powerful reminder that your worth is inherent, not something that needs to be earned or proven. This belief can help you live more authentically, build meaningful relationships, and free yourself from the burden of seeking validation from others.

These mantras are more than just words; they've been lifelines that I've clung to in moments of doubt and despair. In your darkest moments, when hope seems to be slipping away, repeat your chosen mantra to yourself. It can serve as an anchor, grounding you when everything else feels chaotic. Whether it's reminding yourself that you are not defined by others' actions, focusing on building a life filled with joy and purpose, or affirming your inherent worth, these mantras can help you regain your balance and move forward with resilience.

When you feel silenced or overwhelmed by your circumstances, use these mantras as tools to reclaim your power. They can help you find the strength to speak your truth and stand up for yourself, breaking free from the chains of past trauma or current challenges. These words, or your own chosen mantras, will guide you out of the darkness, empowering you to step into your full potential and live authentically.

The release I experienced was profound. My vision is to reach out to those who, like me, have faced significant adversities and feel trapped by their pasts. Through sharing my story, I intend to offer hope and guidance, a reminder that it is possible to overcome even the most harrowing experiences and emerge on the other side as a survivor and thriving individual.

I am dedicated to being a source of strength and inspiration for others. The scars of the past will never fully fade, but they no longer dictate the course of the future. We all have the power to build a future free from the past; a future filled with resilience, purpose, and endless possibilities.

* * *

Speaking up is necessary. Every year, at least ten million people in the US (which includes children, adults, and elders) experience domestic violence.[1] This includes physical, sexual, and emotional abuse, and neglect. And although the number of cases that go unreported can't be known for certain, it has been estimated that nearly 50 percent of survivors do not speak about their abuse.[2] These aren't just statistics. They're stories—untold, unheard, unresolved. The silence doesn't protect them; it protects the pain.

When we raise our voices, we don't just heal; we interrupt the cycle, and name what was hidden, and in that naming, we begin to set each other free. When survivors remain silent, the consequences ripple far beyond the individual. The mental health toll is staggering. Survivors are significantly more likely to struggle with depression, anxiety, and post-traumatic stress disorder.[3] Suicide attempts are common among survivors as well. It has been reported that over half of the battered women who attempt and fail will try

---

1 Huecker, Martin, William Smock, Kevin King, and Gary Jordan. 2023. "Domestic Violence." National Library of Medicine. StatPearls Publishing. 2023. https://www.ncbi.nlm.nih.gov/books/NBK499891/.

2 Tapp, Susannah, and Emilie Coen. 2024. "Criminal Victimization, 2023." https://bjs.ojp.gov/document/cv23.pdf.

3 Huecker et al. 2023, 14 &15.

again; and they are usually successful the second time.[4] The weight of unspoken pain can disrupt daily life, impair judgment, and make hope feel entirely out of reach.

At the same time, the body doesn't forget what the mind tries to bury. Chronic stress from unresolved trauma can lead to real and lasting health issues. Survivors are at greater risk for heart disease, diabetes, and widespread inflammation. The emotional wounds they carry often manifest in physical form, eroding both quality of life and longevity. In the absence of healthy tools for healing, survivors may turn to destructive behaviors. Substance abuse, self-harm, and risky choices can become temporary escapes from the emotional pain, but they often prolong suffering and delay recovery. These coping strategies mask the hurt but rarely resolve it.

And then there is trust, which once broken by abuse, is hard to rebuild. Emotional trauma can make it difficult to open up, form close bonds, or believe in the safety of love. Many survivors withdraw, keeping others at arm's length to avoid being hurt again. This protective distance can increase loneliness and prevent connection at the very moment it's most needed.

When abuse is hidden in silence, society suffers. Stigma goes unchallenged. Resources go underfunded. Cycles of violence continue. The long-term societal effects include higher healthcare costs, increased rates of homelessness among survivors, and a lack of accessible support systems. Silence doesn't just harm individuals, it fuels a public health crisis.

* * *

Just last week, I got a call from someone I've known for more than twenty years, an accomplished leader who reached out for advice.

---

4 Huecker et al. 2023, 15

He sounded tired. Burnt out. Worn down by everything he was carrying.

As we talked, I didn't jump into solutions. I didn't coach or teach. I shared my story. It wasn't the first time I'd spoken it. I've shared it for years with close family and the dearest of friends and for more than a year now, I've been telling it publicly, online, at conferences, in spaces where silence still has a grip.

That said, it was the first time I shared it with him.

After a long pause, he said quietly, "I had no idea. I'm so sorry that happened to you."

I told him what I've come to believe with everything in me: "I'm not sorry anymore. Because now, I'm using it—to help others, to encourage them to end their own silence. We all carry trauma. And much of it still hides in our bodies. It needs a voice before it can be released."

That conversation didn't rewrite the past. It transformed the moment in its own quiet way. It reminded me that we don't help others by being perfect. We help them by being real. That's the legacy I want to leave. One that comes from showing up fully, speaking the truth without flinching, and staying on the path of healing, no matter how long it takes.

Speaking out shifts the narrative. It fosters compassion, encourages others to share, and builds a culture where healing is possible. The stories we tell create ripples of change, break barriers, dismantle shame, and empower others to reclaim their voices. Let's create a world in which trauma isn't hidden, but held, with care, courage, and community.

One voice at a time. The silence ends here.

CHAPTER 26

WHAT'S NEXT FOR YOU AND ME?

Change does not roll in on the wheels of inevitability but comes through continuous struggle.
—DR. MARTIN LUTHER KING, JR., 1959

If you've walked a path like mine, or are walking it right now, I want you to know this: you are not alone.

If you're surviving in silence, if your voice has been dismissed, if your truth has been buried beneath shame or fear, your story still matters. It always has and it always will.

I know this because I've lived it.

At *seven*, I had already endured more than many adults ever will. A fire that nearly killed me. Skin grafts. A dog attack while I was still healing. A home full of tension, where the air was always heavy with unspoken fear. I hid behind the bed and scratched into the wall:

I'm not crazy; he is!

That wasn't rebellion. That was survival.

Somehow, my heart stayed open. I never stopped feeling. I never stopped hoping.

At *seventeen*, I was already in college, "brilliant" on the outside, but fractured on the inside. I wore my achievements like armor—good grades, early graduation, perfect manners. I thought if I just worked hard enough, acted grateful enough, and smiled wide enough, I could escape the wreckage behind me. Trauma doesn't stay in the past; it seeps into the present. I wasn't missing who my father was—I was wrestling with who he never became.

What saved me then was connection. Jay, my best friend, saw me. Really saw me. He proved that not all men hurt others. Some love. Some stay. Some heal. That was the beginning of my voice finding its way out—first as a whisper, then as truth.

At *forty,* I was at Booz Allen, leading global projects, training and mentoring talent around the world. To the outside world, I was thriving—respected, accomplished, seen. However, behind all that success, I was still wearing the mask. I knew how to perform. What I hadn't yet learned was how to let myself be seen without the mask. I told everyone's story but my own.

At *fifty,* everything shifted. After four years in India, I stopped performing and started becoming. I slowed down enough to hear what had always been inside me. I carried with me the voices of those who had shaped me—Mom, Audre, Blanche. Their wisdom wasn't something I had to hold onto; it was something I could walk with.

Now, at *sixty-six,* I understand that healing doesn't arrive all at once. It unfolds in layers, in whispered truths, in brave choices, in staying when it would be easier to run.

If you've endured the unimaginable—or love someone who has—your presence, your patience, and your belief are lifelines. You may never fully know the impact of your compassion, but trust me: it matters more than you think.

Some of us are just beginning to name what happened. Some are deep in the work of healing. Some are holding others through it. Some, like you, may be ready to use your voice, your story, and your strength to help others find theirs.

If you are living in fear right now—if every day feels like survival, if your voice has been silenced, or if you are enduring pain that no one else sees—I want you to know something deeply important: *you are not alone.*

What is happening to you is not your fault.

You did not cause this, and you do not deserve it. Abuse thrives in silence, in secrecy, and in shame. It can convince you that you are powerless, that you have to stay quiet to stay safe, or that your story doesn't matter. I promise you, it does. You matter.

You do not have to have it all figured out. You do not need to be ready to leave or ready to speak. You only need to know that hope is not a lie. A different life is possible, even if you cannot see it yet. Sometimes healing begins not with action, but with belief—the belief that something better could exist and that you are worthy of it.

If no one else has told you today:

I believe you. I believe in your strength. I believe in the life that is still waiting for you, one that is not defined by fear, silence, or shame. There is a way forward, even if it begins with the smallest step.

This is not the end of your story.

This is the beginning of something braver.

Join the Movement

> ***A dream you dream alone is only a dream.***
> ***A dream you dream together is reality.***
> —JOHN LENNON / YOKO ONO

Movements aren't built by perfect people, they're built by people who care, act boldly, and show up consistently. Whether you're a survivor, a therapist, an advocate, or an ally, you have a place in this movement.

Every small act, listening to someone's story, creating space for honest conversations, holding your own truth, is part of this transformation.

This isn't about shouting the loudest. It's about showing up with courage, again and again, and saying: "You matter, your pain matters, and your healing is possible."

If I'm fortunate enough to reach *eighty,* I hope I'm still learning, loving, and laughing.

Whatever happens, I will still be walking beside that seven-year-old boy who survived, the seventeen-year-old who thought he needed to be perfect, the forty-year-old who wore the mask, the fifty-year-old who came home to himself, and the sixty-six-year-old who finally spoke the truth out loud.

Healing isn't the end of the story. It's how we live it fully, honestly, and bravely, one breath at a time. It's how we grow through what we go through. When we live that way, our stories don't just heal us; they make space for others to begin.

Share the Book and Spread the Message

This book isn't a solution, it's a *companion.* A conversation starter and a seed.

- Gift the Book: To a survivor, a therapist, a friend, or a colleague. Not because it has all the answers, but because it opens the door for understanding.
- Start Conversations: Use it to begin the hard talks, between parents and children, within therapy groups, at community centers, and in classrooms. Let it spark stories that have waited too long to be told.

- Amplify Online: Share a passage. Post a quote. Reflect aloud. The more we speak, the less shame has room to grow.
- Use #EndTheSilence: Or start your own hashtag. Build a community. One voice becomes many. Many voices change everything.

Live the Message

You may encounter many defeats, but you must not be defeated.
—MAYA ANGELOU, *CONVERSATIONS WITH MAYA ANGELOU* (1989)

Living this message is a daily decision. Some days it roars. Other days, it whispers. Sometimes it means drawing boundaries. Sometimes it just means getting out of bed. There's no right way to heal, only your way.

Say What's True: Create Your Mantras

Mantras are quiet anchors. Small truths that remind you of the bigger one: you are worthy. Whether whispered before sleep or written on your mirror, let these become familiar:

- "The best revenge is living well."
- "I am enough, I have always been enough."

Choose what resonates. Repeat them until they feel like home.

Practice the Principles

Healing isn't about perfection, it's about alignment. The five principles that anchor this book are not checklists or rigid steps. They are lived truths. They show up in the way we respond to pain, in how we ask for help, in the relationships we build, and in the purpose we pursue. Each one is a guidepost, gently reminding us how to return to ourselves when life gets loud. As you move forward, revisit them often, not to measure your progress, to ground your path. You have seen them echoed in every chapter of this book:

1. Grow Through What You Go Through
2. Value the Support of Others
3. Pursue Lifelong Learning and Adaptability
4. Cultivate Meaningful Relationships
5. Stay Purposeful and Relevant

Build Your Network: Healing Isn't Solo Work

You don't have to do this alone. There are:

- *Therapists* who specialize in trauma and wholeness.
- *Friends and family* who listen without judgment.
- *Retreats and workshops* that give space to breathe.
- *Online communities* where vulnerability is welcome.

Find the voices that remind you you're not alone. Stay close.

Ground Yourself / Mindfulness & Visualization

Close your eyes. Breathe in. Breathe out. You are here and that is enough.

Try grounding through your senses: five things you can see. Four you can touch. Three you can hear. Two you can smell. One you can feel.

Then: visualize the you who is free. Safe. Fully alive. That version already exists inside you. Walk toward them.

Let Something Move Through You

Healing isn't always loud. It doesn't always arrive in language. Sometimes it comes through your hands in the soil, your feet on a trail, or your body on a mat. Gardening taught me patience. Travel reminded me there was more to the world than my past. Practicing yoga helped me come back into my body.

Those were my beginnings; my ways back to myself.

You may have your own or you may still be looking. Either way, know this: outlets for expression are not luxuries, they are lifelines. They are places where the unspeakable finds form, where the body speaks without apology, and where healing becomes something you can feel.

Here are a few options to try. See what stirs, and stick with what feels right for you:

Creative Outlets:

- Painting or drawing: letting your hands speak when words can't
- Writing: journaling, poetry, letters you may never send
- Music: playing, singing, or simply feeling rhythm move through you
- Movement or dance: not for performance, just for presence
- Photography: seeing yourself and the world in new light

Nature-Based and Physical Outlets:

- Walking or hiking: letting the earth steady your steps
- Swimming: surrendering to something larger than yourself
- Rock collecting or beachcombing: meditative, simple, grounding
- Herb gardening or foraging: learning to nurture and be nurtured

Community and Somatic Outlets:

- Drumming circles: syncing your heartbeat with others
- Theater or improv: stepping into voice, into play, into power
- Martial arts or Emotional Martial Arts: where strength and stillness meet

Spiritual and Reflective Outlets:

- Meditation or breathwork: letting silence hold you
- Ritual or ceremony: honoring what was, what is, and what's next
- Candle-making or incense crafting: marking time with scent and flame

You don't need to master any of these. I have never mastered yoga, which is why it's called "practicing" yoga. You only need a place where your emotions can move through you—grief, joy, memory, hope.

Even a single deep breath is a beginning.

Reflect with Intention: A 26-Week Path

> ***Owning our story and loving ourselves through that process is the bravest thing that we'll ever do.***
>
> —**BRENé BROWN, The Gifts of Imperfection (2010)**

Healing doesn't just happen. It unfolds when we pause, reflect, and reconnect. The *Vulnerable A–Z Healing Challenge* offers a weekly rhythm to help you do exactly that—twenty-six themes, each with a prompt, a practice, and a path inward.

You'll find the full challenge in Appendix A. Whether you're just beginning or already deep in the work, this journey meets you where you are and invites you to keep going.

Turn Pain into Power: Get Involved

Your voice doesn't just matter; it can shape change:

Join or lead support networks.
Share your story with purpose.
Volunteer in spaces that need empathy.
Push for policies that protect and empower survivors.
End the Silence.

As you turn the last page, carry this truth with you: healing isn't about erasing the past. Healing is about learning how to live with it out loud without shame. You don't have to roar to be heard. Sometimes strength is a whisper that holds steady. Sometimes it's simply staying when everything in you wants to run.

You've read my story; I know you carry one too. Maybe you've shared it. Maybe you haven't. Maybe today is the first time you've let yourself feel it fully.

Wherever you are, know this: you're *not* alone. You never were.

If you're ready to use your voice, not just for yourself, but for someone still finding theirs, we're already walking together.

This book ends here. Healing doesn't. Emotions still live inside me, ones I thought I had outgrown or left behind. As Howard taught me through EMA: "Emotions don't know the calendar." They hide in the places we forget to look. Now when they show up, I see them. I release them. I return to the present. That is the practice. We don't have to do it alone.

With deep respect,
Ed

EPILOGUE

BROTHER TO BROTHER

The silence we carry can lose its power the moment we speak a few words that allow love to enter the space between us.

For the first seven years of my life, my brother Phil and I slept in the same room, yet I have no memory of him there. After our father left, Phil visited a few times in the early seventies. He was a hippie then—long hair, carefree, living by his own rules. I longed for his acceptance, but each visit ended in a fight, and then he was gone. One time, he stood in our kitchen, inhaled deeply, and let out long, piercing screams—Arthur Janov's Primal Scream Therapy, made famous by John Lennon and Yoko Ono.

The sound ripped through me—I was back inside my father's rage—the beatings, the threats, the way his fury swallowed a room. Mom froze, Diane's eyes widened, and I shook with fear. Only now do I realize Phil was really crying out:

"Hold me. Love me. Please see me."

Instead, the moment spiraled, and Phil and his girlfriend left, leaving the raging echo lodged inside me.

Through the years, I longed to be close to Phil. I watched brothers who were best friends and wanted that for us. Our paths pulled us apart, first by age, later by the ways in which we each coped with fear disguised as anger, stubbornness, beliefs, and ideologies. Beneath it all was the unspoken truth: we both carried the same shame.

But many years have passed . . .

When I asked Phil to read the parts of this book that included him, he agreed without hesitation. After he finished, we talked. One conversation led to another. Two brothers, with more days behind than ahead, broke the silence we had carried alone.

It was like opening a window in a long-closed room. At first the air is stale. Then a breeze stirs the dust and carries it away. It's easier to breathe, and silence no longer owns the space.

Phil's thoughts on our conversation

When you're in a broken family, you experience deep pain that never goes away. You can't just write off a family member. It's always there, like a volcano bubbling underground, waiting to erupt.

This dialogue is part of my brother and me finally facing that pain. I've always wanted Ed in my life. Interestingly, we have followed very similar career paths: pouring into leaders and creating organizational structure. I see him as way more intelligent than me; I used to feel threatened by that, and that I never could measure up. But now I see his brilliance as a gift, not a threat.

You're not reading this conversation as "what we talked about." You're reading what we experienced as we started to heal, individually and together.

* * *

I started the conversation by asking Phil if he could remember Mom and Dad ever getting along.

PHIL: Not once. It was always tense, always waiting for the next blowup. They were like two broken radios stuck on different frequencies, screaming into a void where no one was listening. I remembered thinking, *If they just could go back to where all these arguments started, they could have peace.* I suddenly feel sad for Mom and Dad, for what could have been.

His words lingered in the air for a moment, heavy with truth.

ED: More than once I asked Mom why she didn't leave. All I got was, "He made me believe I was nothing without him." It had to be him leaving, because she couldn't go. The fighting felt endless, and I just wanted it to stop. Eventually I stopped wondering.

Phil nodded, then leaned back, as if seeing Dad from a distance all over again.

PHIL: It was like a demon lived inside him, tormenting him through mental breakdowns, ulcers, and migraines. It never stopped, never left him in peace. He tried to manage his demon through drinking, gambling, adultery, and violence against his wife and children. He didn't just drink. He swallowed pills by the handful. Sedatives that were highly addictive with horrendous side effects became household words in our home . . .

I remembered it too. The bottles, the pills, the constant threat of explosion.

ED: Once he claimed he swallowed the entire bottle. Mom had to rush him to the hospital.

Phil's eyebrows lifted, the only outward sign of what was churning inside.

PHIL: I'm not surprised. He was often drunk. He kept a bottle of Scotch in the kitchen corner cabinet. Whenever any of us suggested he had a drinking problem, he flew into a wild rage, like a roaring tiger snarling, "Back off so you don't get hurt." He put a piece of tape on the bottle to track the level, just in case one of us tried to sneak a sip. A few times I outsmarted Dad by taking a couple of swigs and then filling it back with water to the mark.

I remembered all the bottles in the cabinet and the ones he also kept on his nightstand.

ED: I could tell he was home before I even saw him. The air in the house got so heavy with the smell of alcohol and cigarette smoke. We kept the windows closed most of the time because he never wanted the outside world to hear. My heart would start pounding the moment I walked in from school. I tried to slip quietly to my room, hoping I would not cross his path.

PHIL: Listening to you talk about Dad makes me think about how far back this went. From what I knew about Grandpa Phil, Dad's father, he carried the same demon. He beat his wife and sons, got into fights with others, and then he died from a heart attack when he was only forty-one.

ED: It really does go back for generations, Phil.

PHIL: I remember when you told me what Grandma Mary said as she was dying—that when Uncle Bert and Uncle Harold were infants, Grandpa Phil shook Harold so hard that he died. They kept that a family secret for more than sixty years. How many generations does this go back? We may never know. What I do know is I'm planting my flag here, shaking my fist at the demon, proclaiming, "Do whatever you want with me.

The buck stops here. You're not getting to my children and grandchildren."

I agreed, and then we shifted to when I was seven.

ED: Do you remember the day the dog attacked me?

PHIL: Yeah, I remember. I didn't think of it as heroic. I just reacted. I yelled and kicked the dog and pulled it off you before I even realized what I'd done.

His words transported me back to that moment. I was seven, still healing from the fire, when its teeth sank into my face. Stitches closed the wounds, yet what stayed with me was the feeling I later told Phil about.

ED: When you pulled the dog off me, it was the first time, I felt someone there to protect me. On the way to the hospital, I didn't think about my pain. I only could think about how angry Dad would be with me. His rage was always louder than any pain.

PHIL: I get it. Dad always told me if I ever lost a fight, I'd have to fight him when I got home. Truth is, I lied many times. I lost many fights. I never was a fighter; I was more of a romantic, a poet, a thinker, a visionary.

ED: We each found different ways to survive. I hid behind a mask because being fully present felt too painful.

Phil's eyes softened, remembering that at twenty years old, his heart opened up to writing poetry, journaling, and a lifelong hunger to listen to and play music, because he loved that more than sports and fighting—Dad's definition of a man. I sat with how much energy I had wasted pretending. He said the pain sent him searching for someone who would listen to his inner screams, for someone or something to make it stop.

PHIL: Drugs. Sex. Madness. Religion. Dominating and manipulating people. Occasionally I'd see something that made me believe I could find a normal life.

I asked him if he found that when he went to school in Mexico.

ED: Back then, I didn't understand any of that. Part of me thought maybe you had escaped, and I remember wishing you had taken me with you.

PHIL: In Mexico, I saw poor villagers with almost nothing, yet their faces glowed with serene joy. It shattered everything I believed about happiness. I thought happiness came from manipulation, power, and possessions, yet here it was—something deeper and freer. I wept as I watched, knowing I wanted whatever they had, but not knowing how to find it.

I saw it again in 1970, when I was homeless and stumbled into the home of a Mormon family in New Mexico. They welcomed me as one of their own—working, laughing, and worshiping together. The father worked beside me by day and spoke to me by night. More than once, he told me, "If you want this kind of love, get down on your knees and find God."

Hearing Phil say this; I could feel the weight he was carrying.

ED: That must have cracked something open. We never talked about it. For me, the house was never safe. I held my breath, waiting for the next explosion, the next slammed door, the next burst of rage. Like I said before, I believed you had found a way out, and I wished I could too.

PHIL: I wanted the love I saw in that family, but I couldn't accept God. The God of my childhood hadn't saved our family. And Jesus? I believed Jesus hated me because I was Jewish, and that his Christians hated me too.

I asked Phil, since he hadn't found what he was searching for in religion, had he found it in Gina? After all, they've been together for more than fifty years.

PHIL: Gina and I argued like a dog barking at a turtle. The louder I barked, the tighter she locked into her shell. I barked because I was afraid she'd leave. She never experienced adults getting angry in her home, so she locked into her shell because she was afraid I'd hurt her.

His words struck me because I knew that circle of fear and retreat.

ED: Pris and I went through that too. For years we circled the same wounds without healing them. After so many failed relationships, I never believed I'd find a true partner. I'm grateful every day she stayed. Now when tension rises, we pause, breathe, and ask, "Will this matter in five years?" That reminder shifts us from proving a point to protecting what matters most, which is what we've built together.

Phil told me that even though he and Gina stayed together, the fights never stopped the emptiness.

PHIL: I kept searching. If I couldn't find peace in religion and I couldn't find it at home, then where was it? I chased every system, every belief, desperate for something solid that wouldn't break under pressure.

I remembered watching that in him, the way he was always testing the edges.

ED: You were always pushing to see what would hold and what would break. Did anything ever stand up to that kind of pressure?

Phil thought for a moment, then gave me a list, pared down to the essentials.

PHIL: A short list. I've rarely seen it—but when I do, I know it. Everything works until it doesn't. Some things break sooner, some later. Here's what lasts:

- When it gives life, even when no one is looking.
- When it's authentic, not denying reality.
- When people genuinely love each other.

Everything else is noise. Distraction. Empty promises.

His words landed with me differently than they would in the past.

ED: I hear you now in a way I couldn't back then. I thought you were just defiant. I see now you were searching for love and truth strong enough to hold when everything else cracked. I was searching too. I tried to earn approval; to perform so well no one could see the fractures. I survived by becoming who I thought others wanted me to be. Different paths, same question: "Is there anything that still holds when you lean your full weight against it?"

Phil didn't flinch. He named the rage that had chased him for years.

PHIL: I couldn't put my pain into words. I felt like a wounded beast, lying awake night after night with a fiery ball of rage in my gut. I tried to smother it with work, drugs, food, sex—anything. I grabbed onto philosophies and religions, only to watch them crumble. To protect myself, I filled the room with my presence because other people's presence scared me. I became the answer guy, the one in charge, running on anxiety and insecurity. Calm felt like danger. If things got quiet, I stirred them up.

His words could have been mine, except for the drugs. I dabbled in some drugs during college, but never went down that path.

ED: I get that. Stillness felt dangerous to me too. I always waited for something bad to happen. I stirred things up for the same reason, so I could feel some sense of control. If I managed how people saw me, they would never get close enough to see how hurt and scared I really was.

* * *

A few weeks later, we picked up our second conversation. This time, our focus shifted from the past to what it means to live in the present.

PHIL: When my two grandsons and I came to visit you and Pris last year, it was the first time I remember us all just . . . getting along. No forcing, no fixing. Just being together. There was honor, respect, and a kind of peace I didn't recognize at first. I didn't know how much I needed that until I felt it. Three generations in the same space, and nobody had to prove anything.

I told him how much that visit had meant to me.

ED: I'll admit, I was nervous at first, wanting it to go well. What you saw with us is just who Pris and I are now. No pretending, no keeping score. That's the space I want us to keep building, where feeling safe is something we can count on.

Our conversation turned again, this time toward what it meant to stop carrying what had been passed down.

ED: I used to think if I moved fast enough and achieved enough, I could outrun the past. I buried myself in work, but the sound of Dad's voice screaming into me, *"You're useless,"* was always there. My healing came when I broke the silence and stopped being afraid to be seen as vulnerable. That's when it finally lost its grip.

I paused, letting the words settle. Phil leaned forward, his response widening the lens from my personal healing to the larger family story.

PHIL: And unless we find a way to honor our parents, we either become them or spend our lives trying not to. That constant fight creates its own damage.

ED: The way I see it now, honoring means saying, I see it all. The good and the broken. The love that was there and the love that wasn't. It means choosing to stop carrying what was never mine to hold. I can mourn the parents I wanted and never had, while moving forward without being haunted by the hell we went through.

PHIL: I see that each of my kids carries our family story in their own way. My deepest hope is that every one of them will find freedom from the wrong that has been passed down, repair what they can, build on the good they received, and add their own good. Then pass that down to their children who will do the same.

ED: I share that same hope for all of our family, Phil. What you and Gina are choosing as grandparents, and what Pris and I are choosing as parents, are ways of breaking the cycle of generational trauma and creating something better for the ones who come after us.

Phil sat back, reflecting on the years of trying.

PHIL: No parents ever truly get it right. I sincerely thought I was. Looking back, I can see deep things in me that I couldn't see then. I wish I could do it over.

ED: I feel the same way, Phil. We make the best decisions we can with what we know at the time. No matter how hard we try, our kids still grow up needing therapy. I tell my friends and new parents to start saving now to cover the costs. That way, at least their kids can thank them for being prepared.

That made his eyebrows rise, and he almost smiled.

PHIL: Well, with nine kids, I probably gave them enough material to make a few therapists rich. Having grandchildren really does feel like a second chance. When we were raising our children, they didn't have grandparents who could help us carry the impossible load of parenting. During those years, we separated ourselves while we were in the Mennonite community. Our children never had grandparents who were wild about them, who would believe in them and love them unconditionally. Gina and I want to be those grandparents. Every time I'm with our grandkids I tell them they're my favorite people in the whole world. Mom's dad, Grandpa Jim, taught me practically everything I know about how to be a successful businessman. He never said anything. I learned it simply by being with him.

ED: I was so young when Grandpa Jim died that I never really got to know him. I did feel loved by our grandparents, and I always felt loved unconditionally by Mom. With Dad, it was different. I never felt love from him, only judgment. After the divorce, when he even forced his own parents to cut off contact with us, it just drove the point deeper.

Phil shook his head, and his voice got quieter.

PHIL: That's sad for me to hear. I actually felt like Dad loved me. He hugged me and told me he was proud of me, which is why it was so confusing that he could still hurt Mom and me so deeply . . .

ED: For me, the only hugs I remember were in public, and I think they were just for show. At home, all I ever saw in his eyes was disappointment and anger.

PHIL: When we were in the church community in Tennessee, they always seemed to find something wrong with me. They excommunicated me twice, and I never understood why. Once, several months passed and none of the leaders came to me with a complaint. I remember thinking, they must be trying to get rid of me. Abuse from people in authority felt like love. I often got on the wrong side of them because I felt a huge void in me when I wasn't being abused. It wasn't until I could honestly name the wounds and my own bitterness that had become my identity that I could get free from attracting abuse from people in authority.

ED: I can see how that has been true for you. For me, breaking free meant realizing that I am enough, and that I have always been enough.

* * *

Phil told me that one thing keeping him from being present was the constant arguments he carried with people who weren't in the room.

PHIL: Unless I keep my head cleaned out, I can accumulate a truckload of offenses and grudges—rehearsing and rehashing.

I started by clearing out years of trash in my head, then noticing it when new or old trash tried to come back.

I knew that loop all too well.

ED: The story in my head wasn't always reality. It was just a scared voice looking for safety, hiding behind a mask. Now I remind myself to stay present and listen with an open mind.

He nodded, then leaned forward, his voice more measured than before.

PHIL: I see that shift in you. I feel safer in our relationship than I ever knew I could. I also had to face something else. As our business evolved, I became a CEO. I devoured everything I could about leadership. On the outside, I looked strong, but inside I was hurting all the time. Being in charge became my hiding place. I started believing I had to be the smartest guy in every room, even the CEO of everyone. I didn't realize I was driving people away, especially my adult children and their spouses. A friend finally told me, "Your unsolicited advice is driving your family away." That wrecked me, but it woke me up. I found a coach online who taught me how to tame my "Advice Monster." At first it left me feeling unsafe, no longer in charge. I had to make room for other people's thoughts and feelings. I still mess up, but now I pause, get curious, and wait for the invitation. My anxiety no longer fills the room, which leaves space for theirs to show up and still feel loved and embraced.

His words landed close to home.

ED: My whole life was built on solving problems, reading the room, stepping in. It made me feel useful, but it kept me from really seeing people, even the ones I love most. I've learned that sometimes the most loving thing is to stay present without trying to steer the moment.

We ended our conversation for that day and have had several since.

* * *

Phil's Final Thoughts: A Morning of Mercy

It's 5:47 a.m. on Saturday morning. The sun hasn't come up yet. I'm sitting at the dining room table with ten candles lit. There's no significance in ten; I just love the quiet light of candles. Soft instrumental music plays in the background.

I've been awake for a couple of hours. Streams of mercy are flooding my soul, as the conversation with Ed has illuminated dark places in me that I never knew how to access.

Why couldn't we talk about it *then*? Discussing it now from our two perspectives, I now realize Dad was addicted to drugs, alcohol, sex, gambling, and probably more. Those demons drove him to wound the very people who loved him and whom he was supposed to love and protect.

Right now, I'm imagining how our home might have been if Dad had been different. It feels happy. It feels playful. Silence feels safe. I can see Dad, Mom, Diane, Ed, and me around the table, sharing a meal, talking about our day, laughing, and enjoying each other's company. We do things together. When conflict comes, we graciously move through it, instead of turning it into a battleground and fighting until we are too exhausted for anything else.

We're there for each other. Home is a safe haven we return to when the world hurts us. Experts say imagination is as real as reality. What if we could release Dad from his demons, dream of the family that could have been, and choose to live in that dream from today forward?

On March 3, 2003 (333), as Mom was taking her final breaths, the candles Ed and Pris had lit flickered around the room. A CD my wife Gina and the kids had recorded played softly. I held Mom's hand, my other hand stretching up toward heaven, reaching for God's hand. In that moment, there was no bickering, no unforgiveness: only peace and love. My heart broke as I saw the real mother behind all her pain and felt regret for the son I could have been.

One by one, the candles went out. Then the hospice nurse said, "She's gone." A couple of hours later, the rabbi came. At the funeral she told me, "I've never entered a home before that was so peaceful after someone had passed."

So, what does all this mean now? While we're still alive, before the candles start going out, can we light candles of love, hope, and forgiveness? Can we release the past, and instead of living in regret of what could have been, live in the sacred beauty of what still can be?

I still can feel the wounds. They may never go away. Yet they no longer demand from me and the people I love something that none of us could ever give. I can let them be. Maybe in time they'll go away.

Ed's Final Thoughts: Making Space for What's Next

These conversations with Phil are not a neat ending. They give us a mirror to see ourselves more clearly and a bridge that had been missing for decades. We grow through what we go through, learning how to live with it in ways that make space for something new.

Reconciliation is always possible. None of us knows how much time we have, which is why moments like this matter. When we choose to stay in the conversation, listen, and care more about each other than about protecting ourselves, we take a leap into something better.

I have found power in naming the pain out loud. I have found peace in honoring what came before without letting it control what comes next. I have found abundance in showing up with the one person who remembers the same painful story and hearing it from a different perspective.

For so many years, I felt the silence that measured the distance between us. Every time we tried to break it, an argument erupted, and the distance grew wider. After finally speaking the words we carried alone for so long, I see how different it can be. The silence no longer owns us.

As I sit with Phil's words about mercy and candles, I realize healing often comes the same way: quietly, one small flame at a time, pushing back the dark.

Is there someone in your life waiting for you to take the first step to end the silence?

APPENDIX A
THE VULNERABLE A–Z HEALING CHALLENGE

A Twenty-six-Week Journey to Reclaiming Voice, Connection, and Wholeness

Healing isn't a single moment. It's a practice. A path. This twenty-six-week challenge is your invitation to walk that path with presence, courage, and compassion. Each week offers a reflection, a guided action, and a journaling prompt, drawing from the truths woven throughout *Vulnerable*.

As you move through this journey, remember that healing can sometimes bring difficult memories or emotions to the surface. If, at any point, these reflections lead to thoughts of harming yourself or someone else, please pause and reach out for support. Speak with someone you trust, connect with a qualified mental health professional, or seek immediate help from a hospital or crisis service. You do not have to walk this path alone.

There's no rush. No race. Just a steady movement from silence to voice. From surviving to living. From being hidden . . . to becoming whole. Let's begin.

Phase 1: Foundations of Awareness (Weeks 1–5)

You begin where healing begins, with truth. These early weeks are about reclaiming your voice, settling your nervous system, and creating emotional safety.

Week 1: Acknowledge the Truth

Healing begins with honesty. Naming what happened is not weakness, it's the foundation of strength.

Try this: Write down one truth you've never admitted, not to anyone else, just to yourself.

Journal: What truth am I finally ready to stop avoiding?

Week 2: Breathe Through the Fear

Fear lives in the body. Sometimes your nervous system still reacts to things that are no longer threats. Breathing brings you back to the present.

Try this: Practice box breathing for three minutes when anxiety surfaces. (Inhale through your nose for four seconds, hold your breath for four seconds, exhale through your mouth for four seconds, then hold again for four seconds, and repeat.)

Journal: When has fear shown up for me recently and what did it want me to protect?

Week 3: Cultivate Connection

You are *not* meant to heal alone. Connection with others invites compassion, safety, and perspective.

Try this: Reach out to someone who makes you feel seen. Tell them something real.

Journal: Who are my lifelines and how do I let them know?

Week 4: Drop the Mask

You wore the mask to survive. Healing begins when you allow yourself to be seen.

Try this: Speak one truth today instead of saying what's expected.

Journal: What mask am I ready to set down and what do I hope to receive in its place?

Week 5: End the Silence

Silence doesn't heal, it hides and what hides, harms. Choosing to speak breaks the cycle.

Try this: Share one part of your story with someone safe or write it down just for you.

Journal: What part of my story is asking to be heard?

Phase 2: Strengthening Self-Worth (Weeks 6–10)

Now that you've begun to speak, it's time to remember who you are. These reflections focus on resilience, imperfection, and your right to joy and growth.

Week 6: Find Meaning, Not Perfection

The goal isn't flawlessness, it's alignment. Growth happens when we seek meaning, not approval.

Try this, then Journal: Reflect on a time when imperfection taught you more than success.

Journal: Where have I been trying to be perfect and what's the cost?

Week 7: Grow Through What You Go Through

Growth doesn't always feel triumphant. It often arrives through pain and persistence.

Try this: Name three ways hardship has helped you grow.

Journal: What part of me was strengthened by what once hurt?

Week 8: Hold Space for the Hurt

Healing takes time. You don't need to fix your pain, just acknowledge it.

Try this: Sit quietly with a hard memory. Breathe. Just stay.

Journal: What pain have I been trying to outrun and what would it mean to simply feel it?

Week 9: I Am Enough. I Have Always Been Enough.

This mantra is a truth your healing deserves: "You were never too broken to be whole."

Try this: Stand in front of a mirror. Say this mantra out loud.

Journal: What would change if I truly believed I am enough?

Week 10: Journey, Don't Sprint

Healing isn't linear. It unfolds step by step, not all at once.

Try this: List five small signs of progress you've made recently.

Journal: Where have I grown, even if it's not obvious to others?

Phase 3: Brave Expression (Weeks 11–15)

This phase builds emotional courage. You'll deepen your honesty, honor grief, listen to your body, and open yourself to help and joy again.

Week 11: Keep Telling the Truth

Your voice is powerful. Every time you share your story, you reclaim a piece of yourself.

Try this: Tell one more truth than you told yesterday.

Journal: What part of my truth still feels risky and why?

Week 12: Listen to Your Body

Your body holds memories. Its wisdom can guide your healing.

Try this: Scan your body and write down what you notice. Tension? Calm?

Journal: What messages is my body trying to send me today?

Week 13: Make Room for Joy

Joy doesn't erase pain, it balances it. You deserve both.

Try this: Do one thing today just for joy. No justification.

Journal: When was the last time I allowed joy without guilt?

Week 14: Name the Grief

Grief isn't only about death. It's about every loss, every unmet need.

Try this: Write a letter to something or someone you've lost.

Journal: What grief have I silenced and how can I honor it?

Week 15: Open the Door to Help

Letting others support you is an act of courage, not weakness.

Try this: Ask someone for a kind favor. Let them in.

Journal: When has someone shown up for me and how did it feel?

Phase 4: Releasing and Rebuilding (Weeks 16–20)

With strength and trust growing, you're ready to let go of what no longer serves you and replace it with grounded presence and reclaimed beliefs.

Week 16: Practice Presence

When you're fully present, you reconnect with what's real.

Try this: Take sixty seconds to notice five things you can see, hear, or feel.

Journal: When do I feel most alive and what takes me away from that?

Week 17: Question the Old Rules

Not every belief you inherited belongs to you. You get to choose what stays.

Try this: Identify one old rule you're ready to break.

Journal: Whose voice taught me that and do I still believe them?

Week 18: Release What No Longer Serves

Healing often means letting go of what once helped you survive.

Try this: Choose one behavior, object, or habit to release this week.

Journal: What am I carrying that's no longer mine?

Week 19: Speak Up

Even a whisper matters. Your voice is part of your power.

Try this: Say something today that matters no matter how small.

Journal: What part of me comes alive when I speak from truth?

Week 20: Trust the Process

You don't need all the answers to take the next step.

Try this: Reflect on a time when not knowing still led somewhere good.

Journal: Where can I choose trust over control right now?

Phase 5: Integration and Expansion (Weeks 21–26)

Here, your story starts to widen. You affirm your worth, rewrite your narrative, recognize patterns, and rise into the now with clarity and vision.

Week 21: Unlearn the Shame

Shame was taught. You can unlearn it.

Try this: Write down five messages you're ready to stop believing.

Journal: What would life feel like without that shame?

Week 22: Validate Your Own Experience

You don't need permission to believe yourself. Your truth matters.

Try this: Affirm your truth aloud: "What happened mattered. What I felt was real."

Journal: Where have I waited for the validation I already deserve?

Week 23: Who is Behind the Mask?

Naming what your mask was hiding brings it out into the open.

Try this: Draw a mask and label how you wanted people to see you when you were wearing it. Now draw another mask and label is as you felt inside and never wanted others to know.

Journal: What will it take for you to remove your mask and truly be authentic?

Week 24: X-ray Your Patterns

Patterns repeat until they're seen. Gently name what's asking for change.

Try this: Notice one emotional reaction this week and trace its origin.

Journal: What keeps showing up and what's it asking from me?

Week 25: Yield to the Now

Stop fixing. Stop performing. Just be here.

Try this: Sit for five minutes doing nothing but breathing.

Journal: What do I notice when I stop trying to manage everything?

Week 26: Zoom Out

You are not where you started. Your story has shape.

Try this: Create a visual timeline of your healing and mark the turning points.

Journal: What proof do I have that I'm becoming whole?

You Made It!

This isn't just the end of a challenge. It's the beginning of a new relationship, with yourself.

You've spoken truth. Released shame. Built connection. Made space for joy. You've done what many avoid their whole lives: the brave, slow work of healing.

Take a deep breath. Look at how far you've come. You didn't just survive.

You chose to live out loud. You are healing and you are *never* alone.

ACKNOWLEDGEMENTS

This book, this movement, would not have been possible without my global village of family, friends, and colleagues.

To my wife and life partner, Pris, my gratitude and love. Your unwavering support and belief in me, even when I doubted myself, have been the foundation of my growth. Together, we have built a life filled with love, adventure, and shared experiences. From navigating the challenges of our early relationship to exploring more than seventy countries, your patience, understanding, and resilience have made our partnership unbreakable. Whether in your successful interior design work or your commitment to our family, you continue to inspire me every day. I am forever grateful for your presence in my life. I love you deeply.

To our daughter, MacKenzie, I am immensely proud to be your father. Your passion for holistic healing and your commitment to helping others are a continual source of inspiration. Your strength and adaptability, especially during our time in India, amazed me. The bond we share, symbolized by the hearts we traded at the airport, remains one of the most profound sources of strength in my life.

Elana and Michael, you are more than cousins, you are like siblings to me. Thank you for your constant love, wisdom, and support. Elana, your guidance through Emotional Martial Arts helped me reclaim my voice and turn pain into purpose. Michael, your humor, encouragement, and steady presence bring joy and comfort. Aunt Audre's influence was profound; she taught us the value of resilience and the importance of family. Her legacy lives on through all of us.

Jay, my lifelong friend and brother in spirit, thank you for being my anchor. From childhood through every stage of adulthood, your support has never wavered. Our friendship has spanned four generations, providing not just stability but shared joy between our families. Thank you for making your family our family: Heather and Andrew, along with Jace; Josh and Mary-Beth, along with Charlie; Danny and Gabriela. Your brother Gary and his family have also brought light and laughter into our lives.

Vina, your friendship has been a cherished part of my life since 1992. From Florida to Southern California and beyond, we've shared memories that mean the world to me. Through celebrations and challenges, your presence has remained constant. You are our oldest daughter in spirit, and I treasure the love and connection we share.

To my brother Phil, you have shown great resilience on your path through the shadows of abuse, supported by Gina by your side. I deeply appreciate your nine children: Noah, Daniel, Anna, Gloria, Josh, Ben, Naomi, Rachel, Nate, and their growing families who bring joy and inspiration.

To my sister Diane, who passed in 2021, your journey was different from mine, but it mattered just as much. You faced your struggles with quiet strength. Your memory lives on, and I hope you have found peace.

My heartfelt gratitude to those who stayed with us from around the world: Tony from Hong Kong, Kyl from China, Christine from Germany, and Nicolene from South Africa. You expanded our awareness and brought us joy.

Charlotte, your steadfast friendship and role as MacKenzie's godmother mean the world to us. Josh Craver, Kathy V., Sheina L., John Chen, and Michael Rosenthal, thank you for your collaboration and friendship over the years across many companies and countries.

To Jennifer, JJ, Britt, Leo, V, Parker, and Djedly, your strength and resilience have inspired me time and again.

During our seven years in India, I had the privilege of working with extraordinary colleagues who became dear friends: Anil, Kritya, Rahul, Ravi Shankar, Sirisha, Amit, Sudha, and many others. Sunita, Kishore, Satish, and Deepika, you are like our children and a constant source of love. Pragnya, you are our sister.

To Prashanth and the children we met at the orphanage, your spirit and resilience touched us deeply. We cherish the bond we formed and the experiences we shared.

I also want to acknowledge the Booz Allen and Satyam teams for your collaboration and commitment. To all the colleagues from organizations where Pris and I have worked or consulted through Nelson Cohen Global Consulting, thank you for trusting us to help grow your leaders and teams.

At SprintRay, I was fortunate to work alongside a brilliant, purpose-driven group: Abby, Amir, Ana, Elias, Erika, Hossein, Jing, John Cox, John Fernandez, John van Dyck, Julissa, Leah, Liang, Matt, Sina, and Tim. Special thanks to Erich, a trusted colleague since 2009. Your support and the friendship between our families have meant so much.

To my Literary Agent, Gary Krebs of GMK Writing and Editing, Inc., thank you for your perseverance and for making it your personal mission to find the right publisher. Your belief in this story and your dedication to bringing it into the world made all the difference.

To Ashley Calvano, my editor, whose thoughtful guidance helped shape this manuscript with care and clarity, I offer my deepest gratitude. Your belief in this story and your patience throughout the process meant a great deal. To Meghan Kilduff, who led production and copyediting with such dedication, thank you for the meticulous attention that strengthened every page. My appreciation also extends to the talented team at Westchester Publishing Services, whose expertise brought the manuscript to life through its elegant layout. I am grateful to Jennifer Stimson for the cover design, which captures the spirit of this book with both beauty and sensitivity. Finally, my sincere thanks to Jarred Weisfeld, president of Start Publishing, and the team at Evan and Nathan Publishing, a Start Publishing imprint, for believing in this work and supporting it so thoughtfully from the beginning. I remain deeply grateful for the care and commitment each of you brought to this book.

Tony Bingham, CEO of the Association for Talent Development (ATD), and the entire ATD team, thank you for your unwavering support since 1986. Your leadership and commitment to talent development have shaped my professional journey.

Vineet Nayar, your book *Employees First, Customers Second* profoundly influenced my approach to leadership. Working with you at HCL helped bring those principles to life in powerful ways.

Dr. Justin Yanuck, your guidance during my ketamine-assisted healing was transformative. Each session felt like a thousand hours of traditional therapy. You helped me complete a healing journey I once thought impossible.

Jeevan, your insight into childhood abuse and its impact gave me deeper understanding and strengthened my resolve to make the invisible visible through Igniting Resilience.

To those who have influenced my life and are no longer with us, I am forever grateful: Grandma Irene and Uncle Burt; my first-grade teacher, Mrs. Hanson; Sandi Thomas, who introduced me to Pris and changed my life; colleagues like Nishi Levitt and Nicola Klein; and to Roy White, wherever you are, I have searched for you for many years. Thank you for saving my life.

To Arvind Krishna, Dinesh Neelakandan, and Hari Ankem, your enduring friendship and now partnership in bringing this book and movement to life means more than I can say.

To my mother, Bernice, who passed in 2003, your unconditional love and quiet strength carried me through more than you ever knew. You stood by me in moments I barely stood myself. I miss you every day. Knowing you were proud of me still brings strength.

To my father, Jerry, your pain was too big to contain, and it spilled into everything around you. I hope, wherever you are, you have finally found peace.

This book, and this movement, would not exist without both of you.